FOOD STUDIES IN LATIN AMERICAN LITERATURE

OTHER TITLES IN THIS SERIES

Rooted Resistance: Agrarian Myth in Modern America

A Rich and Tantalizing Brew: A History of How Coffee Connected the World

To Feast on Us as Their Prey: Cannibalism and the Early Modern Atlantic

Forging Communities: Food and Representation in Medieval and Early Modern Southwestern Europe

Inventing Authenticity: How Cookbook Writers Redefine Southern Identity

Chop Suey and Sushi from Sea to Shining Sea: Chinese and Japanese Restaurants in the United States

Aunt Sammy's Radio Recipes: The Original 1927 Cookbook and Housekeeper's Chat

Mexican-Origin Foods, Foodways, and Social Movements: Decolonial Perspectives

Meanings of Maple: An Ethnography of Sugaring

The Taste of Art: Food, Cooking, and Counterculture in Contemporary Practices

Devouring Cultures: Perspectives on Food, Power, and Identity from the Zombie Apocalypse to Downton Abbey

Latin@s' Presence in the Food Industry: Changing How We Think about Food

Dethroning the Deceitful Pork Chop: Rethinking African American Foodways From Slavery to Obama

American Appetites: A Documentary Reader

Food Studies in Latin American Literature

PERSPECTIVES ON THE GASTRONARRATIVE

EDITED BY ROCÍO DEL AGUILA
AND VANESA MISERES

The University of Arkansas Press
Fayetteville
2021

ISBN: 978-1-68226-181-1
eISBN: 978-1-61075-754-6

25 24 23 22 21 5 4 3 2 1

Manufactured in the United States of America

♾ The paper used in this publication meets the minimum requirements of the American National Standard for Permanence of Paper for Printed Library Materials Z39.48-1984.

Library of Congress Cataloging-in-Publication Data

Names: Aguila, Rocío del, 1975– editor. | Miseres, Vanesa, editor.
Title: Food studies in Latin American literature: perspectives on the gastronarrative / edited by Rocío del Aguila and Vanesa Miseres.
Description: Fayetteville: The University of Arkansas Press, 2021. | Series: Food and foodways | Includes bibliographical references and index. | Summary: "Collection of essays analyzing a wide array of Latin American narratives through the lens of food studies"—Provided by publisher.
Identifiers: LCCN 2021022881 (print) | LCCN 2021022882 (ebook) | ISBN 9781682261811 (paperback) | ISBN 9781610757546 (ebook)
Subjects: LCSH: Food in literature. | Latin American literature—History and criticism. | Food habits in literature. | National characteristics, Latin American, in literature. | LCGFT: Essays. | Literary criticism.
Classification: LCC PN56.F59 F684 2021 (print) | LCC PN56.F59 (ebook) | DDC 860.9/3564—dc23
LC record available at https://lccn.loc.gov/2021022881
LC ebook record available at https://lccn.loc.gov/2021022882

Vice of habituation. Wonder of childhood,
magical feeling of raw materials and elements:
flour, salt, oil, water, fire.
Moments of pure vision, pure hearing, pure touch.

Consciousness of life at one moment.
All the memories revolve around bread.

It carries an intense sense of life, and also,
through I don't know what internal association,
an equally strong sense of death.
The thought of life turns banal from the moment
it isn't blended with the thought of death.
The pure essentials are superficial giants
or little pagans.
The pagan paid attention to both.

Gabriela Mistral, "Bread," 1938

Cinnamon Ice Cream

Since literature seeks solace in the kitchen, why can't educators, whose mission is to teach what's good, do so as well? What I have here is delectable on the palate and satisfying for the belly.

Break some good quality cinnamon sticks into small pieces and simmer for an hour in the amount of water needed for the ice cream, along with an ounce of ground cinnamon placed inside a cloth pouch (flannel or gauze works nicely).

Remove from heat and strain through a sieve. Sweeten with sugar and, before freezing, add a few drops of cinnamon extract to heighten the aroma.

Recipe by Enriqueta Lund (Lima),
in Juana Manuela Gorriti's *Cocina ecléctica*, 1890
(Translation by Julie Henderson)

CONTENTS

ILLUSTRATIONS

SERIES EDITORS' PREFACE

The University of Arkansas Press series on Food and Foodways explores historical and contemporary issues in global food studies. We are committed to representing a diverse set of voices that tell lesser-known food stories and to opening up new avenues for interdisciplinary research. Our strengths are works in the humanities and social sciences that use food as a critical lens to examine broader cultural, environmental, and ethical issues.

Feeding ourselves has long entangled human beings within complicated moral puzzles of social injustice and environmental destruction. When we eat, we consume not only food on the plate, but also the lives and labors of innumerable plants, animals, and people. This process distributes its costs unevenly across race, class, gender, and other social categories. The quotidian processes of food production and distribution can obscure the significance of these material and cultural connections, impeding honest assessments of our impacts on the world around us. By taking these relationships seriously, Food and Foodways provides a new series of critical studies that analyze the cultural and environmental relationships that have sustained human societies.

In *Food Studies in Latin American Literature: Perspectives on the Gastronarrative*, Rocío del Aguila and Vanesa Miseres have assembled thirteen essays that illustrate, as the editors so eloquently state, "what comes in and out of our mouths, whether food or words, will always reflect what we are, what we are made of, what we reject or hide, or what we find irrepressible." This important collection was inspired, as the very best scholarship is, by a sense of intellectual urgency. The contributors are united in their interest in the connections between the fields of Latin American literature and food studies as well as by their conviction that food—like literature—functions as a narrative as deserving of sustained analysis as textual sources. Until now, this group had not seen their intellectual questions adequately addressed by the scholarship in either field. They begin to fill this void by bringing their work to the common table of this collection with the hope that their efforts will both highlight current research on these subjects and inspire others to join this vibrant conversation.

Although shared concerns and thematic threads bind this volume together, it is also sweeping in its chronological and geographical scope.

The various authors engage with food stories taking place in locations ranging from Peru to New York, occurring from pre-Columbian times to today. In these pages, readers see how food can be used to unite people around a shared sense of identity or alternatively to distinguish one group from a purportedly undesirable "other." They witness historical and literary subjects using food as a metaphor and as a substance to tell stories of home, to navigate the unfamiliar spaces of travel, and to construct a multiplicity of ideas about nationality, gender, and race. The editors compellingly argue that across time and space "few great Latin American writers escaped the call of food." This collection validates the significance of listening to that call, providing a fresh lens for surveying the rich culture and histories of this complex, multifaceted region.

JENNIFER JENSEN WALLACH AND MICHAEL WISE

ACKNOWLEDGMENTS

After years of discussing how to teach our "food classes," we finally came to the realization, as Latin American literature professors, that there was little scholarship that supported our common interest in connecting food and literature, especially regarding Latin America. *Food Studies in Latin American Literature: Perspectives on the Gastronarrative* is the result of those conversations. Once we developed the concept for the book and what we envisioned for this volume, we moved on to the *mise en place*. Like the nineteenth-century women writers who have been the subject of our passionate research and publications, we reached out to our scholarly networks and convened an outstanding group of collaborators who brought our volume on literary food studies to life. After receiving their essays, we became convinced that this project would be a significant contribution to academic studies on both food and Latin American literature. We wish to express our appreciation to the brilliant scholars who have patiently worked with us to assemble the collection.

We would also like to acknowledge the diligent work of the editors of the Food and Foodways series at the University of Arkansas Press, who initially expressed their interest in our book and later answered all of our inquiries during the publication process: Jennifer Jensen Wallach and Michael Wise, history professors at the University of North Texas; and D. S. Cunningham, editor in chief at the University of Arkansas Press, who worked with us in reviewing the manuscript.

We both wish to thank our departments and institutions, the Department of Modern and Classical Languages and Literatures at Wichita State University, and the Department of Romance Languages & Literatures at the University of Notre Dame, respectively, for supporting us as we designed and now continue to teach our food studies courses. Both "Cooking Communities" at WSU and "From Texts to Table" at ND are courses where students and instructors alike always find intellectual discovery and growth. At Wichita State we would also like to recognize Wilson Baldridge for his heartfelt comments and Julie Henderson, whose style corrections have been invaluable. At Notre Dame, we offer our thanks to the Institute for Scholarship in the Liberal Arts for providing funds for editing the volume and to Omar Hamal for helping with translations.

We are deeply grateful to the wonderful women who have helped us reach our personal and academic goals. Some of them chose to work within the domestic space, while others felt trapped in it; still others we met within academia, but they all taught us how to put food on the table, literally as well as metaphorically. Your *saberes* keep nourishing our lives. We especially note Karina Vázquez's encouragement through scholarly comments, knitting patterns, and cake recipes. As feminists, we perceive the kitchen as a complex space that can be both constraining and liberating, and we will keep exploring its multiple meanings and power.

We offer our heartfelt thanks to our partners, Enrique and Juan, both of whom are also scholars, and to our children, Adrian and Isabella, for allowing us the time to work on this project and for their unwavering support. We will continue to research narratives related to food and cooking, and to incorporate culinary and social practices into our studies. To our future food historians who inspire us daily: once again, thank you!

FOOD STUDIES IN LATIN AMERICAN LITERATURE

INTRODUCTION

Toward the Construction of a Latin American Gastronarrative

ROCÍO DEL AGUILA AND VANESA MISERES

Food and eating are constantly used in metaphors throughout literature and our daily language to refer to topics such as life, death, love, and hate. How many times have we expressed that we cannot *stomach* someone? Or that we couldn't *digest* the news or the *unpalatable* truth? Who hasn't *devoured* a book in a couple of hours? Or has not *swallowed* his or her own words? These are not *cheesy* idioms or images at all. In his essay "Edible Écriture," Terry Eagleton offers a series of images and examples in which food, language, and literature appear inexorably intertwined.[1] The author mentions Francis Bacon's essay "Of Studies," in which the philosopher classifies books according to their ability to be tasted, swallowed, chewed, or digested. Eagleton also refers to *anorexic* texts such as Samuel Beckett's, "in which discourse is in danger of dwindling to a mere skeleton of itself," and analyzes Roland Barthes's structuralism as a *food menu* from which one has to select between linguistic axes (paradigmatic and syntagmatic), just as one would do with main courses and desserts.

Both Barthes and Eagleton confirm that food is never *just* food. The act of eating, according to the former, involves "a system of communication, a body of images, a protocol of usages, situations, and behavior."[2] Food, like literature, is an affective link and a communicative system. Eating and writing connect us with others, and depictions of food and culinary metaphors in literary works help to explain the complex interconnection among the body, subjectivity, and social structures. Looking at the connections between food and literature allows us, therefore, to analyze power structures, coloniality, the paradoxes of modernity and, in short, our own complexity as humans in terms of exchange: what comes in and out of our mouths, whether food or words, will always reflect what we are, what we are made of, what we reject or hide, or what we find irrepressible.

Warren Belasco has explained that food, being traditionally associated with concrete and corporeal experiences, was therefore not worthy of serious academic attention or philosophical inquiry. Belasco affirms that academia has inherited the Victorian tendency to the separation of spheres, the private versus the public, and that within this "institutionalized bias," food became a subject of study for the domestic disciplines that, given their nature, did not receive much academic prestige, "particularly dietetics, home economics, social work, and nutrition education."[3] Despite the feminist movements that began to challenge this private-public separation in the 1960s, scholars have perpetuated the "Victorian-era blinders and prejudices" and even now associate cooking and food matters with female enslavement and, therefore, consider them not to be "serious pursuits" for intellectuals.[4]

In this book, we view food as a narrative in and of itself, one that expresses aesthetic, political, and cultural statements. With chapters analyzing food and its connections to race, gender, politics, and national identity, the term *gastronarrative* serves as an overarching concept and method for contemplating food in relation to the literary text. In his classic study of the linguistic sign, Ferdinand de Saussure claimed that "it is the point of view which creates the object"; hence, in order to deconstruct this disdainful attitude toward food within the literary field, we need to start by creating our own *gastrolinguistic* sign. This is a relational sign that, like Saussure's, arbitrarily connects the signifier with the signified and will establish food and language as a point of departure for the creation of a narrative that defines itself in that very association. We can trace a gastrolinguistic sequence that goes beyond language, and it is in this surrounding space where meaning is created. The language of food takes place out of the mere verbal, in the semiotic field where it brings manifold significance even in the symbolic sphere, but remains discourse as it is expressed and represented through language. That is, we propose "gastronarrative" as a term both to describe our object of study (the connections between food and literature) and to refer to our methodology, which consists of analyzing literary texts as aesthetic and political formulations of a culinary and linguistic sign that is, at the same time, a channel for the expression of a specific period, society, or movement. In this sense, a gastronarrative is also semiotic, conveying all the cultural meanings and impacts of the written and the culinary worlds. It does not matter how brief the incidence of food is in the text, it is usually immensely vital to the narrative logic because the language of food tends to constantly resemanticize itself, and its mere presence implies meaningful connections to other discourses. Therefore, minutiae that might have been overlooked are brought to the nucleus of the analysis, and narrative examination is centered on the gastronomic.

Inspired by the concept of *gastrocriticism*, a term coined by Ronald Tobin to designate readings based on food and its concomitants, we believe that the correlation between what one eats and who one is can be seen as the very premise of gastronarratives.[5] Food systems inform literature. For this reason, we believe it is important to present some key moments in Latin American traditions in which foodways are central to the shaping of the continent's identity politics. What follows in the coming pages, then, is not just anecdotal references to food in Latin American literatures, but rather a reading exercise or, as Willa Zhen names it with a culinary term, a *mise en place* that brings food into the center of the literary scene.[6] As we arrange, select, and combine ingredients to create a dish, we take similar steps in order to approach and understand the essence of literary food studies in Latin America.

Food in Time and Place: Latin American Culinary Traditions and Narratives

In Latin America, the presence of food and food rituals is central in most visual and contextual expressions of culture and, since colonial times, edibles have served as a symbolic marker of identity. Pre-Columbian texts such as the *Popol Vuh* recount the legend of how man was created from corn, whose several varieties are the quintessential ingredient of numerous Latin American culinary specialties. Later, in the twentieth century, Guatemalan Nobel Prize winner Miguel Angel Asturias would delve into a clash between Western civilization and Mayan myths in his novel *Men of Maize* (1949). Similarly revealing are such stories as that regarding the cocoa beans Montezuma gave to Hernán Cortés, the roots that Cabeza de Vaca devoured to stave off hunger and starvation, and several others. In his first voyage to America, Christopher Columbus's description of the incredible diversity of fruits, vegetables, and tubers that indigenous people prepared in countless ways represents the difference and exuberance of this yet-to-be-named New World. For Columbus, food is also one of the reasons underlying his exploration—the search for spices—and constitutes a vital need to ensure his crew's survival.[7]

From the very first moment European and African populations set foot on the American continent, the foundations were established for new types and choices of foods and new patterns of consumption and preparation. European, indigenous, and African traditions all left their mark on New World cooking and eating, revealing the cultural exchange that occurred as well as the violence, negotiations, and power relations involved. Slavery gives rise to new economic systems and the continent takes its first early steps toward modernity and capitalism, all as a consequence of what anthropologist Fernando Ortiz calls the "counterpoint" (*contrapunteo*) between European and American commodities (sugar and tobacco in Ortiz's work).[8] Conquistadores' accounts, indigenous codices, and religious texts all refer to food as an intermediary and a regulator of social relationships.

With viceroyalties established, colonial societies demonstrated their sophistication through intricate cuisines, and convents jealously guarded their secret recipes for pastries and desserts. All the while, indigenous populations continued to use their traditional ingredients, and African slaves contributed their own techniques and flavors to the mix. The use of entrails, for instance, provided these communities with some animal protein intake even as it forced them to create new dishes. With help of native informants Fray Bernardino de Sahagún's *Historia general de las cosas de Nueva España* (General History of the Things of New Spain)—written, edited, and published between 1540 and 1585 and known as the *Florentine Codex*—offered a detailed account of the region's indigenous diet, food preparation, and markets, a vital space for both pre-Columbian and colonial foodways. One final telling example reflects the importance of food in society: *casta* paintings produced during colonial times portrayed people of specific races with particular types of food, inextricably linking the racial categories that were established to control and organize colonial society through the food that they consumed.[9]

During the nineteenth century, both before and after the wars of independence, food was central to shaping a modern concept of citizenship. It became crucial to distinguish not only what people ate but also how, where, and when they did so. Rituals around family meals helped to define the cultural separation between the domestic and public spheres and accompanied the rise of the middle class. For this reason, the inhabitants of the newly created countries witnessed the proliferation of manners and etiquette manuals that circulated transnationally between Europe and Latin America, whose rules were purposed to align the continent with the "modern" and "civilized" international (mostly French and Anglo-American) context. Among the most popular versions of these books on civility and refinement—*urbanidad*—are *Lecciones de urbanidad* (1877?) by Peruvian Bartolomé Trujillo and the *Código completo de urbanidad y buenas maneras* (1844) by Mexican Manuel Díez de Bonilla. The best example of this trend, however, is the best-selling book popularly known as *El manual de Carreño*, written by Venezuelan Manuel Antonio Carreño and first published in 1853. This manual educates the individual on "decent" behavior and elaborates on the moral and religious standards of nineteenth-century Western societies.

Essays, novels, and journal articles followed this pattern and stressed the importance of food preparation and consumption to convey key aspects of nineteenth-century everyday life, such as social classes, racial distinctions, and political struggles.[10] Education in etiquette was, of course, gender specific, and along with books dictating male conduct came an abundance of texts for the education of women, such as Soledad Acosta de Samper's "Consejos a Señoritas."[11] They extracted their models from Victorian society and introduced a modified version of an "angel in the house" as the ideal for feminine conduct. As the role of women was vital and constrained within the domestic sphere, their education on how to prepare and serve a proper meal, for instance, provided a marker of the whole family's social status. We see this portrayed in novels such as *María* (1867) by Jorge Isaacs, *Cecilia Valdés* (1882) by Cirilo Villaverde, and *Aves sin nido* (1889) by Clorinda Matto de Turner.

Travel writing was also important for transnational exchanges and to increase awareness of the many cultures within Latin America in the nineteenth century, even for Creole intellectuals, criollos, who shaped their ideas about their own nations following the models and descriptions proposed by foreign travelers. Figures such as the German explorer Alexander von Humboldt or the French Peruvian writer and socialist activist Flora Tristan used food discourse in different ways, but frequently it served to reinforce their own European subjectivity from which they judged the location and people they visited. During this period in particular, Latin Americans would also start traveling more frequently to Europe. In the Old World, and in France in particular with Jean Anthelme Brillat-Savarin's influential gastronomical study *The Physiology of Taste*

(1825), the ruling elites would seek culinary inspirations even as they proudly expounded on their own customs, or *costumbres*, including some indigenous traditions.[12] *Cocina ecléctica* (Eclectic Cuisine, 1890), by Argentine writer Juana Manuela Gorriti, perfectly exemplifies how the relevance of food, manners, transnational exchanges, and gender expectations intertwined in this type of work.[13] In her cookbook, Gorriti subversively adheres to a domestic narrative of the above-mentioned "angel of the house" as she calls on a wide range of women writers, cooks, and ladies from the Latin American elite to submit a recipe of their preference. The selections present us with patriotic and nationalist elements ("dorado a la San Martín," a fish recipe in honor of South American independence leader José de San Martín) combined with cosmopolitan taste, as seen in "gallina a la persa" (Persian hen), a recipe brought by a contributor's father from a world's fair. We also find local adaptations using traditional Western ingredients such as oysters; the influence of African servants in *sollito mojarra* (another fish recipe), whose authorship is ascribed to a Black woman ("la negrita Encarnación"); and indigenous techniques and recipes including Quechua names such as *chicha*, *humintas*, or *huatia*.[14]

The "food plot" in the twentieth century was the next development, serving as a metaphor for political dissent and a way of proclaiming civil rights and gender equality.[15] In her testimonial account, indigenous leader Rigoberta Menchú establishes the dichotomy between bread (*pan*) and tortilla to express the ignorance of Guatemalan politicians with respect to indigenous communities and their traditions. As General Kjell Laugerud promised the peasants land and bread in return for their vote on his electoral campaign, Menchú, indignant, recalled: "They have to say bread, they can't even say tortilla. Most of them don't even know what Indians eat."[16] On another note, some women writers resisted and others found an alternative language to express themselves in the space of the kitchen. This tension, which had already appeared decades before in Gorriti's culinary project, reemerges in *Like Water for Chocolate* (1989) by Mexican author Laura Esquivel. Each chapter of Esquivel's novel begins with a recipe for a dish that Tita, the main character, cooks during that section. Food is, therefore, central to the novel's structure and meaning as it expresses the developments in both the plot and the characters' lives. The relationship of women with food and the kitchen seems to constrain them within traditional female domestic roles but, at the same time, it provides them with a sphere in which they can find freedom and cultivate their creativity and sorority.

Few great Latin American writers escaped the call of food and, consequently, it is possible to find not only memorable food-related literary moments, but also complicated food abstractions in many of their works. The classic novel *One Hundred Years of Solitude* (1967) by Gabriel García Márquez devotes its first page to the moment when a main character touches a block of solid ice for the first time. The surprise that this new technology produces engages the reader from the very first page and allows us to understand the complexity of modern times in Latin America. In the current context, food in the region persists as a manifestation of all of these relationships, and it also works as a reflection on contemporary phenomena such as immigration, consumerism, political and economic violence, and the role of the continent in the Global South. In Argentina, writer and poet Washington Cucurto offers a pan-Latino consciousness by centering his poems and stories in the poor neighborhoods of Buenos Aires, taking up the narrative of a new wave of immigrants who come to the country from Peru, Bolivia, Paraguay, or the Dominican Republic. Cucurto revises nineteenth-century parameters of national identity and debunks the myth of a white Argentina, portraying instead a "tropicalized" country no longer shaped by European models but by Latin American immigrants with their food, music, and other cultural practices. Food and immigration are also connected in Elizabeth Acevedo's *With the Fire on High* (2019), a novel that narrates the dreams and burdens of a young Afro-Latinx woman through cooking. In Peru, Gustavo Rodríguez echoes the global boom of Peruvian cuisine with his novel *Cocinero en su tinta* (2012). The book was involved in a huge controversy after writer Ivan Thays invoked it in an article in which he criticized Peruvian cuisine, confirming that citizens view national identities as closely connected to each nation's food.[17] A similar rationale is the backbone of "Marca Perú" (Peru Brand), the branding of the country itself launched by a branch of the government; it is similar to other nation-branding strategies in that it relies heavily on its culinary strength and multicultural identity perception.

Numerous scholarly works on Latin America have focused on the relationship between food and several aspects of its societies such as agriculture, labor movements, food industry, consumption policies, indigenous and mestizo foodways, inequalities and poverty, dietary issues such as diabetes and malnourishment, internal and external migrations, and national cuisines. Within the cultural perspective, a particular interest in Latin America has been noted through the impact on Latinx habits and traditions in American society. *Taco USA* (2012) by Gustavo Arellano, *Latino Food Culture* (2008) by Zilkia Janer, An van Hecke's articles on Sandra Cisneros's work, *Latin@s' Presence in the Food Industry* (2016) edited by Meredith Abarca and Consuelo Carr Salas, or *Decolonize your Diet*, the blog and cookbook project created by Luz Calvo and Catriona R. Esquibel, to name only a few, evidence the interdisciplinary academic interest in tracing the historical Latinx presence in American foodways, food industry, and culinary traditions.[18] Additionally, María Claudia André and Meredith Abarca have adopted a gendered perspective to study the role of the kitchen as an empowering space for Chicanas and Mexican American women.[19]

In the field of history, significant contributions have come from Rebecca Earle (*The Body of the Conquistador: Food, Race and the Colonial Experience in Spanish America, 1492–1700*, 2012; and *Potato*, 2019), Jeffrey Pilcher and his numerous studies on food in Mexico and the Mexican American population, Rebekah Pite (*Creating a Common Table in Twentieth-Century Argentina: Doña Petrona, Women, & Food*, 2013), Deborah Toner (*Alcohol and Nationhood in XIX Century Mexico*, 2015), Cruz Miguel Ortiz Cuadra (*Eating Puerto Rico: A History of Food, Culture, and Identity*, 2006), and Arnold Bauer (*Goods, Power, History: Latin America's Material Culture*, 2001). Although some of these works take literary texts as sources for their analysis, we found the need to publish a volume in which literary matters and food connect beyond the representational level and lead us to the creation of a gastrocriticism specific to the Latin American context.[20]

Our Scheme: Connecting Food, Narrative, and Identity

Food Studies in Latin American Literature: Perspectives on the Gastronarrative is the first English-language volume to offer an overview of literary food studies focusing exclusively on Latin America. Similar works in Spanish that precede it include *Conquista y comida: Consecuencias del encuentro de dos mundos* (1996), devoted exclusively to the period of the conquest, and *Comidas bastardas* (2013), a collection of essays that focuses on racial issues such as *mestizaje*, as well as such traditional topics in Latin American literature as cannibalism through food identities of the continent.[21] Other works by Renée Sum Scott, Maite Zubiaurre, Rita de Maeseneer, and Nina Scott have addressed literature and food in specific regions, time periods, and/or authors.[22] In this book, we do not limit ourselves to literature, but rather insert literary topics, metaphors, and strategies as vital to discussions on food within the humanities. We analyze manuscripts, magazine articles, cookbooks, menus, etiquette manuals, popular advertising, material and visual cultures, and of course, literature from pre-Columbian times to the present. We offer narratological and historiographical inquiries; analyses of the intersection of race, gender, and class; consumption and consumerism; and culinary imaginaries, origins, and mapping of culture based on food and foodways on the continent.

Although the expansion of food studies is novel in the field of the humanities—and certainly extremely limited in relation to literary studies—the emergence of the discipline can be traced back to the 1960s, and it has evolved thanks to anthropology (Claude Lévi-Strauss and Mary Douglas), history (Marc Bloch, Jean-Louis Flandrin, and Massimo Montanari), and sociology (Norbert Elias, Pierre Bourdieu, and Claude Fischler). With this interdisciplinary base in mind, our goal is to address food topics and the cultural phenomena surrounding them in order to consolidate basic concepts that will encourage the conversation of how to analyze the role of food in Latin American narratives, as well as the importance of doing so. Hence, this volume opens up the literary field to unexplored expressions and materials (the language of food) while expanding food studies to aesthetic discourses and practices that are not usually incorporated as an object of study by other disciplines.

Each contributor offers a fundamental step toward a gastronomic discourse of *latinoamericanidad*, what Latin America represents as a continent in its narratives and culinary traditions. The essays address the political and ideological implications of connecting language, aesthetics, and food. They prove that food is not only an effective linguistic tool, but also a political metaphor and communicative system; it is, as previously mentioned, the gastrolinguistic sign created by our point of view, one through which to read Latin America. It is not feasible to understand the Central America that Columbus encountered without understanding the concept of the banana republics and how the fruit companies helped shape these countries. Sugar, tobacco, and the sweat of the Black population will become part of the production of these countries. Language and food are even connected in the Caribbean islands, which were named after the Caribs, a dominant tribe in the region that Columbus mistook for cannibals and therefore feared becoming their food.

The chapters that follow are organized thematically into four different sections, since we consider it equally important to describe the main cycles experienced in the continent with respect to these issues and to propose a more nuanced view of food and narratives, one that simultaneously challenges both national boundaries and time periods. Thus, the thematic sections add another distinctive characteristic to our work. Differing from previous historical approaches, we do not limit the project to one single nation, ethnicity, cultural group, tradition, or era. Part I focuses on indigenous traditions, food legacies, and exchanges from colonial Mexico and Peru and their impact on the contemporary cultural and political issues of the two nations that were, at one time, centers of their corresponding indigenous civilizations and later the oldest viceroyalties. Studying pre-Columbian and colonial diets represents, for example, a significant contribution toward understanding concepts such as decolonization—that is, the undoing of the colonial matrix in societies and thinking paradigms—which can be recently found as a trend of studies not limited only to Latin American food studies. The debates around a "modernized" Latin American table, and between national identities and transnational relations, are the focus of Part II. The significance of defining concepts and perceptions is crucial to the chosen authors within their zeitgeist and allows the reader to understand Latin American nation-states from their formation to the present, passing through a history of wars, appropriation, and economic paroxysm. The articles provide different approaches to understanding food representation, biopolitics, and cultural contacts within narratives of discord and tragedy. Part III echoes the debates around gender currently flourishing in Latin America, especially after local movements such as Ni Una Menos (Not One Less), offering a wide range of readings about women and their complex connections with food and the domestic space of the kitchen. If some sectors of feminism felt confronted by culinary studies, it could be due to the aforementioned perception that the kitchen was a containment space for women, part of the "gilded cage," and that these studies would constitute a setback. The truth is quite the opposite. Analyses of the private space and of material culture have brought to light women's strategies of resistance and empowerment. To an extent, we could affirm that food studies are a pillar supporting gender studies. It is relevant to understand that some feminist groups take advantage of unusual places and use different strategies for enfranchisement. Therefore, trying to understand the kitchen as a place from which power emerges can open up new reading options such as the ones suggested by our contributors in this section. Questions that are pending within the feminist agenda could be addressed in this field: the authority of the male chef versus the knowledge of the female cook, mapping sororal spaces through the kitchens and recipes, supposedly "natural" activities for women, and so on. The last section, Part IV, provides us with some ideas on how to read food from aesthetic and historiographical discourses, as well as the importance of doing so from a pedagogical point of view. It constitutes, in consequence, a solid contribution to the creation of the field of Latin American gastrocriticism and the design of a unique gastronarrative for the continent.

Part I begins with Alison Krögel's analysis of the significance of cultivating, preparing, and consuming food in Andean narratives and verse. She argues that descriptions of food and cooks creatively encode natives' resistance to marginalizing power(s) in colonial and contemporary Andean contexts. In chapter 2, Regina Harrison offers an interdisciplinary approach to the history of potatoes, examining the intrinsic connections between botanical research, local and global perspectives, native peoples, knowledge systems, and the image of the tuber in popular written and visual culture. The third and final chapter of the section discusses the intricate world of Sor Juana Inés de la Cruz and her love of food. Paola Jeannete Vera Báez and Ángel Tuninetti study Sor Juana's recipe manuscripts and other culinary comments from colonial convents in New Spain. The study of cooking manuscripts from convents opens a window to understanding how culinary practices and traditions created a mestizo cuisine during the New Spain Viceroyalty. It shows, at the same time, that Sor Juana transformed the kitchen from a place of penance to a place of learning and reflection, as she expressed in her well-known text *Response to Sor Filotea*, written in 1691.

Part II follows with Lee Skinner's "Immigrants, Elites, and Identities: Representing Food Cultures in Nineteenth-Century Latin America." Skinner examines representations of food and eating in Mexico and Peru, countries that experienced waves of immigration from France, Germany, Italy, and China. As the continent began to open up to free trade, with the proliferation of restaurants owned and operated by immigrants and the increasing business of food and beverage imports, food and eating habits were used to comment on and to represent individuals' and nations' relations to modernity, progress, and elite status. In chapter 5, Mercedes Lopez Rodriguez focuses on alimentary encounters in nineteenth-century travel writing on Colombia, including those of Jean-Baptiste Boussingault, Elisée Reclus, and Latin American authors such as Manuel Ancízar and José María Samper. Delving into emotions, Lopez Rodriguez analyzes male travelers' attitudes when confronted with native food: disgust, fear, discomfort, and even frustration. Food as a cultural artifact, concludes the chapter, allows for the exploration of awkward materialities (sticky, dusty, among many others), and the emotional reactions that they trigger can be interpreted as a way of exploring fears of racial and class contamination. Vanesa Miseres also addresses nineteenth-century Latin American foodways with a reading of Eduarda Mansilla's travel to the United States. In the second half of the century, when the United States' expansionist policies were threatening the rest of the American continent, Mansilla makes use of manners and food habits as a mark of differentiation of Latin American identity while traveling around North America.

Part III, which is devoted to gender relations with food, opens up with Sandra Aguilar-Rodríguez's contribution "Homemaking in 1950s Mexico: Women, Class, and Race through the Kitchen Window." In this chapter, she explores gender and race in Mexico between 1930 and 1960 from the perspective of cookbooks and appliance brochures by analyzing both the content and images in such publications. Aguilar-Rodríguez studies how traditional knowledge and culinary practices continued to be deemed as inferior to European and US practices, under a discourse of modernization and *mestizaje*. Elizabeth Montes's work focuses on Mexican writer Rosario Castellanos's short story "Cooking Lesson." Her theoretical approach draws from the cultural geographer Doreen Massey on the sense of place, and from Nancy Duncan on the public and the private. Montes examines the construction of roles and spaces through focalization and irony in order to illustrate how Castellanos defies the cartographies assigned to her gender in the 1960s, particularly in the private spaces of the bedroom and the kitchen. In chapter 9 Nina Namaste focuses on "Marina y su olor" by Puerto Rican author Mayra Santos Febres. In this story, Namaste discovers an expression of power conflicts derived from racial, class, and gender struggles. As with Lopez Rodriguez's nineteenth-century travelers, emotions and senses are likewise important. Relying on a cultural studies approach and a detailed textual analysis, Namaste proposes that olfactory control of both foodstuffs and emotions directly contributes to the development of main character Marina's identity as a Black Hispanic woman. Lastly, chapter 10 closes the section with Karina Vázquez's reading of "El budín esponjoso" by Argentine writer Hebe Uhart. In this essay, Vázquez analyzes how this emblematic short story cooks up a critique of the consumption that governs gendered class relations and class prerogatives and transforms the Argentine middle-class concept of taste.

The last section, Part IV, is no less groundbreaking than the previous ones. Here, Ignacio Sánchez Prado analyzes Mexican writer Salvador Novo's perception of Mexico City cuisine. Dialoguing with the work of Caroline Levine, this essay proposes the idea of a poetics of gastronomic history to account for the ways that writings about food may be read within literary criticism. For Sánchez Prado, the literary genre of the *crónica* provides Novo a window to perform a type of culinary critique that neither anthropologists nor chefs could achieve. Therefore Novo's *Cocina mexicana* proves that gastronomic history is a cultural form very closely intertwined with literary forms and styles. Similarly, Ángel Tuninetti explores the different dimensions of the politics of food in the work of Argentine writer and chronicler Martín Caparrós. Tuninetti addresses the relationship between metafiction, abundance, and hunger using the concept of *pornocrónica*, an adaptation of the term "food porn" created by Rosalind Coward in *Female Desires: How They Are Sought, Bought and Packaged* (1985). Tuninetti argues that the attitude of the *cronista*, and by extension the reader, when confronted with the literary recreation of the realities of hunger, reproduces the "pleasure in looking at the supposedly forbidden," a reminiscence "of another form of guilty-but-indulgent looking, that of sexual pornography."[23] The last study in this section is Russell Cobb's "American Counterpoints: *Barbacoa* and Barbecue beyond Nation," in which he develops a translational and literary history of this dish across the Americas. From its etymology to the nationalist ideas surrounding it, Cobb discusses how even today we can perceive through this food cultural traces persisting through the centuries from the time of Columbus. María Paz Moreno closes this collection with an epilogue that reflects on the relevance of studying food-related texts and other aesthetic expressions from Latin American traditions. Why, in other words, this gastronarrative matters.

While we wanted to be comprehensive, there are some authors, literary genres, and concepts dealing with foodstuffs and food consumption that we could not include in this work. José Lezama Lima and Tununa Mercado, Pablo Neruda's odes to food, the enormous field of Brazilian literature itself, and the topics of cannibalism and anthropophagy, whose numerous references and meanings in Latin American cultural, social, and political history have been addressed several times in a wide range of critical analyses; these are just a few of the sources we have had to omit. We have also purposely left out Latinx cuisine because it is precisely the area that has enjoyed more critical production recently in terms of analyses of identity and power through culinary culture. The volume, however, addresses this vital topic tangentially, as some of the studies touch on the subject of the Mexican American people and the African diaspora.

We believe that the area of food studies, particularly when focused on regions such as Latin America, matters more than ever. In our current political climate, studying food and its representations inspires critical thought, inclusiveness, and hope. The academic interdisciplinary experience of food studies has been productive and has provided new understandings of old subjects.

We need to bring these interdisciplinary practices to our work as educators and scholars. Nevertheless, we don't want to appeal only to scholars; rather, we would encourage students and general audiences to read this book. Through proper critical analysis, we wish to shed light on the immense language that is food and, to repeat a term used in our first paragraphs, we would like everyone to *devour* these pages. The emotional value of words and food are always intersecting. Food brings emotions back to our palates and souls. Food conjures up memories, brings places to mind, simultaneously evokes both flavors and sorrows. Whether you read and cook in the classroom or at home, in a large group or alone, *Food Studies in Latin American Literature: Perspectives on the Gastronarrative* aspires to be a path for both experiences and to make them available to everyone in the field of food studies and beyond. ¡Buen provecho!

Notes

1. Terry Eagleton, "Edible Écriture," in *Consuming Passions: Food in the Age of Anxiety*, ed. Sian Griffiths and Jennifer Wallace (Manchester: Mandolin, 1998), 204–5.
2. Roland Barthes, "Toward a Psychosociology of Contemporary Food Consumption," in *Food and Culture*, ed. Carole Counihan and Penny Van Esterik (New York: Routledge, 2008), 29.
3. Warren Belasco, *Food: The Key Concepts* (London: Bloomsbury, 2008), 2–3.
4. Belasco, *Food*, 3.
5. Maria Christou, *Eating Otherwise: The Philosophy of Food in Twentieth-Century Literature* (Cambridge: Cambridge University Press, 2017), 7.
6. Willa Zhen, *Foods Studies: A Hands-on Guide* (London: Bloomsbury, 2019), 4.
7. Nina M. Scott, "La comida como signo: Los encuentros culinarios de América," in *Conquista y comida: Consecuencias del encuentro de dos mundos*, ed. Janet Long (Mexico City: Universidad Nacional Autónoma de México, Instituto de Investigaciones Históricas, 1996), 145–47.

8. See Fernando Ortiz, *Contrapunteo cubano del tabaco y el azúcar* (Havana: J. Montero, 1940).
9. Nina M. Scott, "Measuring Ingredients: Food and Domesticity in Mexican Casta Paintings," *Gastronomica* 5, no. 1 (Winter 2005): 70.
10. For an analysis focused on the concept of a national cuisine during the nineteenth century, see Rocío del Aguila, "Cocinando la nación. Representaciones del capital cultural en *Cocina ecléctica*," *Diálogo* 18, no. 1 (2015): 67–78, where she analyzes Juana Manuela Gorriti´s work and the network of women intellectuals in South America. In another article, she discusses the gastronomic concepts that Clorinda Matto uses in her first book to represent the Andean traditions of the new nation-state of Peru. See Rocío del Aguila, "Una mirada al pasado culinario en *Tradiciones cuzqueñas*," *Comida y bebida en la lengua española, cultura y literaturas hispánicas*, ed. Andjelka Pejović, Mirjana Sekulić, and Vladimir Karanović (Kragujevac, Serbia: University of Kragujevac, 2012), 375–87.
11. See Soledad Acosta de Samper, *La mujer: revista quincenal exclusivamente redactada para señoras y señoritas*, January–June 1880, May 1881, https://soledadacosta.uniandes.edu.co/items/show/638.
12. Gastronomy in France came to prominence, as almost a cultural field of its own, during the nineteenth century. The gastronomic writings of critics, epicures, and gastronomes who adopted the responsibility of formalizing this phenomenon were crucial in the mechanism that allowed the culinary to become culture. The fascination with the French tradition was possible in part by the textual production of many authors such as Grimod de la Reynière, Marie-Antoine Carême, and, of course, Anthelme Brillat-Savarin, whose book *Physiologie du goût* [The psychology of taste] (1825) was extensively mentioned by his contemporary Spanish American intellectuals.
13. Elisabeth Austin studies the tensions between patriarchal thinking and a feminist glimpse in *Cocina ecléctica*. See Elisabeth Austin, "Reading and Writing Juana Manuela Gorriti's *Cocina Ecléctica*: Modeling Multiplicity in Nineteenth-Century Domestic Narrative," *Arizona Journal of Hispanic Cultural Studies* 12, no. 1 (2009): 31–44. For an analysis of cookbooks and their impact in regional formulations of national identity, see Arjun Appadurai.
14. Juana Manuela Gorriti, *Cocina ecléctica*, in *Obras completas* (Salta, Argentina: Fundación del Banco del Noroeste, 1994), 3:233; 179–80.
15. Michael Parrish Lee, *The Food Plot in the Nineteenth-Century British Novel* (London: Palgrave Macmillan, 2016).
16. Quoted in Nina Scott, "Rigoberta Menchú and the Politics of Food," *Revista Harvard Review of Latin America*, Spring 2001, https://archive.revista.drclas.harvard.edu/book/rigoberta-mench%C3%BA-and-politics-food.
17. Daniel Alarcón, "Contra la gastronomía peruana," January 3, 2017, in *Radio Ambulante*, produced by Daniel Alarcón, podcast, accessed January 19, 2020, http://radioambulante.org/audio/contra-la-gastronomia-peruana-2.
18. See Gustavo Arellano, *Taco USA: How Mexican Food Conquered America* (New York: Scribner, 2012); Zilkia Janer, *Latino Food Culture: Food Cultures in America* (Westport, CT: Greenwood Press, 2008); An Van Hecke, "'As Black as Huitlacoche.' La comida mexicana en *Caramelo* de Sandra Cisneros," *Foro*

Hispánico 39 (2010): 161–79, and "Sabores y aromas de México: la comida en la obra de Sandra Cisneros," *The Shade of the Saguaro: Essays on the Literary Cultures of the American Southwest* 18 (2013): 333–42; Meredith Abarca and Consuelo Carr Salas, *Latin@s' Presence in the Food Industry* (Fayetteville: University of Arkansas Press, 2016).

19. See María Claudia André, *Chicanas and Latin American Women Writers Exploring the Realm of the Kitchen as a Self-Empowering Site* (Lewiston, NY: Edwin Mellen Press, 2001); Meredith Abarca, *Voices in the Kitchen: Views of Food and the World from Working-Class Mexican and Mexican American Women* (College Station: Texas A&M University Press, 2006). On Chicano literature, see also Nieves Pascual Soler and Meredith Abarca, *Rethinking Chicana/o Literature through Food: Postnational Appetites* (New York: Palgrave MacMillan, 2013).
20. Ronald Tobin, "Qu'est-ce que la gastrocritique?," *Dix-septième siècle* 217, no. 4 (2002): 621–30.
21. See Janet Long, *Conquista y comida: Consecuencias del encuentro de dos mundos* (Mexico City: Universidad Nacional Autónoma de México, 2003); Ángeles Mateo del Pino, *Comidas bastardas: Gastronomía, tradición e identidad en América Latina* (Santiago: Cuarto Propio, 2013).
22. See Renée Sum Scott, *What Is Eating Latin American Women Writers? Food, Weight, and Eating Disorders* (Amherst, NY: Cambria Press, 2009); Maite Zubiaurre, "Culinary Eros in Contemporary Hispanic Female Fiction: From Kitchen Tales to Table Narratives," *College Literature* 33, no. 3 (Summer 2006): 29–51; Rita de Maeseneer, "La comida en Cecilia Valdés," *El Festín de Alejo Carpentier. Una lectura culinario-intelectual* (Geneva: Librairie Droz, 2003), and *Devorando a lo cubano. Una aproximación gastrocrítica a textos relacionados con el siglo XIX y el Período Especial* (Madrid: Iberoamericana Vervuert, 2012); Nina Scott, "Measuring Ingredients," *Gastronomica* 5, no. 1 (Winter 2005): 70–79. Some other edited volumes have intended to cover similar topics, see Rita de Maeseneer and Patrick Collard, eds., *Saberes y sabores en México y el Caribe* (Amsterdam: Rodopi, 2010); Anđelka Pejović, Mirjana Sekulić, and Vladimir Karanović, eds., *Comida y bebida en la lengua española, cultura y literaturas hispánicas* (Kragujevac, Serbia: University of Kragujevac, 2012), a trilingual volume in English, Spanish, and Serbian; and the bilingual English and Spanish volume "Mestizaje and Gastronomy: What Latinos Eat," *Diálogo* 18, no. 1 (Spring 2015). In a similar fashion, *Cualli*, the journal of Latin American and Iberian Food Studies Review from Kennesaw University, produced one digital volume in 2012. Rebecca Ingram (University of San Diego), who usually focuses on Spanish literature and culture, has been working with Lara Anderson (University of Melbourne) on an edited volume on Transhispanic food cultural studies that should see light in the near future in the *Bulletin of Spanish Studies*.
23. Rosalind Coward, "Naughty but Nice: Food Pornography," in *Ethics: A Feminist Reader*, ed. Elizabeth Frazer, Jennifer Hornsby, and Sabina Lovibond (Oxford: Blackwell, 1992), 101.

PART I

Culinary Fusion

Indigenous Heritage and Colonialism

CHAPTER 1

Food, Power, and Discursive Resistance in Tahuantinsuyu and the Colonial Andes

ALISON KRÖGEL

Sapachallaykim / kanki / urway saracha jina . . . / Mamayki/ Pachamamam / huk weqe qochata . . . / taytaki / Apu intiña-taqmi / wayrata / paskirqamurqa/ rimayniyki / kay pachapi uyarikunampaq / ¡wamanchallay! (All alone / you are / like a solitary maize stalk . . . / your Mother / the Earth Mother / unleashed a lagoon of tears / your father / Father Sun / unleashed the wind / so that in this world / your voice / might be heard / Wamanchallay!)

—Dida Aguirre, "Sapachallaykim" ("All alone," in Jarawi)

The use and application of power frequently enter into changes in a society's food consumption habits. Where this power originates; how it is applied and to what ends; and in what manner people undertake to deal with it, are all part of what happens when food habits change.

—Sidney Mintz, *Tasting Food, Tasting Freedom*

For centuries, food has played a symbolic role in Andean ritual practices: as a sacrificial offering, a medium of communication, or as an amulet meant to bring future prosperity. Pizarro's arrival to South American shores in 1532 precipitated the conquest of one of the world's great empires—the Inca "land of the four *suyus* [regions]" known in the Quechua language as Tahuantinsuyu.[1] Colonial documents suggest that both before and during the Inca reign throughout the Andes, food served as an indispensable element of the religious ceremonies and incantations performed by Andean ritual specialists. Under Inca rule, the planting, harvesting, and distribution of food was closely monitored and controlled by authorities in Cusco, and the local headmen or curacas of conquered provinces were required by Inca overlords to extract labor tribute from their communities in the form of crops or textiles.[2] The Quechua verb used to designate the offering of a sacrifice to a deity is *mikhuchiy* or "to feed," and Inca rulers highly valued both women and food as tribute and sacrificial "items." Conquered groups were required to send to Cusco their most precious food (high-quality crops—particularly corn—destined for sacrifice to the sun god Inti) and "chosen women" (dedicated to Inti as his "wives," or *aqllakuna*). Occasionally, during celebrations such as the Capacocha festival, women and food were fatally joined as sacrificial gifts offered to Inti.[3] Vanquished groups who rebelled against their new Inca overlords were also required to send both food and women to Cusco as reparations for their insubordination.[4]

In the royal quarters known as *aqllawasi*, which housed and trained the tribute women in Cusco and throughout Tahuantinsuyu, the precious "wives of the Sun" would receive annually allotted portions of the sacred corn grown on the islands of Lake Titicaca. The colonial chronicler Inca Garcilaso de la Vega relates:

> [From the sacred island located in Lake Titicaca workers] harvested some cobs in a limited quantity which were taken to the King as a sacred thing . . . and of these he sent some to the chosen virgins [*aqllakuna*] who were in Cusco and he ordered them to be taken to the other convents and temples [*aqllawasi*] which were located throughout the kingdom . . . so that they might enjoy that grain which was like a thing brought down from the heavens.[5]

The Incas believed that deities such as their creator god Wiracocha and the sun god Inti, as well as their sacred ancestors, controlled the viability of their empire's crops. Since Andean deities decided whether to bestow or withhold food from human believers, the Inca royalty in Cusco devoted an incredible amount of ritual energy to performing food-centered incantations, ceremonies, and sacrifices for these divine power holders. As Irene Silverblatt points out, as the Incas successfully expanded their vast territorial holdings—surprisingly, in just over one hundred years—they were "continuously sparring to impose their economic and cultural ways, just as those ways were unevenly resisted, distorted, resigned to, or accepted by [conquered peoples]."[6] The reciprocal and ritual exchange of food, food labor, and women as gifts, tribute payments, or as religious offerings played a key role in these processes.[7]

In the sixteenth-century Andes—as in many other regions of the world throughout history—conquistadores, priests, and colonial administrators attempted to realize their respective ambitions through a combination of military, spiritual, linguistic, and gastrocolonization of indigenous peoples and their cultures. Although historians and linguists have made important inroads into the study of the sociocultural and political impacts of colonial-era language policies, scholars of the colonial Andes are just beginning to come to understand the important implications of gastrocolonization in the Viceroyalty of Peru.[8] Food practices, like language, possess important symbolic and pragmatic functions and features—attributes that a colonized or subjugated people must often aggressively defend in the face of the destructive ambitions or homogenizing intentions of a hegemonic power. Similar to their attempts to restrict the use of the Quechua language for purposes not directly linked to the church, Spanish colonial policies also sought to reorient Andean agricultural production practices toward the cultivation of European crops.[9] During the era of the colonial Viceroyalty of Peru (1542–1824), indigenous and mestizo visual and verbal artists often integrated representations of food into their work as a tool for obliquely critiquing the excesses of an oppressive colonial regime. Moreover, references to certain Andean foods allowed colonial-era writers and visual artists to venerate symbolically and ritually significant victuals within a society that actively sought to repress indigenous Andean cultural and religious practices.

The Andean "food-landscape"—a term I use to refer to the multitude of nuanced details involved in cultivating, preparing, serving, and consuming different foods—became one of the many spaces where Spanish colonial power holders sought to exercise dominance, while also serving as a medium for both the conquerors and the conquered to express their own cultural, religious, and political identities and loyalties. The term

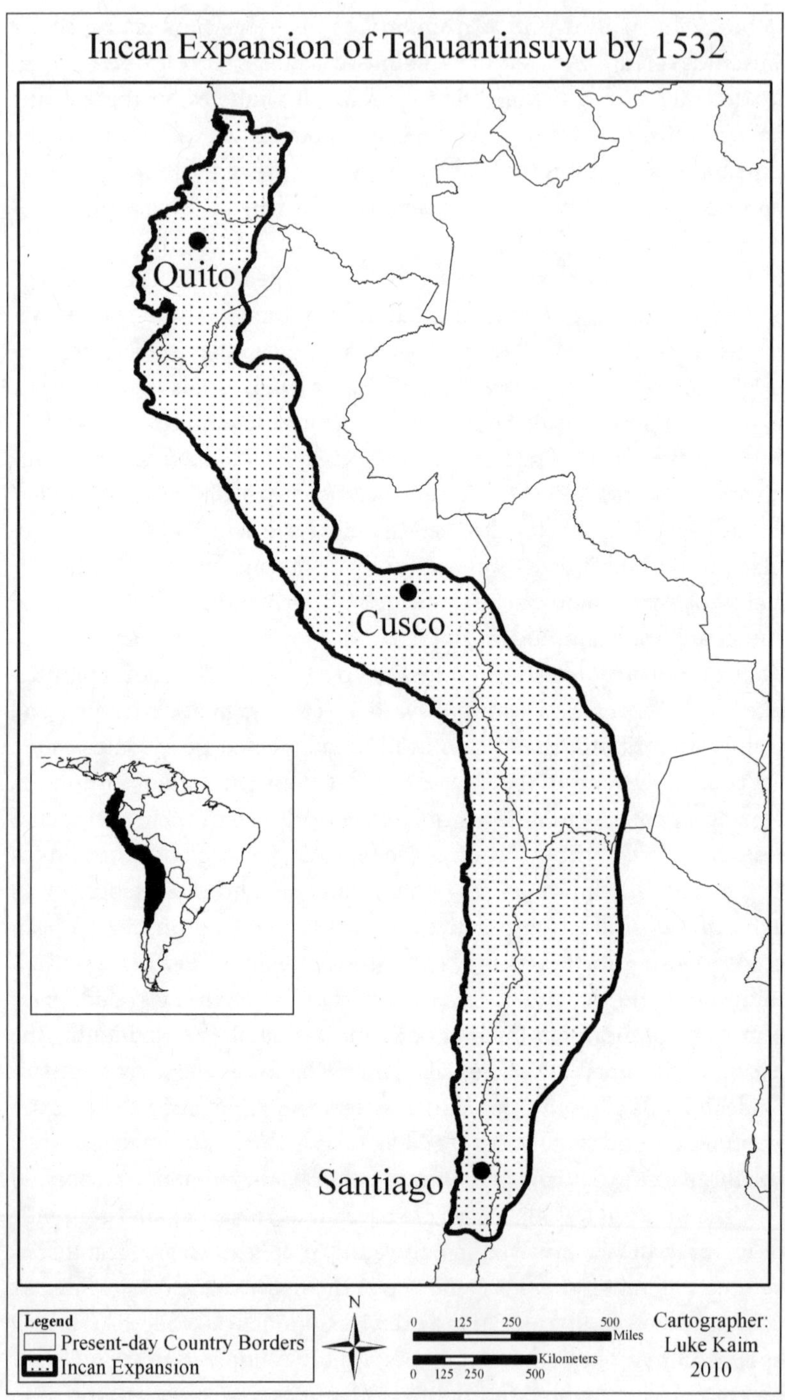

Map of Tahuantinsuyu, Inca Expansion by 1532. *Courtesy Luke Kaim.*

"food-landscape" reinforces the important connection between alimentary and agricultural practices, and in my discussion of food production, consumption, and identity politics in Tahuantinsuyu and colonial Peru, I use the term to refer to the ways in which both discursive meanings associated with food as well as pragmatic food practices were altered or redefined within the colonial context.[10] During the early years of the conquest and throughout the colonial era, the unbridled chaos and violence; devastating epidemics; cultural trauma; methodical destruction of Andean religious practices, sites, and relics; and general plundering of Andean institutions and economic, political, and social structures greatly disrupted the carefully administered and ritually vital food-landscape of Tahuantinsuyu. Moreover, colonial Spanish administrators disturbed intricate cultural and religious aspects of Andean alimentary practices and cycles by disrupting preconquest production and distribution systems and by controlling or inhibiting the consumption of certain food items.

Although indigenous communities in the Andes beyond Cusco were already accustomed to paying tributes to their Inca overlords, unlike the Spaniards, Inca rulers had demanded food tributes from fields designated for the production of state crops. Thus if harvests were poor in a particular year the state absorbed the loss; communities were never asked to pay tribute in food produced on lands designated for their own subsistence.[11] Yet it is interesting to note that evidence from colonial-era documents suggests that after the conquest, Andean indigenous communities (or ayllus) continued to designate a portion of their agricultural land for state tribute payments (now handed over to the Spanish), while primarily cultivating native Andean crops on lands allocated for ayllu subsistence.[12] Since colonial sources rarely discuss the role of domestic food production, scholars are mostly left to speculate about how the shift from Inca to Spanish colonialism affected the daily lives of Andean commoners within provincial ayllus. We do know, however, that with the discovery of silver in Potosí in 1545 (and to a lesser extent, the mercury deposits found in Huancavelica in 1560), the Andean highlands were rapidly transformed into an active, international marketplace. Quechua farmers, cooks, and weavers from the Cusco region produced and transported many of the food crops and textiles purchased in the Potosí marketplace and these men and women quickly became adept participants in the interregional mercantile economy of the early colonial era.[13] As the Spanish colonial chronicler Pedro de Cieza de León disapprovingly remarks, many of the indigenous men working in Potosí spent their daily wages indulging in their cravings for any number of dishes sold by the Quechua cooks in the plaza: "And since they earned daily wages, and since these Indians are such friends of food and drink . . . they spent all their wages on the [foods] which were brought to market."[14]

Although this emerging market economy in colonial Spanish America encouraged the exploitation of indigenous labor, it also created economic opportunities for indigenous women who worked as independent sellers, market merchants, cooks, owners of dry goods stores, or even long-distance traders.[15] Indeed, the economic and social opportunities and relative freedom of movement that often accompanied an indigenous or mestiza woman's employment in colonial maize-beer taverns (*chicherías*), market food stalls, and restaurants remained beyond the reach of higher-class women whose social position precluded them from working in public spaces.[16] Moreover, market participation often served as a tactic by which Quechua families managed to accumulate enough currency to satisfy Spanish tribute requirements without having to pay with their own agricultural products.[17] Ironically then, indigenous Andeans' participation in the mercantilist economy instituted by the Spaniards seems to have oftentimes alleviated further outside interference in their ayllus' economic, political, and cultural practices.

Clearly then, indigenous Andeans did not passively accept Spanish attempts to impose changes on their alimentary and agricultural practices and preferences and they often found creative ways to resist colonizing efforts to disrupt or stigmatize their food-landscapes. For example, the association between the Spanish military conquest and the Spaniards' subsequent efforts at gastrocolonization were so inextricably linked in the minds of many indigenous Andeans that one of the central prohibitions for participants of Taqui Onqoy—the indigenous rebel movement that swept through the Andes in the 1560s—included a pledge to shun any foods of Castilian origin.[18] Moreover, sixteenth- and seventeenth-century accounts of the food-landscapes of early colonial Peru written by indigenous, mestizo, and Spanish chroniclers often reveal indigenous Andeans' deep pride and preference for their own food-landscapes, as well as their frustration with colonial attempts to interfere with Andean food culture.[19]

Following the conquest, the Andean food-landscape became one of the many spaces where colonial powerholders (both Spaniards, as well as indigenous or mestizo curacas) sought to exercise dominance. For instance, in the *Comentarios reales* (the Royal Commentaries of the Incas)—Inca Garcilaso de la Vega's best-known text—the author refutes, critiques, and corrects the work of Spanish chroniclers writing during the conquest of Peru and the early colonial era, prior to the arrival of viceroy Francisco de Toledo in 1569.[20] Born in the former Inca capital city of Cusco, just seven years after Pizarro's arrival in Peru, Garcilaso was a self-conscious narrator. Throughout the *Comentarios* he repeatedly asserts that his unique family tree, with its maternal branches of Inca royalty and paternal roots in Extremadura, provides him with singular qualifications "as an Inca Indian" for accurately describing Inca rites and customs.[21]

Writing from Córdoba some twenty-five years after having left his homeland for Spain at the age of twenty-two, in his account of Inca history and society, Garcilaso takes great care to present the inhabitants of Tahuantinsuyu as intelligent, hardworking, and benevolent people living in a society more sophisticated in many aspects than that of Renaissance Europe. Interestingly, in many instances throughout the *Comentarios reales*, descriptions of the Andean food-landscape serve as a narrative device for introducing Garcilaso's European readers to positive aspects of Tahuantinsuyu, and to unseemly traits of the Spanish. In this way, the intricately crafted representations of food in the *Comentarios reales* serve as a valuable window into the complex and often devastating sociopolitical, economic, and cultural aftershocks felt throughout the Andes in the years following the conquest of the Incas.

Monstrous Radishes and Gold-Eating Spaniards: Food Metaphors in the Chronicles of the Inca Garcilaso and Guaman Poma de Ayala

Throughout the *Comentarios reales*, Garcilaso uses his representations of food as a tool for presenting Inca rulers as capable administrators and benevolent conquerors, while indirectly presenting Spanish conquistadores as inept and irrational in their attempts to disrupt the Incas' methods for administrating the Andean food-landscape. For instance, when chronicling precolonial military practices, Garcilaso explains that Inca soldiers often overtook their poorly equipped adversaries quite easily. In order to spare their wives and children from the threat of death or starvation, the ill-prepared and vanquished enemy would often quickly surrender. As the son of an Inca noblewoman, Garcilaso was always eager to present the Incas as benevolent colonizers (in contrast to the Spanish), and he asserts that once enemy soldiers laid down their arms, "The Incas . . . gave them gifts and soothed them and fed them."[22]

In the fifth book of the *Comentarios reales*, Garcilaso explains that as soon as a new territory had been conquered, the Inca ruler would dispatch engineers from Cusco to begin the construction of irrigation canals.[23] Census takers would appear soon afterward in order to determine the new province's population. An Inca ruler and his provincial administrators could then use this demographic data to make decisions regarding the quantity and type of agricultural infrastructure required in the region, the amount of tribute payments that could be expected, as well as the number of manual laborers needed to complete the arduous process of creating arable, mountain terraces.[24] While Inca rulers did require subjects to divide agricultural plots into three sections belonging to Inti, the Inca ruler/Cuzco, and the local ayllu, Garcilaso insists that this practice was always carried out with careful attention to the needs of each local community

> so that they would have a surplus rather than be in want. And when the people of the town or province increased in number, they [the rulers] would take away the Sun's portion and the Inca's portion for the [benefit of the] vassals; in this way the King did not take anything for himself, nor for the Sun except for the lands that would have remained deserted, without an owner.[25]

As in many parts of the *Comentarios*, here Garcilaso leaves unsaid what may have been his principal point: that, in contrast to Inca policies, Spanish colonial agricultural administration and taxation practices often left many indigenous Andeans in want, while the Spanish Crown (and its Spanish, mestizo, and indigenous local administrators) profited handsomely from the land and labor of indigenous commoners.[26]

Garcilaso dedicates chapters IX–XVI of the *Comentarios*' Book 8 to a description of the varieties of fruits, vegetables, grains, and livestock native to Peru. He carefully describes each foodstuff, notes any medicinal value it may possess, and details the necessary steps for preparing each item. Garcilaso scoffs at the careless manner in which the Spanish desecrated the original names of various foods to the extent that "nothing remains but a corruption of all the other names they have given them."[27] He also chastises himself when he cannot recall the names of certain fruits, "because of the distance of the place and the absence of my people I will not be able to find out the answer very easily."[28] Garcilaso enthusiastically praises Andean foodstuffs such as llama meat and the *uchu* pepper as finer than similar foods available in Europe; even the Spaniards, he tells us, realized that the Peruvian *uchu* is superior to the "oriental varieties."[29]

Garcilaso dedicates several chapters of the *Comentarios reales* to outlining the competition between Andean foods and those brought from Europe.[30] He sardonically relates the "anxiety" that plagued the Spaniards until they were able to cultivate their own Iberian fruits, vegetables, and grains.[31] In order to illustrate his portrayal of Spanish colonizers' dreams of achieving a large-scale agricultural and gastronomical transformation in the Andes, Garcilaso cites a royal decree in which Carlos V offered two silver bars of three hundred ducats each to the first Spaniard who could successfully produce *medio cahíz* (approximately nine and a half bushels) of wheat or barley, or *cuatro arrobas* (approximately twelve gallons) of olive oil or wine:

> The Catholic Monarchs [Ferdinand and Isabella] and the Emperor Charles V had declared that the first who, in any town of Spaniards, could reap a certain quantity of new Spanish fruits such as wheat, barley, wine or oil would be given from the royal treasury a jewel and two bars of silver worth three-hundred ducats each.[32]

While Garcilaso admits that the new Spanish crops initially impressed indigenous Andeans, he primarily emphasizes the Europeans' amazement at the astonishing abundance and high quality of the Iberian crops that they soon began to harvest in Peru.

The introduction of Spanish seeds into Andean soils, however, could also wreak havoc on native species. Garcilaso laments that many Spanish flowers and herbs proliferated to such an extent that

> now there is such abundance that many of them are now very damaging . . . they have spread so much in some valleys that they have defeated human force and diligence, everything possible has been done to pull them out, and they have prevailed to such an extent that they have erased the name of the valleys and forcing them to be called by their name, such as the Valley of Mint [*yerbabuena*] on the seacoast which used to be called *Rucma*, and other [valleys are] the same.[33]

Immediately following this tale of botanical and appellative assault, in which the Spaniards' *yerbabuena* mint plant supplants both the valley's native name and crop (the fruit called *rucma* or *lúcuma*), Garcilaso relates the shocking case of a disproportionately large radish. He describes the root as being "of such strange greatness that in the shade of its leaves five horses were tied up . . . a monstrous thing."[34] Garcilaso corroborates his report by citing the testimony of a "gentleman" named Don Martín de Contreras, "nephew of the famous Governor of Nicaragua Francisco de Contreras" who declared to the chronicler, "I am an eyewitness to the greatness of this radish from the valley of Cuzapa."[35] Garcilaso's witness even suggests that such gigantic vegetables are not particularly unusual in colonial Peru, affirming that he once "ate from a head of lettuce that weighed seven and a half pounds" and that in the Ica valley he once witnessed a melon so huge that its size was recorded by a notary "in order to document such a monstrous thing."[36]

As Roberto González Echevarría points out, in the *Comentarios reales* Garcilaso almost always uses the adjective "monstrous" to refer to inordinate size.[37] Yet his use of the adjective also reflects the negative, unnatural connotations that have been associated with the word since Roman times and are evident in the definition of "monster" provided by Sebastián de Covarrubias Orozco's early seventeenth-century Spanish dictionary (*Tesoro de la lengua castellana, o española*), published just five years before Garcilaso's death in 1616. In his dictionary, Covarrubias defines "monstro" as "any birth which goes against natural law and order."[38] While one may argue that Garcilaso's descriptions of the "strange greatness" (*extraña grandeza*) of these giant cultivars can be interpreted as an example of his admiration of the great scale of Spanish cultivars harvested in Peru, this seems unlikely given that his testimonies of the unnatural births of these monstrous vegetables immediately follow his account of the "damaging" abundance of many Iberian plants that "have vanquished human strength and diligence in spite of all efforts to uproot them."[39] Moreover, the juxtaposition of the noun "greatness" with the adjective "monstrous" in this chapter creates the clever effect of linking these two qualities in the reader's mind in order to suggest that at some point the enormous sizes of these vegetables leads one to deem them as "frightening and incredible" (*espantables e incréibles*).[40]

Julio Ortega refers to these same passages as part of Garcilaso's "discourse of abundance," arguing that descriptions of the "abundance of Spanish transplants" (gigantic radishes, lettuces, and Spanish herbs) growing in the Andes reflect the chronicler's attempts to present "more proof of historic providentialism" resulting from a fertile mixture of European seeds and Andean soils.[41] According to Ortega's analysis, gigantic vegetables and rapidly spreading herbs signal a new "abundance" that resulted from a mixture of the new and the old world, and that Garcilaso's descriptions of vegetable abundance serve as a natural model for hybrid cultural processes and reinforce his argument that the mixing, or *mestizaje*, of plants, humans, and cultures can breed positive results.[42] I would argue that Garcilaso—undoubtedly aware of the censorial powers of the Inquisition—took advantage of these pages of seemingly innocuous alimentary descriptions in his *Comentarios* to laud the virtues of the Andean food-landscape and to focus attention on the stark reshaping of Andean cultural practices following the arrival of the Spaniards. It seems quite plausible that in these passages from the *Comentarios*' Book 9, monstrous radishes and lettuce and the insatiable spreading of mint plants serve as a metaphor for the greedy appetites of Spanish conquistadores and colonists whose plants caused great destruction to the food-landscape of many regions throughout the colonial Andes. As with other Golden Age writers such as Calderón de la Barca, Garcilaso's use of the adjective "monstrous" to describe Spanish cultivars likely served to signify the chaos and confusion of the sociohistorical context in which the plants took root in New World soil.[43]

Like Garcilaso's *Comentarios reales*, many passages in Felipe Guaman Poma de Ayala's nearly twelve-hundred-page chronicle, *El Primer nueva corónica i buen gobierno* (1615), also feature alimentary descriptions that critique the greedy excesses of Spanish colonial policies and practices. The indigenous chronicler and artist Guaman Poma praises the stunning variety of crops cultivated in the Andes and denounces the Spaniards' callous destruction of the Inca alimentary infrastructure in a much more direct and caustic tone than that used by Garcilaso. One of the key critiques of Spanish colonialism advanced by Guaman Poma centers around his denunciation of what he perceives as the Iberians' excessive greed and dishonorable treatment of indigenous Andeans and their cultural practices and values. He often uses descriptions of food to illustrate Spanish injustices perpetuated against indigenous Andeans.

One of the more humorous of the 398 illustrations included in Guaman Poma's *Nueva corónica* depicts an encounter the author imagines as having taken place between the Inca ruler Huayna Capac (father of Húascar and Atahualpa) and a Spanish explorer who preceded Pizarro's arrival. Through both words and image, Guaman Poma highlights Huayna Capac's observation of the Spaniards' insatiable interest in gold. In the chronicler's representation of the exchange, the words of the Inca ruler reveal his assumption that the strange, bearded man's voracious appetite for the gleaming metal can only be explained by the fact that he can, in fact, *eat* gold. This hypothesis leads the dignified-looking Inca to ask the Spaniard kneeling before him, "Do you eat this gold?" ("Kay quritachu mikhunki?") The oafishly depicted Spaniard replies with a vacant expression, "We eat this gold" ("¿Este oro comemos?").[44] Huayna Capac's logic reflects the fact that in Tahuantinsuyu—a civilization whose strength and well-being depended heavily on abundant, reliable harvests and healthy herds—food, not gold, was the most prized commodity.[45]

Yet clearly, Guaman Poma also seeks to demonstrate that the Spaniards were interested in pillaging more than just the precious metals of Tahuantinsuyu. The chronicler denounces, in great detail, the manner in which the Spaniards abused the Inca system of *tambu* (storehouses, alternatively spelled *tanbo*), and he enumerates all of the goods and services nabbed from the indigenous custodians of these food depositories:

> Said Spanish travelers, even if they are priests who pass along the royal roads and tanbo, how they arrive angrily at said tanbos, seize the Indian custodians of the tanbos . . . and ask for Indians whom they might force into mitayos [servitude] and much camarico [a coveted product], and so on with maize and potatoes and llamas and chickens and eggs . . . and ch'uñu [preserved potato], quinua [highland seed], chiche [small fish] and chicha [maize beer] and blankets of chuci and pots.[46]

In this and similar passages, Guaman Poma creates a rhythmic mesodiplosis (the repetitive use of a word in the middle of successive sentences) by preceding the name of each food item seized by the Spaniards with the conjunction "and." This technique serves to emphasize the extent of the exploitation inflicted upon indigenous Andeans within the reader's mind, while simultaneously demonstrating the rich diversity of the Quechua food-landscape.[47] As Ortega has pointed out, these critiques of the disorder and abuses propagated by colonial officials serve as a primary image and symbol of colonial violence and pillaging.[48] In this way, Guaman Poma's descriptions of food become one of his central metaphors and serve as a "powerful version of the violence, and of the irrationality of colonial practices which destroy other knowledges and instead, disseminate want."[49] Thus, Garcilaso and Guaman Poma, two of the best-known chroniclers of colonial Peru and Tahuantinsuyu, both utilize the trope of food to critique Spanish colonial excesses, as well as the colonizers' destruction of Andean alimentary infrastructures and the subsequent

“Conquista: Gvaina Capac Inca, Candía Español,” from Felipe Guaman Poma de Ayala, *Nueva corónica y buen gobierno (Codex péruvien ilustré). Travaux et Memoires de L’Institut d’ethnologie* (1615; repr., Paris: L’Institut d’ethnologie, 1936), 23:369. The 1936 edition is based on the original manuscript GkS 2232, 4to, Royal Library of Denmark, Copenhagen.

disease, destitution, and death that afflicted indigenous Andeans throughout the Viceroyalty of Peru.

■ ■ ■

This chapter's consideration of the manner in which Inca Garcilaso de la Vega and Felipe Guaman Poma de Ayala describe particular aspects of the Andean food-landscape within colonial Peruvian society serves as an example of the numerous ways in which food (and descriptions of food) became a medium for expressing cultural, ethnic, and religious identities and loyalties, while also serving as a tool for denouncing the perceived shortcomings (or abuses) of other groups. If representations of food in Tahuantinsuyu's religious rituals and hymns primarily focused on creating a balance of praise and petitions directed toward Inca deities, in post-conquest colonial Peru, representations of food by Guaman Poma and Garcilaso often served as subtle, low-risk tools for disseminating positive depictions of indigenous Andean culture, history, and traditions and for celebrating Andean agricultural bounty and innovation. In the incredibly tumultuous context of the sixteenth- and seventeenth-century colonial Andes, food preferences, practices, and policies became a multivalent discursive space wherein Spanish attempts to devalue and dismantle certain aspects of the cultural, religious, and community identities associated with indigenous Andean food-landscapes were continually contested.

Notes

1. Beginning in the early fifteenth century until the conquest of the Spanish in the 1530s, the Incas expanded their empire from their political center in the city of Cusco to encompass parts of present-day Ecuador, Bolivia, northern Chile, southern Colombia, and northwestern Argentina. Tahuantinsuyu eventually extended more than 350,000 square miles (906,500 square kilometers) and included such varied terrains as high-altitude grassy plateaus (*punas*), low-lying jungles, deserts, coastlines, and fertile river valleys. See John V. Murra, *La organización económica del estado Inca* (Mexico City: Siglo XXI, 1983), 57–82.
2. Murra, *La organización*, 3–14. Elizabeth Ramírez also discusses the complexities of preconquest reciprocity politics in Tahuantinsuyu's provinces as they relate to the roles played by local curacas and the food tributes they were required to pay to Cusco. See Susan E. Ramírez, *To Feed and Be Fed: The Cosmological Bases of Authority and Identity in the Andes* (Redwood City, CA: Stanford University Press, 2005), 59–112. Following the Spanish conquest, local curacas from ethnic groups recently vanquished by the Incas often allied themselves with Spanish colonizers in an interethnic collaboration they hoped would help them attain

greater provincial sovereignty. In this way, the provincial curacas' "appropriation of intrusive Spaniards both challenged and generated colonialism, and defies reduction to either tendency alone." Peter Gose, *Invaders as Ancestors: On the Intercultural Making and Unmaking of Spanish Colonialism in the Andes* (Toronto: Toronto University Press, 2008), 15. Rebecca Earle also highlights the importance of avoiding analyses which describe colonial power structures in terms of fixed and disconnected categories of the "European" and the "indigenous." Rebecca Earle, *The Body of the Conquistador: Food, Race and the Colonial Experience in Spanish America 1492–1700* (Cambridge: Cambridge University Press, 2012), 1–18.

3. Peter Gose, "The State as a Chosen Woman: Brideservice and the Feeding of Tributaries in the Inka Empire," *American Anthopology* 102, no. 1 (2000): 84.
4. Irene Silverblatt, *Moon, Sun, and Witches: Gender Ideologies and Class in Inca and Colonial Peru* (Princeton, NJ: Princeton University Press, 1987), 92.
5. Inca Garcilaso de la Vega, *Comentarios reales* (1609; repr., Mexico City: Porrúa, 1998), 138. Translations from the Spanish and the Quechua in this essay are my own.
6. Irene Silverblatt, "Imperial Dilemmas, the Politics of Kinship, and Inca Reconstructions of History," *Comparative Studies in Society and History* 30, no. 1 (1988): 99.
7. Gose, "The State as a Chosen Woman," 84–86.
8. See Earle, *The Body of the Conquistador*, for a sweeping study of the importance of food to the colonial project in Spanish America, as well as how anxieties about the foods of the "other" shaped constructions of race and difference in the New World.
9. George Kubler, "The Quechua in the Colonial World," in *Handbook of South American Indians: The Andean Civilizations*, ed. Julian H. Steward (Washington, DC: Smithsonian Institution, 1946), 2:355; Nathan Wachtel, *The Vision of the Vanquished: The Spanish Conquest of Peru through Indian Eyes, 1530–1570*, trans. Ben Reynolds and Siân Reynolds (New York: Harper and Row, 1977), 143; Earle, *Body of the Conquistador*, 158–186.
10. For a more extensive discussion of the notion of the Andean food-landscape as it relates to colonial and contemporary Quechua verbal and visual art, see Alison Krögel, *Food, Power, and Resistance in the Andes* (Lanham, MD: Lexington Books, 2011). For an extended version of several of the analyses presented in this essay, see also Alison Krögel, "Food Production, Consumption, and Identity Politics in Tahuantinsuyu and Colonial Perú," in *Routledge History of Food*, ed. Carol Helstosky (New York: Routledge, 2014), 19–41.
11. Karen Spalding, *Huarochirí: An Andean Society under Inca and Spanish Rule* (Redwood City, CA: Stanford University Press, 1984), 159–63.
12. Steven J. Stern, "The Variety and Ambiguity of Native Andean Intervention in Markets," in *Ethnicity, Markets, and Migration in the Andes: At the Crossroads of History and Anthropology*, ed. Brooke Larson and Olivia Harris (Durham, NC: Duke University Press, 1995), 81–82.
13. Stern, "The Variety," 73.
14. Pedro Cieza de León, *Crónica del Perú: el señorío de los Incas*, ed. Franklin Pease (1550; repr., Caracas: Biblioteca Ayacucho, 2005), 273.

15. Susan Migden Socolow, *The Women of Colonial Latin America* (New York: Cambridge University Press, 2000), 41.
16. Socolow, *The Women*, 114.
17. Stern, "The Variety," 90.
18. Sara Castro-Klarén, "Dancing and the Sacred in the Andes: From Taqui-Oncoy to Rasu-Ñiti" in *New World Encounters*, ed. Stephen Greenblatt (Berkeley: University of California Press, 1993), 168–69.
19. Garcilaso, *Comentarios reales*, 416; Kubler, "The Quechua in the Colonial World," 346; Wachtel, *The Vision*, 142–44; Marcos Jiménez de la Espada, *Relaciones geográficas de Indias: Perú, 1577–1586*, ed. José Urbano Martínez Carreras (Madrid: Atlas, 1965), 1:234.
20. Scores of scholarly studies examine the life, work, and intellectual and historical milieu of Inca Garcilaso de la Vega. See Margarita Zamora, *Language, Authority, and Indigenous History in the Comentarios reales de los incas* (New York: Cambridge University Press, 1988); José Antonio Mazzotti, *Coros mestizos del Inca Garcilaso: resonancias andinas* (Lima: Fondo de Cultura Económica, 1996); and D. A. Brading, "The Incas and the Renaissance: The Royal Commentaries of the Inca Garcilaso de la Vega," *Journal of Latin American Studies* 18, no. 1 (1986): 1–23.
21. Garcilaso, *Comentarios reales*, 4–6, also 13.
22. Garcilaso, *Comentarios reales*, 237, also 37–38.
23. Garcilaso, *Comentarios reales*, 169.
24. Garcilaso, *Comentarios reales*, 169–70.
25. Garcilaso, *Comentarios reales*, 170.
26. See Gose, *Invaders as Ancestors*, 14–35, for an astute discussion of the fact that the Spanish could not possibly have conquered Tahuantinusyu or administered it throughout the colonial period without the significant assistance of mestizo and indigenous collaborators. As Gose points out, "colonial incorporation was (and still remains) a two-way street. Colonizers subsumed the colonized by definition, but the reverse was no less true. European colonists depended on indigenous practices to recruit labour and to govern. . . . Such practices were not just sites of colonial power but also points of European vulnerability, where indigenous people could encompass them with their own sociability and assimilate them to their own institutional norms," (15).
27. Garcilaso, *Comentarios reales*, 350.
28. Garcilaso, *Comentarios reales*, 349.
29. Garcilaso, *Comentarios reales*, 351, also 357.
30. Garcilaso, *Comentarios reales*, 406–24; see also Julio Ortega, "Discourse of Abundance," trans. Nicolás Wey Gómez, *American Literary History* 4, no. 3 (1992): 374–81; and Julio Ortega, *Transatlantic Translations: Dialogues in Latin American Literature* (London: Reaktion Books, 2006), 57–58.
31. Garcilaso, *Comentarios reales*, 416.
32. Garcilaso, *Comentarios reales*, 417.
33. Garcilaso, *Comentarios reales*, 420.
34. Garcilaso, *Comentarios reales*, 421.
35. Garcilaso, *Comentarios reales*, 421.
36. Garcilaso, *Comentarios reales*, 421.

37. Roberto González Echevarría, *Celestina's Brood: Continuities of the Baroque in Spanish and Latin American Literature* (Durham, NC: Duke University Press, 1995), 101–2.
38. Sebastián de Covarrubias Orozco, *Tesoro de la lengua castellana, o española* (Madrid: Imprenta Luis Sánchez, 1611), 554r, http://fondosdigitales.us.es/fondos/libros/765/16/tesoro-de-la-lengua-castellana-o-espanola/. See also González Echevarría, *Celestina's Brood*, 96–97.
39. Garcilaso, *Comentarios reales*, 420.
40. Garcilaso, *Comentarios reales*, 422.
41. Julio Ortega, "Leer y describir: el Inca Garcilaso y el sujeto de la abundancia," in *El hombre y los Andes: homenaje a Franklin Pease G.Y.*, ed. Javier Flores Espinoza and Rafael Varón Gabai (Lima: Pontificia Universidad Católica del Perú Fondo Editorial, 2000), 1:402; and Ortega, *Transatlantic Translations*, 56.
42. Ortega, "Leer y describir," 402; Ortega, "Discourse of Abundance," 377; and Ortega, *Transatlantic Translations*, 56–57. Earle also discusses the Spanish discourse of abundance as it related to a belief in providentialism in early colonial Peru, as well as the Spaniards' interconnected projects of evangelization and transforming indigenous dietary habits in *The Body of the Conquistador*, 17–26, 156–59. Among other fascinating documents, Earle quotes a royal order from 1573 stating Spaniards should regularly remind indigenous peoples that they had certainly benefitted from colonization since in this way they had come to know "bread and wine and oil and many other foods." "Ordenanzas de su magestad hechas para los nuevos descubrimientos, conquistas y pacificaciones," July 13, 1573, quoted in Earle, *The Body of the Conquistador*, 166.
43. I am indebted to González Echevarría for this reading of Garcilaso's representation of vegetable abundance in Peru. In chapter four of his book *Celestina's Brood*, he demonstrates how the figure of the monster in Calderón's play *La vida es sueño* (1635) becomes an emblem of chaos and confusion and a means for the playwright's conveyance of shock and surprise to his audience; *Celestina's Brood*, 82–83.
44. Felipe Guaman Poma de Ayala, *El Primer nueva corónica y buen gobierno*, ed. John Murra and Rolena Adorno, trans. J. L. Urioste (1615; repr., Mexico City: Siglo XXI, 1980), 2:342–43.
45. See also Ortega, *Transatlantic Translations*, 68–69. The Incas' appreciation of the aesthetic effects produced by gold and silver ornaments is evident in the descriptions of the gold leaved walls of Qoricancha (the "Temple of the Sun"), as well as the many sacred objects that Inca artisans fashioned from the precious metals. Indeed, the Incas honored their staple foodstuffs by creating golden replicas of each crop within Cusco's Qoricancha temple (Garcilaso, *Comentarios reales*, 135).
46. Guaman Poma de Ayala, *Primer nueva corónica*, 2:500.
47. As proof that there is "more than enough bread in this kingdom," Guaman Poma's "First Chapter of the Christian Indians" includes an even longer and more detailed list of foods cultivated and enjoyed by indigenous Andeans; see *Primer nueva corónica*, 2:840–41. Hamilton suggests that Guaman Poma's penchant for exhaustive lists such as these may reflect his familiarity with quipus,

the knotted cords used by the Incas for recording Tahuantinsuyu's history, as well as its military, political, and agricultural administration; Felipe Guaman Poma de Ayala, *The First New Chronicle and Good Government: On the History of the World and the Incas up to 1615*, trans. Roland Hamilton (Austin: University of Texas Press, 2009), xix.

48. Julio Ortega, "Guaman Poma y el discurso de los alimentos," in *Reflexiones lingüísticas y literarias: Literatura, II*, ed. Rafael Olea Franco, James Valender, and Rebeca Barriga Villanueva (Mexico City: Centro de Estudios Lingüística y Literatura, Colegio de México, 1992), 145; and Ortega, *Transatlantic Translations*, 73–76.
49. Ortega, "Guaman Poma," 145.

CHAPTER 2

The Potato

Culture and Agriculture in Context

REGINA HARRISON

Too often the potato is disparaged for its lowly origins and referred to with derisive slurs: spud, couch potato, potato head, hot potato, small potatoes.[1] Nevertheless, the humble potato has gained in stature because millions of people depend upon this staple in their daily diet; the tuber is the most important non-grain crop in the world. The United Nations declared a "Year of the Potato" in 2008 to acknowledge the Andean origins of this underground rhizome that is now cultivated in vast expanses. Global dependence on the tuber has called for renewed scientific interest: pinpointing the domestic hearth of the potato, analyzing the potato blight of past centuries, noting nutrient contents and agricultural crop yields. Similarly, writers, filmmakers, and indigenous community leaders have also documented the considerable cultural importance of the Andean tuber in songs and poems, colonial histories, narratives, and films.

Potato Origins: Spanish Chronicles

References to the potato in the early colonial period are hybrid texts of scientific and cultural descriptions; all note it as an important foodstuff. The Spanish encounter with new geographies, civilizations, and foods was often expressed with prose of awe and wonder as well as accurate attention to botanical detail. One early description of a truffle-like underground plant is narrated by Juan de Castellanos, who lived in Nueva Granada (now Colombia) as a priest and was ordained in Cartagena in 1553. He notes the dependence of the indigenous populations on this food as a staple in their diet. In the northern Andes it is called a *yoma* (not a *papa*), but acute readers understand from his description of the leaf and details of the tuber that it must be the potato:

> Houses are all stocked with corn, beans, *turmas* [truffles] (rounded roots that are planted and produce a stalk with branches and leaves), and rarely flowers of a soft purple color. And attached to the roots of that plant, which is some three *palmos* of height [sixty centimeters] under the earth, are [truffles] about the size of an egg, some round and others long in shape, white and purple and yellow, [having] floury roots with a good taste, a welcome gift among the Indians, and even among Spaniards seen as an exquisite dish.[2]

Another enthusiastic soldier-chronicler, Pedro de Cieza de León, traveling in the Viceroyalty of Peru in the mid-sixteenth century, rightly calls them *papas* (or potatoes) and gives us details based on comparisons with European plants:

> They call [them] *papas*, a thing that is sort of a testicle of the earth [*turma de tierra*], that after cooking are soft inside like a chestnut. They do not have an outside shell or a fruit stone inside . . . because it is born under the earth like a *turma*. This fruit produces an above-ground growth more or less like a field poppy.[3]

A chestnut, a field poppy, and a truffle-like tuber are the closest comparisons Cieza de León can come to identifying the plant that is, as he recognized, "the principal sustenance among the Indians."[4]

In the seventeenth century, Bernabé Cobo devoted an entire chapter of his *Historia del nuevo mundo* (1653) to the *papa*. A resident of Peru, he also noted the widespread consumption of potatoes by native inhabitants of the Andes: "half of the indigenous have no other bread."[5] He provided a thorough botanical description of the above-ground plant as well as the underground tubers:

> The plant attains a height of two *palmos* [about forty centimeters]; the leaves . . . are similar to the leaves of lemon balm. The flower is bell shaped, a little bigger than the *alhelí* . . . some are purplish and others are white as well as other colors. After flowering, a little fruit emerges that is of no use, like *alcaparrones* [capers].[6]

He then waxes on about the potato tuber itself, alluding to the many varieties: "Potatoes differ from each other in size and taste; the large ones are the size of a fist and others the size of a chestnut, but the common ones are the size of a chicken egg. They are of all colors: white, yellow, purple, and red."[7] Cobo must have enjoyed culinary delights. He notes that Spanish women prepare delicious *buñuelo* (biscuit) fritters and all sorts of gift-worthy sweet desserts filled with almonds and sugar and made from *chuñu* (dehydrated potato) flour as well as from the common potato.[8]

Cobo was aware of the importance of the freeze-drying techniques common to *chuñu* potatoes, and he devoted descriptive passages enthusiastic about the process developed in the Andes:

> [*Chuñu*] is dried in this manner. Harvest time for potatoes is in the months of May and June, when the harshness of cold and frost begins in these lands; well, then they harvest them and spread them out on the earth, where they get sun in the daytime and frost in the nighttime, and at the end of twelve to twenty days they are wrinkly but still watery. Then, to squeeze out the rest of the water in them, they stomp on them very well and leave them in the sun and frost another fifteen or twenty days. At the end of that time, they become as dry and as lightweight as cork—dense, stone-like and solid so that from four or five bushels of raw potato only one *chuñu* results. The *chuñu* is so well preserved that, even though it is stored for many years, it does not rot or decompose and Indians eat it as their bread.[9]

The principles of dehydration were long understood by Andean natives. Cobo also extols the curative properties of potatoes: raw potato consumed after a meal cures indigestion, gout is cured with application of a warm tuber paste. He notes that *chuñu* in powder form heals up the most persistent of wounds.[10]

These scientific chroniclers of the seventeenth century provide us with a means of tracing the mysterious introduction of the potato to the Old World. Legends abound: most notably, credit is bestowed on Sir Walter Raleigh or Sir Francis Drake for bringing the potato to Europe. However, this supposition was disproved by the potato specialists J. G. Hawkes and J. Francisco-Ortega, who searched the archives of a hospital in Seville (La Sangre) and discovered bills of lading listing bags of potatoes bought for consumption in 1573.[11] In pursuit of even earlier dates, these researchers found conclusively that potatoes were being grown in the Canary Islands by 1567 and from there were shipped to Europe.[12]

Potato: An Everyday Staple Receives Scant Praise

While some chroniclers offered abundant commentary praising the potato, in reality other early modern writers gave little heed to the plant and instead waxed enthusiastically about corn. Similarly, indigenous peoples in the Inca territories seemed to prize corn more: corn was the item frequently offered in rituals, corn was the high-status food, and corn was valued because of its superior storage qualities. Much more attention was devoted to the growing of corn, which demanded elaborate irrigation systems, terraces, and fertilizer to grow in the protected areas of the Andean terrain. Corn attracted notice; corn (the "wheat of the Indies") was conceptualized as God's gift to the Europeans in many of the reports written for Spanish administrators.[13]

The drawings sketched by the Amerindian writer Felipe Guaman Poma de Ayala, in his one-thousand-page-long chronicle, reveal this value system at work in the Inca territories. He illustrates the agricultural and ritual cycles for an entire year and abundantly mentions corn in prose descriptions and in illustrations for eight of the months. Only two months are centered on the potato: the digging up of the tubers (June) and the ritual planting (December). In both illustrations, a specialized Andean instrument, the foot plow (*chaquitaclla*) perforates the earth to loosen the soil. In the harvest drawing (June) large sacks of potatoes are carried off for storage by women agriculturalists, and in the ritual ceremony of December seed potatoes are taken out from a carrying sash wrapped around the female specialist to be planted in the fertile ground.[14] More revealing of the status and valuation of these two crops is found in the sketch for February; Guaman Poma draws two potato plants crowded into the left-hand corner of the picture, whereas eight rows of corn fill the remainder of the visual space.[15]

Although Guaman Poma rarely illustrates potatoes, he frequently mentions them in the titles of his calendar and in prose descriptions of Inca agricultural practices. He writes "Zara, papa hallmai mit'a" (time to mound up the earth around the corn and potatoes) in bold letters for his drawing for January, when in fact corn is the only crop illustrated.[16] Numerous varieties of corn appear in the texts, yet for potatoes he only mentions the generic large or small potato along with naming the potatoes of the early harvest (*chawcha papa*, *maway papa*). There is no indication of the existence of thousands of native varieties domesticated in the Andes before the arrival of the Europeans.

“Time to Stand Watch Over the Corn at Night” (February), from Felipe Guaman Poma de Ayala, *Nueva corónica y buen gobierno (Codex péruvien ilustré). Travaux et Memoires de L’Institut d’ethnologie* (1615; repr., Paris: L’Institut d’ethnologie, 1936), 23:1035. The 1936 edition is based on the original manuscript GkS 2232, 4to, Royal Library of Denmark, Copenhagen.

Another well-known writer, mestizo Inca Garcilaso de la Vega, lauded the biodiversity of foods domesticated in the Indies, as found in his history of the Incas written in the early colonial period. As a fluent Quechua speaker with a noble Inca mother, he had intimate knowledge of customs and tradition in the Andes. Yet he, like Guaman Poma, devoted a chapter with long descriptions to corn: the grinding of corn in the Andes, the fashioning of soft sacrificial corn breads, the manner of toasting corn, and mention of the numerous flat corn patties eaten daily in the households. He asserts that he was an eyewitness to Andean corn processes and adds that he was nourished with corn until he was about nine or ten years old.[17] However, the next chapter, titled "Vegetables That Grow Underground," only devotes two sentences to the potato plant. He states that it is eaten like bread, cooked and roasted, as well as added to stews. He mentions the freeze-drying process and notes its importance to the indigenous peoples; it "sustains them, especially in areas devoid of corn."[18] After that description he moves on to write about other underground plants: *oca*, peanuts, calabashes, and sweet potato.

In a seventeenth-century collection of Quechua myths in the province of Huarochirí (near Lima) we find another instance of the expression of the lowly status of the potato. In the narrative, the figure of Huatyacuri is specifically called a potato eater. He is also dressed in rags, like a beggar, which indicates his low-status position in the society; thus, he only eats potatoes.[19] Similarly, Andean indigenous peoples are disparaged for what they eat, even by another Andean Indian writer. Guaman Poma refers to the Collas as "chubby and lazy," people rich in herds and silver but "poor in corn and wheat." They are potato eaters, feasting on dehydrated potatoes as well as the more common types of tubers.[20]

There are early accounts of Spanish resistance to the inclusion of the potato in their diet. It is said that when Pedro de Valdivia's forces were starving during the conquest of Chile no one chose to eat potatoes abundant in the lands. Instead they prized daily measured out rations of "a few score grains for each man." Valdivia, after the smoke of battle cleared away, also wrote that he planted corn alongside fields of Old World wheat to feed his men, but he makes no mention of potatoes in a letter to Charles V dated 1551.[21] As Carl O. Sauer has noted, "Spanish colonists in the New World did not take readily to native foods if they could provide themselves with the familiar Spanish food items."[22]

The fate of the potato in Europe reflects a pattern of both acceptance and resistance. The early aversion to the potato stems from its characteristics: it grew beneath the ground, it was the first edible plant to not be grown from seeds, and it was the first plant to have white or flesh-colored nodules on its underground stems.[23] The status of the potato was reflected in accepted culinary knowledge: "Those who eat only the food of savages, the roots, the nuts, the berries, that which the earth produces, will be like savages."[24] The early botanists recognized that the potato should be included in the nightshade family, *Solanaceae*, which includes plants such as tobacco, jimson weed, belladonna, eggplant, and the tomato. The characteristic leaves and flowers identified the poisonous and narcotic properties of potato.

Acceptance was also partially stymied because of the doctrine of signatures, a system of classification that functioned in the belief that humans could read the healing properties of the plants from their outward appearance. Thus, the yellow sap of an herb might cure a "yellow" disease, jaundice. Crops that grew underground were classified as aphrodisiacs in accordance with the doctrine of signatures; mandrake root was believed to cure sterility and ginseng root might be a cure for impotence. Certainly the deeply gnarled skin and shape of the potato were easily compared to testicles, as we saw in the early accounts mentioning the *turmas de tierra*.[25] The early herbalists further disseminated the belief in the "lusty" attributes of the potato, although they frequently confused the sweet potato with the common Peruvian potato. Clusius (Jules Charles de L'Ecluse), author of a history of rare plants, provides us with an early depiction of the potato in 1601, which defines its knobby attributes and opines: "they are flatulent . . . some use them for inciting Venus."[26] Similarly, Gaspard Bauhin writes in his *Prodromus theatri botanici* (1619) that people eat potatoes for increasing semen.[27] By the early 1600s, the potato featured prominently in the dialogue of plays in the city of London: "I have fine potatoes, Ripe potatoes. Will your Lordship please to taste a fine potato? 'Twill advance your withered state, Fill your Honour full of noble itches."[28] Thus we glean detailed observations, rather unappreciative of the underground tuber, written by Spaniards and indigenous authors who prefer the more high-status crop, corn.

Potato Lore: Indigenous Communities Express Respect and Affection

In thinking about the potato, John Murra, in his well-known anthropological study "Rite and Crop in the Inca State," calls attention to the framing devices which shape both European and Amerindian conceptions of the potato.[29] He cautions us to not depend entirely on sources of chronicles and official reports mailed to Spain; the constant mention of maize and its rituals and the relative silence concerning the potato came about from a Spanish preference for wheat-like grains. He reminds us, however, that Andean indigenous people relied heavily upon tubers as a staple foodstuff and that with persistence we can uncover embedded references to the potato in writings of the colonial period.

Ecclesiastic literature and colonial field reports are valuable sources. For instance, prayers in Quechua recorded by Cristóbal de Molina accord equal importance to both maize and potatoes. Mindful of the need for a staple food to feed large populations, these ritual prayers call forth abundance:

> Oh Lord, ancient Lord, expert creator, thou who maketh and establisheth, saying: "In this lower world let them eat, let them drink," increase the food of those whom thou hast established, those whom thou hast created. Thou who commandeth and multiplieth, saying: "Let there be potatoes, maize, and all sorts of food," so that they shall not suffer and, not suffering, do thy will; let it not freeze, let it not hail; keep them in peace.[30]

Murra acknowledges the absence of potato rituals as compared to abundant descriptions of corn ceremonies. No doubt, rituals are important; these ceremonies serve to shape perceptions of collective unity and also serve as a means of communication with varied regional ethnicities. One description of an Andean potato ritual has survived from the early modern period. A report by Cieza de León provides excellent ethnographic details for an indigenous ritual observed by a Spanish-born priest, Marcos Otaço, in the month of May 1547. The indigenous converts to Christianity had requested permission to perform a traditional ceremony in a time of full moon and the potato harvest; the priest agreed to it, with some reservations. It is recorded that the indigenous leaders were seated on layers of weavings in the plaza and a procession of young boys and then young girls ceremoniously passed in front of them. Everyone was dressed in fine clothing, displaying quantities of gold and silver on their clothes or on the richly woven coca bags. Six male farmworkers came out, with their digging tools on their shoulders, followed by six more young boys, drumming, bearing sacks of potatoes. After a ritual bowing of heads, the laborers plunged their foot plows in the earth and hung "large and specially chosen sacks of potatoes" on them.[31] A year-old llama—unblemished and of one color—was sacrificed. The entrails were taken to the Andean priests to observe; other participants "hurriedly scooped up all the blood they could manage with their hands and dribbled it on the potatoes in the sacks."[32] Most certainly, this descriptive report of an elaborate potato ritual is indicative of the high esteem the plant garnered as a life-sustaining foodstuff in the high mountain ranges.[33]

Contemporary myth and narrative in Andean communities attest to the prominence of the potato. It is evident in the care with which the farmers observe and tend the potato crop; daily ritual practices often are carried out in the fields of potatoes to ensure plentiful yields. The oral tradition reveals a potato image rich in mythical symbolism and imbued with lyrical affective expression. A myth from the indigenous community of Huanusco El Rosario in Peru reveals the importance of the existence of numerous varieties of potatoes, to guarantee human sustenance:

> After the potato is planted, just about when the flowers are emerging, they come out at night. Flowers change into people and begin a dance called tupanakuy ["the meet-up"]. The large potatoes become men and the little round potatoes become women and thus they couple up. They visit from *chacra* to *chacra* [small plots] in these groups until they become mature plants. Sometimes in the middle of their fiesta, when the group is distracted, they become scared and scatter, fleeing away in every direction. Then they get confused as to where their patch was and from this time on a new variety appears.[34]

Similarly, in the Bolivian area, many origin myths about the potato have been collected in the Aymara language through an ongoing oral narrative project.[35]

An explicit emotional attachment to the potato is found in the Quechua words of a contemporary song from the Cuzco region in Peru, sung by Maxmiliano Cruz Ch'uktaya. He describes an intimate relationship with the potato plant; he speaks directly to it and he remembers when he covered it tenderly with clods of earth:

> Of the potatoes I planted (*tarpurikushyani*)
> I ask a question, carefully, respectfully: (*tapupayashyani*)
> "Are there any tiny roundish potatoes yet?
> Are there any leaves bursting forth yet?"
> "Do you still remember?
> Do you, I wonder?"

> How, with our hands and our feet
> we planted [potatoes]?[36]

An intense respectfulness colors the questioning and the wondering; the Quechua language has morphemic forms to indicate verbal modalities of admiration and supplication (*paya* in the second line). A Quechua esthetic principle is conveyed, as seen in the parallelism of similar verbs "to plant" (*tarpuy*) and "to question" (*tapuy*) made structurally repetitive throughout the lyrics. This song is fashioned into an Andean reverie, a recounting of potatoes sown by hand in moments when the earth was perforated by the foot plow.

This song and the many myths told in Andean communities attest to the centrality of the crop in daily life. As keen agriculturalists, Andean Indians categorize and prioritize the varieties that they will plant in their plots. As many as forty-six varieties of potato are planted in a typical potato field, chosen according to criteria of taste and texture, storage capabilities of the potato, the altitude where it is to be planted, which ones serve as gifts to friends and family, and which ones have potential as a seed potatoes.[37] Ancient Quechua names for potatoes persist, such as the *huira ppasña papa* (the fat woman potato) and the *aya papa* (the ancestor potato) or the *moro kohui sullu papa* (the spotted guinea pig fetus potato).[38] A glossy display of potatoes, recently published to exhibit the agricultural knowledge of Quechua speakers from the Canchis province in Peru, depicts some eighty-one varieties of potato, all recognized and labeled with their common regional name.[39]

Potato Plaudits in Contemporary Andean Prose, Poetry, and Film

José María Arguedas, the Peruvian author who grew up speaking Quechua as his first language, was sensitive to emotional as well as practical attachments to the land and crops in the Andes. Arguedas often defended an Andean way of life and knowledge of agriculture that differed in expression from scientific formulas and molecular analyses. One of his poems written in Quechua highlights the contrast between the Western conceptions of the world as opposed to those of the indigenous people who are descendants of the Incas. In the poem "Huk doctorkunaman qayay" (Telling Truths to Those Know-It-All Personages [Big Shots]) he calls out the "educated" elite; he protests against racial prejudice and conceptions

Papa allay (potato harvest) in the region of Sarhua, Peru, 1990. ADAPS Peru 90. *Personal collection. Photo by Regina Harrison.*

of the indigenous as unlettered and backward. He builds an argument for valuing Andean ways of knowing, and he points out the potato:

> Five hundred potatoes grow where your eyes do not reach
> in the mix of golden night, in the silvery day, in the land.
> That's where my intellect is, that's where my heart is.[40]

César Vallejo, the esteemed Peruvian poet, was similarly motivated by the inspirational content of the Andean landscape in his "Telúrica y magnética," praising the Indian, the *vicuña*, firewood, leaves of *coca*, the "intellectual terrain of the mountain range." Similar to Arguedas he looks to the fields and rural scenery to reveal "a taxonomy by which man orders the world around him and his moral and intellectual life."[41] Vallejo's sensory-filled lyric proclaims that nature is the source of thought and feeling, as even furrows are deemed intelligent. And, of course, the potato lies in that furrow, another product of human and botanical interaction:

> Technologies, sincere and Peruvian,
> those of the henna color hill.
> Soil of the earth, theoretical and practical.
> Intelligent furrows: the monolith and its celebratory followers.
> Fields of potatoes, barley, alfalfa, so wonderful!
> Crops that mingle with an astonishing hierarchy of farming tools.[42]

Originally written as a "lyric engagement with Marxism,"[43] the poem was reworked in 1937 to include a strong element of Peruvian context and reveal the poet's sincere declaration of allegiance to the Andes, "one of his most explicit meditations in his work on Peru."[44]

We similarly rejoice by digging into the earth for potatoes in Julio Ortega's short story "Avenida Oeste," written in 1981 and set in an urban cityscape. The young Peruvian father caring for his son alone actually plants a potato under a tree near his apartment complex, after peeling and slicing and cooking the tuber in a special Peruvian dish for noontime lunch. The act of preparing the potato bought in the United States leads the protagonist to compare this potato (from Wyoming? from Idaho?) to the ones he has known in the Andes: gritty potatoes with the flavor of the earth, royal purple ones and delicate yellow ones, and varieties that have been lost. He is aware of how much he does not know about his country and the potato.

Now appreciative of the crisp white pulp in the slices, he is conscious of his former aversion to potatoes. For him, they represented the provinces, meager resources, and underdevelopment in the land he has left behind to move north. Yet, here in the kitchen, he senses that the potato has been transformed, right in his hands. Perhaps he has found one of the lost varieties, one that belongs to him.

Not content to merely narrate the history of the potato in an effort to teach his young son about his Peruvian ancestry, the father in this story tenderly nestles the potato in his hand as he realizes the symbolic importance of the tuber's resistance of oppression:

> He was not surprised that the misshapen form of the swollen tuber adapted to the contour of his hand; he knew the potato adapted to different lands, true to its own internal form as if it occupied stolen space. The entire history of his people was here, he said to himself,

> surviving in a territory overrun and pillaged several times, growing in marginal spaces, under siege and waiting.[45]

This act of planting the potato with his bare hands merges both his Peruvian identity with the new life he is forging as an immigrant. The plant will grow underground and survive in its new circumstances; the potato mediates his estrangement.

A discussion of the potato in literary contexts must necessarily include Pablo Neruda's "Ode to the Potato," from *Nuevas odas elementales* (1956). A gourmand, Neruda has been described appropriately as a "Renaissance Pope: gluttonous and refined" and in his odes he turns his attention to the everyday items we consume.[46] Yet his focus in not in the eating, he instead provides a historical profile of the plant. His description of the potato recalls similar prose found in the colonial chronicles; he writes that it is an almond of the earth, it flowers under the earth, it possesses a soft pure pulp. His understanding of the agricultural stages is informed by looking at the plant in the fields:

> your flower
> quite undistinguished
> announces
> the dense and tender
> birth of your roots.[47]

Indeed, the flowering indicates the growth of the tubers that are ready to harvest when the vines turn yellow. Neruda is proud of the Chilean potato; his verses situate the early tubers in the damp islands of Chile and in the coastal shores of Chiloé Island. How prescient his poetics—recent studies from the herbarium collections begun in the 1700s have confirmed that both Andean and Chilean landraces were separately introduced into Europe. Although the Andean potato predominated in the early specimens, after 1811 the DNA markers reveal the dominance and spread of the Chilean species.[48]

A committed Communist and a onetime candidate for the presidency in Chile, Neruda does not disparage the tuber; he highlights and praises the potato as food for the masses, found there among the common man. The potato is "dark like our skin," is definitely not called *patata* (as the potato is known in Spain) but always revealing its Quechua origins expressed in the name *papa*. In so doing Neruda alludes to the networks of Iberian invasion and colonization, of pillage and plunder, the "War of Darkness / Spain of the Inquisition." In the midst of this turmoil the potato survived, underground and waiting, to eventually become the "subterranean / unceasing treasure / of the people [the *pueblos*]."[49]

The Bolivian poet Eduardo Mitre carries us right to the consumption of the potato, after a brief description of its characteristics. At first, he centers on the sinuous curves of the potato skin, with the inevitable comparison to the white skin of a woman. Yet abruptly he changes course, as Neruda did before him, alluding to the ethnic component of the tuber:

> Daughter of this America,
> dark skinned like these people
> you possess a supple resilience.[50]

Pleased with the poetic lines and the aptness of the description, he ends, inviting the reader to enjoy the feast:

> Just enjoy it, it's ready right now
> on the plate
> and on the page.[51]

While many of the poets' verses aptly detail the visual aspects of the potato by means of words and rhythm, filmmakers have the good fortune to actually zoom in and focus closely on the cultural metaphors inherent in the tuber. Alex Rivera brought a personal connection to the potato before he started filming. His father was born in Peru, and his cousins migrated north to avoid the ravages of terrorism in the Andes. As a political science major in college, his senior video project was an effort to link the potato diaspora with the stages of his father's migratory progress, resulting in the award-winning *Papapapá* (1995).[52] Rivera uses documentary footage to inform the viewer of the prowess of the Incas, as master agriculturalists who specialized in irrigation and terracing and also perfected methods of storing and preserving potatoes. The historical segments of what he calls an "experimental documentary" are intercut with a humorous depiction in Claymation of the potato leaving on a galleon for Europe, with the route traced on vintage maps and stop-motion animation. Significantly, though, the perspective deepens. Only the uniform white potatoes make a flying leap toward a voyage to Europe aboard the sailing ship. The brown potato had not been loaded on board.

The theme of exclusion and migration becomes more pronounced as we view a cutout of Alex's father, mounted on a giant potato, making his way north, morphing into a "couch potato" glued to the television set six to seven hours a night.[53] Peruvian father and Peruvian potato both are reduced to commodity status as they accommodate to modernity; Rivera collapses maps and kinship diagrams.[54] The human *papá* (his father) is a migrant worker physically laboring long hours but emotionally grounded in Peru and the vegetable *papa* is transformed from a sacred object into a commodity status of French fries and bags of potato chips.[55] Rivera, as the director of *Sleep Dealer* (2008), is fascinated by border crossings and post-national spaces; the potato animated his first creative impulses.

A gruesome image of the potato looms figuratively in Claudia Llosa's film *The Milk of Sorrow* (2009) when a medical doctor explains to a young woman, bleeding and fainting in a state-run Lima hospital, that she "has a tuber (*tubérculo*) in her vagina. A potato to be more exact."[56] The diagnosis is shocking. Fausta Isadora Janampa Chauca, the young woman protagonist, finally explains the circumstances. Years ago, she was told a story by her mother: a neighbor woman in her remote village made this insertion to avoid being raped during the traumatic years of the Shining Path in Peru. This explanation is further augmented in song. Fausta's lyrics reveal that the potato serves her as a shield, a coat of arms, a bottle stopper. Post-traumatic stress is not explained in medical and scientific imagery here; instead, the voices of the Quechua-speaking villagers reveal their means of survival in the context of rape and violence with the aid of the potato.

Lore of the countryside also positions the potato in a scene of merriment and laughter in the film as when the bride-to-be is forced to peel a potato to show her domestic prowess. The future bride deftly wields her knife in front of the assembled extended families and in the end a single long strip of potato peel is held up and displayed to the guests. This scene well captures the traditions of the highland populations of the Andes. J. G. Hawkes wrote of this popular custom in his fieldwork of the 1940s; he recorded the name *cachan huacachi papa* as "the potato that makes the daughter-in-law cry."[57] According to Quechua tradition, "this potato was used to prove potato peeling skills of the newly wed daughters-in-law."[58]

Fausta, with the potato still inside her body, is traumatized.[59] Significantly, the sympathetic gardener, Noé, befriends and counsels her as they work together as landscaper and maid for the owner of an opulent, gated mansion. In the end, it is he who carries her to the hospital to undergo an operation to remove the tuber. Her grief, for her own life and that of her deceased mother, seems to fade away with Noé's nurturing presence after the medical procedure. The last scene pointedly depicts two potato stems growing out of one flowerpot. As Fausta leans into this last frame the symbolism is overt; she has overcome her fears. The possibility of a future marriage for her is cued visually by interpreting the symbolism of the two little potatoes growing out of the potted plant. This "potato conclusion" redeems the film for Cynthia Vich, who is critical of the overt exoticism of the residents on the outskirts of Lima seen in the film; they have been turned into an image commodity manufactured and sold to international fans of cinema. Better the vitality and growth of the potato flower and the two stalks in the last frame as Fausta survives and makes use of the quintessential Andean symbol.[60]

Potato Agri/Culture

The care with which the Andean farmer has tended the potato over the centuries is testimony to the persistence of agricultural knowledge and practice that was harnessed to sustain the world's population. Contemporary scientists appreciate the work of the early botanists—their classification of the *Solanum tuberosa*, the plotting of agricultural venues most appropriate for high yields, their work to extend the range of the plant from the Andes to the southwestern region of the United States.[61] By means of a thorough examination of 742 landraces (indigenous cultivated potato species) and eight wild species by molecular markers, David Spooner and his team of contemporary scientists determined that there are four species (including Andean and Chilean cultivar groups) and three hybrid cultivated species.[62] More than four thousand native varieties exist; indeed, the potato is the fourth most important food crop in the world.

Redcliffe Salaman writes a penetrating conclusion to his exhaustive book on the tuber; he asks what part the potato plays in the economic scheme of things. He outlines the importance of the potato as one of the cheapest and most efficient single foods cultivated in the temperate zones, just as he acknowledges the potential of the potato crop to enable an exploitation of a politically subordinate laborer.[63] Rebecca Earle similarly notes that potatoes "are part of how we understand famine, or survival, or the experience of being governed." By no means a simplistic symbol, for Earle potatoes provide a means with which to explain the socioeconomic structures of famines in Ireland or the cash income crisis in Russia during the 1990s from a global perspective.[64] Potatoes cheaply feed the masses and, for some scholars, potatoes thus enable these laborers to live and participate in nation-state economic projects planned by the governing classes.

In tracing the intricate route of the potato from the Andes to the far ends of the world, we also appreciate the metamorphosis of the *papa* in its technological, cultural, and esthetic manifestations. Presented steaming hot on a dinner plate, lying in an agricultural furrow or under the scientific microscope, displayed visually in film or inscribed enticingly on the written page, the all-pervasive potato humbly sustains and nourishes the world.

Notes

1. See Andrew F. Smith, *Potato: A Global History* (London: Reaktion Books, 2011), 94–101.
2. Juan de Castellanos, *Historia del Nuevo Reino de Granada*, ed. Antonio Paz y Mélia (1589; repr., Madrid: Imp. A. Pérez Dubrull, 1886), 1:88. Translations are my own throughout the chapter unless noted.
3. Pedro de Cieza de León, *Primera parte de la chronica del Perú*, ch. XL (Antwerp, Belgium: Editorial Juan Steelsio, 1554), 105r–105v.
4. Cieza de León, *Primera parte*, 105v.
5. Bernabé Cobo, *Historia del nuevo mundo*, ed. Marcos Jiménez de la Espada (1652; repr., Seville, Spain: Imprenta de E. Rasco, 1890), 1:360.
6. Cobo, *Historia del nuevo mundo*, 360. *Ahelí* is possibly *alhelí* (carnation).
7. Cobo, *Historia del nuevo mundo*, 361.
8. Cobo, *Historia del nuevo mundo*, 361.
9. Cobo, *Historia del nuevo mundo*, 361.
10. Cobo, *Historia del nuevo mundo*, 362.
11. See J. G. Hawkes and J. Francisco-Ortega, "The Early History of the Potato in Europe," *Euphytica* 70 (1993): 2. Also see investigative dating in J. G. Hawkes, *The Potato: Evolution, Biodiversity and Genetic Resources* (Washington, DC: Smithsonian Institution Press, 1990), 31.
12. Hawkes and Francisco-Ortega, "The Early History," 4–5. See John Reader, *Potato: A History of the Propitious Esculent* (New Haven, CT: Yale University Press, 2009), 89–91, for an expansive summary.
13. Indeed, Rebecca Earle's well-researched book provides more commentary on maize than the potato. See Rebecca Earle, *The Body of the Conquistador: Food, Race and the Colonial Experience in Spanish America* (Cambridge: Cambridge University Press, 2012).
14. Felipe Guaman Poma de Ayala, *El primer nueva corónica y buen gobierno*, ed. John V. Murra and Rolena Adorno, Quechua trans. Jorge L. Urioste, online facsimile, 2001, http://kb.dk./permalink/2006/poma/info/en/frontpage.htm, [1157], [1175]. Corrected page numbers are in brackets as seen in the facsimile. First published in 1615.
15. Guaman Poma, *El primer*, [1145].

16. Guaman Poma, *El primer*, [1142].
17. Inca Garcilaso de la Vega, *Comentarios reales de los Incas*, ed. Aurelio Miró Quesada, bk. 8, ch. 9 (1609; repr., Caracas: Fundación Biblioteca Ayacucho, 1985), 171.
18. Garcilaso, *Comentarios reales*, bk. 8, ch. 10, 173.
19. See *The Huarochirí Manuscript: A Testament of Ancient and Colonial Andean Religion*, trans. Frank Salomon and Jorge L. Urioste (Austin: University of Texas Press, 1991).
20. Guaman Poma, *El primer*, [179].
21. Cited in Redcliffe N. Salaman, *The History and Social Influence of the Potato* (1949; repr., Cambridge: Cambridge University Press, 1985), 69.
22. Carl O. Sauer, *Seeds, Spades, Hearths, and Herds* (1952; repr.; Cambridge, MA: MIT Press, 1975), 152.
23. Salaman, *The History and Social Influence*, 112.
24. Anthony Pagden, *The Fall of Natural Man: The American Indian and the Origins of Comparative Ethnography* (Cambridge: Cambridge University Press, 1982), 177.
25. Salaman, *The History and Social Influence*, 129.
26. Salaman, *The History and Social Influence*, 104.
27. Quoted in Salaman, *The History and Social Influence*, 104.
28. John Fletcher's play, *The Loyal Subject* (1617), quoted in Reader, *Potato*, 77.
29. John V. Murra, "Rite and Crop in the Inca State," in *Culture and History: Essays in Honor of Paul Radin*, ed. Stanley Diamond (New York: Columbia University Press, 1960), 393–408.
30. John Howland Rowe, "Eleven Inca Prayers from the Zithua Ritual," *Kroeber Anthropological Society Papers* 8–9 (1953): 90. Translated by John Howland Rowe.
31. Cieza de León, *Primera parte*, 274v–275r.
32. Cieza de León, *Primera parte*, 276r.
33. Murra alludes to this ritual in his "Rite and Crop," 397. Miriam Doutriaux also analyzes this ritual, see Miriam Doutriaux, "Power, Ideology and Ritual: The Practice of Agriculture in the Inca Empire," *Kroeber Anthropological Society Papers* 85 (2001): 91–108.
34. Asociación de Defensa y Desarrollo de las Comunidades Andinas del Perú and the Instituto de Extensión Agrícola de la Universidad de Hohenheim de Alemania, *Taller campesino sobre la papa: Costumbres y perspectivas, Lima, 4–9 de septiembre de 1989* (Lima: [1989?]), 45.
35. See Denise Y. Arnold and Juan de Dios Yapita, eds., *Madre melliza y sus crías/ Ispall Mama wawampi: Antología de la papa* (La Paz, Bolivia: Hisbol/ILCA, 1996).
36. Maximiliano Cruz Ch'uktaya, "Papa tarpuy," in *La sangre de los cerros / Urcukunapayawarnin: Antología de la poesía quechua que se canta en el Perú*, ed. Rodrigo Montoya, Eduardo Montoya, and Luis Montoya (Lima: Centro Peruano de Estudios Sociales; Mosca Azul; Universidad Nacional Mayor de San Marcos, 1987), 63. My translation is from the Quechua. See the entire song in Regina Harrison's *Signs, Songs, and Memory in the Andes: Translating Quechua Language and Culture* (Austin: University of Texas Press, 1989), 190–91.

37. Stephen B. Brush, Heath J. Carney, and Zózimo Huamán, "Dynamics of Andean Potato Agriculture," *Economic Botany* 35, no. 1 (1981): 80.
38. J. G. Hawkes, "On the Origin and Meaning of South American Indian Potato Names," *Linnean Society of London Botanical Journal* 53 (1947): 231.
39. Raymundo Gutiérrez and César Valencia, eds., *Las papas nativas de Canchis: Un catálogo de biodiversidad* (Lima: Servicios Gráficos JMD, 2010), 29–30.
40. José María Arguedas, "Huk Doctorkunaman Qayay," in *Temblar/Katatay* (Lima: Instituto Nacional de Cultura, 1972), 50, 51, 53. My translation from the Quechua.
41. Jean Franco, *César Vallejo: The Dialectics of Poetry and Silence* (Cambridge: Cambridge University Press, 1976), 175.
42. César Vallejo, "Telúrica y magnética" from *Poemas humanos*, in *Obra poética completa*, ed. Enrique Ballón Aguirre (Caracas: Fundación Biblioteca Ayacucho, 1985), 135.
43. Franco, *César Vallejo*, 173.
44. Michelle Clayton, *Poetry in Pieces: César Vallejo and Lyric Modernity* (Berkeley: University of California Press, 2011), 12.
45. Julio Ortega, "Las papas," trans. Regina Harrison, *Boston Globe Sunday Magazine*, February 28, 1988, SM16; also found in *Global Cultures: A Transnational Short Fiction Reader*, ed. Elizabeth Young-Bruehl (Middleton, CT: Wesleyan University Press, 1994), 30–34.
46. Fernando Velerio-Holguín, "Pilgimage and Gastronomy," in *Gabriel García Márquez in Retrospect: A Collection*, ed. Gene H. Bell-Villada (Lanham, MD: Lexington Books, 2016), 153.
47. Pablo Neruda, "A la papa," in *Obras completas* (Buenos Aires: Losada, 1967), 1:1299.
48. David Spooner, "Roadmaps to the Origins of the Potato," in *International Year of the Potato 2008: New Light on a Hidden Treasure* (Rome: Food and Agriculture Association of the United Nations, 2008), 116.
49. Neruda, "A la papa," *Obras*, 1:1299.
50. Eduardo Mitre, "La papa," in *La luz del regreso* (La Paz, Bolivia: Servicio Gráfico Quipus, 1999), 34.
51. Mitre, "La papa," 34.
52. Alex Rivera, *Papapapá* (1995; United States: SubCine, 1997), DVD.
53. Furthermore, the television set displays the title of a show that he is watching in black and white, "Las papas de mis papas" (The Potatoes of My Parents).
54. See Amy Sara Carroll, "From *Papapapá* to *Sleep Dealer*: Alex Rivera's Undocumentary Poetics," in *Political Documentary Cinema in Latin America*, ed. Antonio Traverso and Kristi Wilson (New York: Routledge, 2016), 211–27.
55. See Laura U. Marks, *The Skin of the Film: Intercultural Cinema, Embodiment, and the Senses* (Durham, NC: Duke University Press, 2000), 99.
56. Claudia Llosa, *La teta asustada* (The Milk of Sorrow) (2009; Lima: Olive Films, 2010), DVD.
57. Hawkes, "On the Origin," 231.
58. Gutiérrez and Valencia, *Las papas nativas*, 37.
59. The theme of trauma and resistance is carefully documented in Adriana Rojas, "Mother of Pearl, Song and Potatoes: Cultivating Resilience in Claudia Llosa's

La teta asustada/Milk of Sorrow (2009)," *Studies in Spanish & Latin American Cinemas* 14, no. 3 (2017): 308.

60. Cynthia Vich, "De estetizaciones y viejos exotismos: apuntes en torno a *La teta asustada* de Claudia Llosa," *Revista de Crítica Literaria Latinoamericana* 40, no. 80 (2014): 343.
61. Larry Zuckerman credits Swiss botanist Gaspard Bauhin with naming the potato *Solanum tuberosum*. Larry Zuckerman, *The Potato: How the Humble Spud Rescued the World* (Boston: Faber and Faber, 1998), 11. See David H. Kinder, Karen R. Adams, and Harry J. Wilson, "*Solanum Jamesii*: Evidence of Cultivation of Wild Potato Tubers by Ancestral Puebloan Groups," *Journal of Ethnobiology* 37, no. 2 (2017): 218–40.
62. Spooner, "Roadmaps," 116. This result differs from earlier studies denoting seven species or as many as twenty-one species previously recognized, with a hearth in southern Peru. However, in the end most taxonomists would argue that absolute classification is difficult because of local nomenclature, hybrid mixing in cultivated plots, and overlapping characteristics in categorization among plants.
63. Salaman, *The History and Social Influence*, 600–601.
64. Rebecca Earle, *Potato* (New York: Bloomsbury Publishing, 2019), 89.

CHAPTER 3

The Culinary World of Sor Juana Inés de la Cruz

PAOLA JEANNETE VERA BÁEZ
AND ÁNGEL T. TUNINETTI

Sor Juana Inés de la Cruz was the most prominent writer in colonial New Spain, a historical period that saw the birth of what is today known as Mexican gastronomy. Her work was written inside the walls of a convent, where the kitchens were the main labs for the development of this new cuisine. This article analyzes the importance of foodways in Sor Juana's work, with special emphasis on the *Recetario de Sor Juana* (Sor Juana's Recipe Book), a collection of recipes from the eighteenth century that is attributed to her.

The foundations of contemporary Mexican culture, including its cuisine, can be placed in the pre-Hispanic world, but the cultural interaction that the diverse regions of current Mexico endured during the times of the Viceroyalty of New Spain generated an astounding mix of flavors, ingredients, and culinary techniques. The different cuisines of Mexico and their foodways represent heterogeneous and polyglot texts that continue to provide new symbolic meanings since the time of their creation.

These culinary texts are result of *mestizaje*, the encounter and fusion of different cultures starting in the sixteenth century with the establishment of the viceroyalty. As we pay special attention to Sor Juana Inés de la Cruz's work in this chapter we need to consider them as part of the material culture of New Spain.[1]

The viceroyalty allowed the Spanish Crown to incorporate and organize the space of the New World according to diverse economic, political, and cultural rules. The integration of the territories required a reordering of the Mesoamerican geopolitical structures under a new project, a goal achieved by the creation of cities that served as political, economic, and social centers that were also models of orderly Christian life.[2] The Spanish Crown added these new territories using a series of mechanisms that regulated culturally and ideologically the relationship between the king and its territories.[3] In the case of New Spain, this project was driven by the Second Royal Court, whose main objective was to consolidate pacts with indigenous groups to guarantee the viability of Spanish domination.[4]

The political and commercial globalization that brought together conquerors, merchants, and slaves from Europe, Africa, and Asia produced a racial, culinary, and linguistic *mestizaje*. In terms of foodways, by the eighteenth century in the country's capital, Mexico City, there were significant social differences related to the buying power of each group.[5] Society was composed of peasants, laborers, craftsmen, and royal officers with significantly different levels of access to the plethora of foodstuffs available in the markets, compounded by the classification of individuals through the caste system. Hispanic Creoles, due to their economic power, had a varied and abundant alimentation.[6] It is precisely this social group that would preserve their recipes in writing, and it is in this tradition that we can place the manuscript attributed to Sor Juana Inés de la Cruz, usually referred to as the *Recetario de Sor Juana*.

Very soon the Viceroyalty of New Spain developed noteworthy culinary traditions, gaining fame and popularity thanks to a wealth of agricultural products (both plants and animals), and some products became important business for their producers and traders. The exploitation of abundant natural resources added to the import of foodstuffs from overseas—thanks to the "Nao de China" or "The Manila Galleons," which were part of the Spanish treasure fleet system—and fueled the development of commercial enterprises based in the main cities such as Mexico City and Puebla and in ports such as Veracruz and Acapulco. These trade ships supplied not only New Spain but also other regions. The exchange and fusion of knowledge and traditions of diverse cultures, directly and indirectly, became part of the culinary fabric of this society, with solid roots in foreign and local traditions.[7] Nevertheless, it is important to mention that such developments were not reflected in the publications of recipe books; as John Super and Josefina Muriel and Guadalupe Pérez San Vicente have studied, there is a dearth of interest in culinary publications in the Spanish viceroyalties.[8]

After the Council of Trent prescribed reformations to monastic life, many monasteries from different orders were founded in the Viceroyalty of New Spain with different rules and constitutions, some of them under diocesan jurisdiction.[9] Convents and monasteries were founded in diverse places such as Mexico City, Puebla, Tlaxcala, Hidalgo, Morelos, Querétaro, Zacatecas, Jalisco, Colima, Michoacán, Guerrero, Veracruz, Oaxaca, Chiapas, and Yucatán, and they are excellent sources to understand the society that created them. The culinary development in these convents was directly related to the spaces in which they were established and served as research and experimentation centers not only for cultivation and foodway development, but also for water management. Looking at conventual documentation such as account ledgers, it is possible to understand the combination of ingredients, utensils, and culinary and preservation techniques that gave birth to this mestizo cooking.

Several aspects of the history of these religious institutions have been the object of historiographical research.[10] On the culinary front, most studies are related to several famous dishes, presumably created in conventual kitchens, such as the *mole poblano*, *chiles en nogada*, and the rich and varied pastries and sweets, such as the ones created at the Dominican convent of Santa Rosa.[11] Most often the origin of these dishes has been explained and recreated in legendary narratives that, while entertaining and interesting, do not have historical validity since they have been transmitted from generation to generation and are full of discrepancies depending on the narrator.

If the origin of some recipes has been of interest to historians, there are fewer studies on topics such as supplies, services, nutrition, and refectories in the convents.[12] Convents in New Spain had spaces devoted to storing, preparing, preserving, and consuming foodstuffs, such as gardens, stables, wells, pantries, kitchens, and refectories.[13] It was precisely around those fires, fueled with coal and wood, where monastic life between monks and nuns developed around certain common rules: meals in the refectory, prayers in the choir, and studies in the cells.[14] All of them, constrained by their temperance and poverty vows, shared a frugal diet enriched by chocolate and wheat bread. To avoid gluttony and other excesses, the consumption of meat was restricted to about one hundred and fifty days a year, observing Lent, Holy Week, and Advent, according to the Catholic Liturgical Calendar.[15]

Nuns' writings in the Hispanic world have received attention by academics in recent years, but literary criticism has paid little attention to culinary writing. Electa Arenal and Stacey Schlau, in one of the most comprehensive studies of nuns' writings, do not even mention them:

> Sisters wrote Lives, letters, chronicles of convent founding, accounts of spiritual experience, and plays. They wrote for the ceremonies of profession—the great event in the life of most nuns. They wrote to decry affronts to sacred images, to lament the death of a king or queen or royal infant. Some nuns who had a flair for poetry participated in contest called certámenes. . . . The writing of the nuns was extremely varied. Some pieces were serious, some humorous. Some were impromptu ditties to accompany gifts or to offer thanks or felicitations; some plumb the depths of spiritual darkness and exalted the heights of union with the divine. Some theatricalized religious celebrations.[16]

As we can see, this lengthy list of texts does not even mention culinary texts.

It is in this context that we must study the most important literary figure of the Viceroyalty of New Spain, Sor Juana Inés de la Cruz. Juana Inés de Asuaje y Ramírez de Santillana was born in San Miguel Neplanta (currently Tepetlixpa, Mexico) on November 12, 1648.[17] In 1669, she changed her name to Sor Juana Inés de la Cruz. Her life as a nun in the San Jerónimo Monastery allowed her to develop her extraordinary literary work and to become one of the most admired writers of her time. Her work is very diverse, but in this occasion we will focus on the few pieces in which there are culinary references.

Around 1664, vicereine Doña Leonor Carreto took young Juana to the palace, where she probably learned about court etiquette and protocol, as well as banquet organization and table settings.[18] The lasting friendship between Sor Juana and Doña Leonor inspired many of the nun's poetic compositions. Moving from country life to the court in Mexico City must have meant a significant change in Sor Juana's dietary and culinary customs, from the simplicity of rural cuisine based on corn, atoles, and maybe chocolate, to the wide variety of ingredients available in the capital.[19]

It is impossible to know for sure the extent to which Sor Juana was involved in the kitchen while at the convent. Conventual kitchens—both the individual kitchens inside the cells and the communal kitchen—were one of the most prolific centers of culinary *mestizaje*; in them, the mix of European, Mesoamerican, Asian, and African flavors as well as different cooking techniques were developed, since the convents had a social stratification clearly defined (for each nun, there were three to five slaves or maids).[20] Their duties would depend on their social status:

> Some order the dishes and supervise their elaboration, in general they are Creoles or Spaniards; the Indians execute them. The Creoles, with their manuscripts, are the ones who left us with the historical legacy of the local gastronomy, but the Indians are the ones who exerted a definitive influence in the formation of Mexican cuisine. Combining different elements, using native and imported ingredients, looking for new flavors and beautiful and suggestive presentations, is an art tied to the spirit of the times, and, consciously or not, it gives style to culinary art.[21]

Maybe Sor Juana practiced the culinary art with her slave,[22] since it was very common for nuns to make special dishes (usually sweets and desserts) as gifts for their sponsors, or to honor the clerical hierarchy and the viceroyalty.[23] While we do not know if she made those gifts, Sor Juana refers to them in poems she exchanges with the world outside the convent.[24] The most direct reference appears in the poem "En retorno de una diadema, representa un dulce de nueces que previno a un antojo de la señora virreina,"[25] written to thank the vicereine María Luisa Manrique, who was pregnant and had given Sor Juana a crown of luxurious feathers as a gift.[26] In the poem, Sor Juana thanks the vicereine for making her a queen, and in return offers her the poem and a walnut confiture.

Sor Juana also shows her knowledge of all kinds of sweets, marmalades, and confitures in poems dedicated to both the Marquise of Mancera, Leonor Carreto, and the Countess of Paredes and Marquise of Laguna, María Luisa Manrique de Lara y Gonzaga y Lujan, as well as to the Countess of Galve, Elvira de Toledo, among others.[27] Their good relationship was based on shared age, sensibility, curiosity, and intelligence, and it was fueled by exchanging gifts that combined words with nourishment, such as chicken stews, bobo mullet fish, walnut confitures, and chocolate candies.[28]

Besides these references to foodstuffs as gifts, the most quoted reference that establishes her knowledge of the culinary arts appears in the famous "Answer by the poet to the most illustrious Sister Filotea de la Cruz," written in 1691 as a response to the bishop of Puebla, Manuel Fernández de Santa Cruz. In this autobiographical letter, she justifies her love of knowledge, and in this eagerness to learn, cooking plays an important role:

> Well, then, my Lady, what can I tell you, about nature's secrets as I've discovered them while cooking? I see that an egg becomes solid and fries in lard or oil, while, on the other hand, it dissolves in syrup. I see that in order to keep sugar in a liquid state it suffices to add to it a very small part of water mixed with quince or another sour fruit. I see that an egg's yolk and white have such opposite characteristics that when one or the other of them is mixed with sugar each one separately works well, but when they are combined they do not. Because I don't want to bore you with which cold facts I'm mentioning them only to give you a full account of my nature—and I think this probably has made you laugh. Nevertheless, my Lady, what can we women possibly know other than kitchen philosophies? Lupercio Leonardo said it quite well: one can philosophize well while preparing dinner. When I see these trivialities I often say this: if Aristotle had cooked stews he would have written a lot more. So, continuing with my mode of cogitation, I tell you that this is constant in me that I have no need for books.[29]

These *filosofías de cocina* (kitchen philosophies), as the Italian scholar Angelo Morino has studied in detail, played a double role when considering gender issues. On the one hand, cooking is a practice that unites Sor Juana with the other women in the convent, as if she were trying to exert her femininity.[30] These philosophies represent a different cognitive experience from men, whose education doesn't include the materiality of everyday life.[31] On the other hand, we can read it as a proposal to overcome the rigid separation between the feminine and masculine worlds, the concrete materiality of cooking with the abstraction of philosophy and a desire for androgyny, an identity that goes beyond gender distinctions and represents a harmonic fusion between male and female elements,[32] and, as Josefina Ludmer has stated in her classic article, there is no distinction between sacred and profane knowledge, between studying in books and in reality.[33]

Sor Juana's most important work related to the culinary arts is known as the *Recetario de Sor Juana*. The manuscript was found in 1979 and includes "some recipes that [the nun] selected and copied from a cookbook at the convent of San Jerónimo."[34] It is a collection of thirty-six recipes, sweet and savory, preceded by a sonnet, and with Sor Juana's signature at the end. The manuscript is a booklet with a total of eighteen leaves, folded. The provenance of the manuscript is not without doubts. A study showed that the paper was made in the eighteenth century, and since Sor Juana died in 1695, some authors have concluded that the manuscript is a copy of the original written by her in the previous century.[35]

As is customary in culinary instructions written before the nineteenth century, the recipes are short and lack precision regarding ingredients, quantities, utensils, cooking techniques, number of portions, and serving directions. Therefore, the recipes cannot be studied from a literary perspective, but as cultural reflections of the time. The manuscript may have been aimed to a limited number of people, not intended for publication or a wider public. More likely it was a recompilation of the cooking knowledge of the convent, as a guide for the future rulers of the kitchen.[36]

Morino sees a feminine hand behind the collection, as they are minimal texts, poorly organized, with a basic and limited vocabulary, intended as flexible notes guiding the cooking process and to be circulated in the private space of the kitchen.[37] No matter how sparse the recipes are, it is possible to find within them a mix of flavors, ingredients, and techniques that reflect the cultural diversity of the society.[38] We can observe the European, Arab-Andalusian, and Mesoamerican influences in the mix of sweet, savory, and spicy. The prevalence of sweet preparations (twenty-six out of thirty-six recipes) shows the importance that sugar would have in the cuisine of the Mexican Baroque, together with vanilla and cinnamon.[39]

Some of the dishes have disappeared from contemporary Mexican cuisine, such as the *ante* (from *antes*: before), sweet dishes that were eaten as appetizers before sweets were relegated just to desserts, and the *gigotes*, stews made with chopped meats and a variety of spices and other ingredients.[40]

A clear example of the complexity of flavors and variety of ingredients—from both the Old and the New Worlds—involved in these recipes can be seen in the *gigote de gallina* (hen stew):

> In a pot spread with pork lard, put a layer of hen and another of tomatoes, chopped onions, clove, pepper, cinnamon, cumin, cilantro, garlic in small pieces, parsley, and saffron, continue this way, and lastly ham slices and vinegar, and cook between two fires. After the broth is cooked as needed, add sausages, raisins, almonds, olives, chilies, and capers.[41]

Another preparation, *manchamanteles* ("tablecloth stainer"), exemplifies the economy of vocabulary and direction, as an elaborate sauce is explained in a short paragraph:

> Deveined chilies soaked overnight, grounded with toasted sesame seeds, everything fried in pork lard, you must water as needed, the chicken, slices of plantain, sweet potato, apple and salt as needed.[42]

The same characteristics could be observed in the sweets, as in this *ante de piña* (pineapple appetizer):

> Use small pieces of candied pineapple, a layer of biscuit and another of pineapple, wine, almonds, pine nuts, cinnamon and the last layer of beaten white eggs, and put fire on top.[43]

Morino has explored in great detail the arguments in favor of and against considering the book an original work by Sor Juana, starting with the introductory sonnet that clearly establishes the author is copying previously extant recipes. This fact explains the lack of consistency in the verb forms, which oscillate between impersonal ("se aparta," "se unta") and personal ("muele," "echa").[44] More surprising than the different verb forms is the number of spelling and punctuation errors, something that we would not expect from a careful writer like Sor Juana, but an explanation could be that she was writing at a time in which there was no spelling normalization, and mistakes could also have been introduced by the copyist.[45] However, what Morino sees as the main obstacle for the attribution of the sonnet (and therefore the manuscript) to Sor Juana is the twelfth line, in which the lack of rhyme ("propicia" doesn't rhyme with "servicio" and "sacrificio") seems very unlikely for a master in versification like Sor Juana.[46]

Another detail that makes this sonnet an unusual one for Sor Juana is to whom it is addressed: another nun (*oh hermana*), as a gesture or homage aimed to circulate between the walls of the convent. This contradicts the rest of her writing, which was always conceived as texts moving outward, leaving the life of the convent behind, as if her daily life inside the cloister was not worthy of her literature.[47] The same conclusion can be reached when the sonnet is compared with what Sor Juana considered her most personal creation, the poem "Primero Sueño." As a woman writer trying to carve out her own space in a world of men, "Juana Inés aspired to impose her presence more from the side of the library than from the kitchen."[48]

After accumulating a series of powerful arguments against Sor Juana's authorship, the Italian critic comes around full circle to find a scenario in which her composition makes sense: seeing this book as a playful creation composed during those times the nun shared with her sisters, freed from the pressure to publish and compete in a masculine world, simply to circulate inside the walls of the conventual kitchen. And Morino even imagines the circumstances in which another nun, many years later, seeing the original manuscript damaged by constant use, decides to make a copy.[49]

In conclusion, we may never know for sure if the *Recetario* was originally written or compiled by Sor Juana Inés de la Cruz. Regardless of the circumstances of attribution of the recipe book, all the culinary references that we find in Sor Juana's literary works—philosophical, sacred and amorous romances, sonnets, letters, and other poetic compositions—add to the well-documented importance of gastronomy in conventual life in New Spain, and make it possible to conclude that Sor Juana's culinary knowledge was no less important than her wisdom on philosophical and scientific issues, or, better yet, was an important part of it.

Notes

1. Marcello Carmagnani, "La organización de los espacios americanos en la monarquía española, siglos XVI–XVIII," in *Las Indias Occidentales. Procesos de incorporación territorial a las monarquías ibéricas (Siglos XVI a XVIII)* (Mexico City: Colegio de México; Red Columnaria, 2012), 333. All translations in this essay are ours unless otherwise noted.
2. Lidia E. Gómez García, "La fundación de la nobilísima Ciudad Puebla de los Ángeles," in *La Puebla de los Ángeles en el Virreinato*, ed. Sigrid María Louvier Nava (Puebla, Mexico: Universidad Popular Autónoma del Estado de Puebla; Fundación Amparo IAP, 2016), 14.
3. Carmagnani, "La organización," 333.
4. García, "La fundación," 14.
5. Enriqueta Quiroz Muñoz, "Del mercado a la cocina," in *Historia de la vida cotidiana en México*, ed. Pilar Gonzalbo Aizpuru, vol. 3, *El siglo XVIII: entre tradición y cambio* (Mexico City: Colegio de México; Fondo de Cultura Económica, 2005), 17–43; Quiróz Enriqueta, "Comer en Nueva España. Privilegios y pesares de la sociedad en el siglo XVIII," *Historia y Memoria*, no. 8 (January–June 2014): 19–58, https://revistas.uptc.edu.co/index.php/historia_memoria/article/view/2616/2427.
6. Quiroz Muñoz, "Del mercado a la cocina," 26.
7. Paola Jeannete Vera Báez, "Viandas para el alma y ayunos para el cuerpo: Del refectorio y la olla de comunidad," in *Los conventos del siglo XVI de Puebla y*

Morelos, ed. Francisco Javier Pizarro Gómez et al. (Puebla, Mexico: Universidad Popular Autónoma del Estado de Puebla, 2018), 191–92.

8. See John Super, "Libros de cocina y cultura en la América Latina temprana," in *Conquista y comida: Consecuencias del encuentro de dos mundos*, ed. Janet Long (Mexico City: Universidad Nacional Autónoma de México, 1996); Josefina Muriel and Guadalupe Pérez San Vicente, "Los hallazgos gastronómicos: Bibliografía de cocina en la Nueva España y el México del Siglo XIX," in *Conquista y comida: Consecuencias del encuentro de dos mundos*, ed. Janet Long (Mexico City: Universidad Autónoma de México, 1996).
9. Vera Báez, "Viandas para el alma," 192.
10. See Asunción Lavrin, "Santa Teresa en los conventos de monjas de Nueva España," *Hispania sacra* 67, no. 136 (2015): 505–29, http://doi.org/10.3989/hs.2015.015; Josefina Muriel, *Conventos de monjas en la Nueva España* (Mexico City: Editorial Santiago, 1946).
11. See some legends on dishes in Paola Jeannete Vera Báez, "Tradición cultural gastronómica de Puebla," in *Encuentro con la Historia. Puebla a través de los siglos*, ed. by Marco Antonio Rojas Flores, Pedro Ángel Palou Pérez, and Víctor Bacre Parra (Puebla, Mexico: Investigaciones y Publicaciones A.C., 2015), 4:367–86.
12. Vera Báez, "Viandas para el alma," 193.
13. Rosalba Loreto López, "Prácticas alimenticias en los conventos de mujeres en la Puebla del Siglo XVIII," in *Conquista y comida: Consecuencias del encuentro de dos mundos*, ed. Janet Long (Mexico City: Universidad Nacional Autónoma de México, 1996).
14. Antonio Rubial García, "Las órdenes mendicantes evangelizadoras en Nueva España y sus cambios estructurales durante los siglos virreinales," *Históricas Digital*, Serie Novohispana 83 (2012): 216, 220, https://www.historicas.unam.mx/publicaciones/publicadigital/libros/iglesiane/iglesia009.pdf.
15. Massimo Montanari, *El hambre y la abundancia. Historia y cultura de la alimentación en Europa* (Barcelona: Crítica, 1993), 82.
16. Electa Arenal and Stacey Schlau, *Untold Sisters: Hispanic Nuns in Their Own Works* (Albuquerque: University of New Mexico Press, 2010), 13.
17. She was also known as Juana de Asvaje or Asbaje, and the year of her birth is still debated, between 1648 and 1651.
18. Daughter of the marquess of Grana and wife of the 25th viceroy of the New Spain (1664–73), Don Antonio Sebastián de Toledo Molina y Salazar, marquess of Mancera. José Luis Curiel Monteagudo, *Virreyes y virreinas golosos de la Nueva España* (Mexico City: Porrúa, 2004), 93–94.
19. Lourdes Aguilar Salas, "Sor Juana, las monjas jerónimas y los deleites de la cocina," *Claustronomía. Revista gastronómica digital*, July 3, 2019, https://www.elclaustro.edu.mx/claustronomia/index.php/investigacion/item/187-sor-juana-las-monjas-jeronimas-y-los-deleites-de-la-cocina.
20. See Mónica Lavín and Ana Benítez Muro, *Sor Juana en la cocina* (Mexico City: Grijalbo, 2010), 18; Rosalva Loreto López and Ana Benítez Muro, "Un bocado para los ángeles: la cocina en los conventos," in *Cocina Virreinal Novohispana II* (Mexico City: Clío, 2000); Rosalva Loreto López, "Prácticas alimenticias en los conventos de mujeres en la Puebla del siglo XVIII," in *Conquista y comida:*

Consecuencias del encuentro de dos mundos, ed. Janet Long (Mexico City: Universidad Nacional Autónoma de México, 2003), 481–503.

21. Josefina Muriel, *Cultura femenina novohispana*, Serie Hist (Mexico City: Universidad Nacional Autónoma de México, Instituto de Investigaciones Históricas, 2000), 476.
22. Octavio Paz (*Sor Juana Inés de la Cruz o las trampas de la fe*) mentions the existence of a slave, and Lota Spell has published the document (*Acervo Histórico del Archivo General de Notarías de la Ciudad de México*, February 25, 1669) stating that Sor Juana received the slave from her mother.
23. Muriel, *Cultura femenina novohispana*, 476.
24. See Juana Inés de Asbaje y Ramírez de Santillana, *Obras completas* (Mexico City: Porrúa, 2018).
25. Asbaje y Ramírez de Santillana, *Obras completas*, poem 23.
26. Her great friend "Lisi." Sor Juana Inés de la Cruz, *Inundación castálida* (Barcelona: Red Ediciones), Kindle; Curiel Monteagudo, *Virreyes y virreinas*, 105.
27. Sor Juana dedicated an extensive poem to the Duchess of Averio and wife of Arcos, María de Guadalupe de Lencastre y Cardenas Manrique. De la Cruz, *Inundación castálida*, 144–49; Asbaje y Ramírez de Santillana, *Obras completas*; De la Cruz, *Obras completas. Comedias, sainetes y prosa*; María Luisa Manrique de Lara y Gonzaga y Lujan was princess of the House of Mantua Gonzaga-Guastalla y del Sacro Imperio Romano Germánico, niece of San Luis Gonzaga, 11th countess of Paredes de Nava and vicereine of New Spain (1680–86), and wife of Don Tomás Antonio de la Cerda y Aragón, 3rd marquess of the Laguna de Camero Viejo, 28th viceroy of New Spain. Curiel Monteagudo, *Virreyes y virreinas*, 101. Elvira de Toledo was the wife of the 30th viceroy of New Spain, from 1688 to 1696, Don Gaspar de la Cerda Sandoval Silva y Mendoza, Conde de Galve. Sor Juana died when they were ruling, on April 17, 1695. Curiel Monteagudo, *Virreyes y virreinas*, 110–11.
28. Bobo mullet fish refers to *joturus pichardi*, fish from the Gulf of Mexico.
29. Sor Juana Inés de la Cruz, "Answer by the poet to the most illustrious Sister Filotea de la Cruz" (1691), trans. William Little, 2008, 18, https://docplayer.net/34355203-Answer-by-the-poet-to-the-most-illustrious-sister-filotea-de-la-cruz-1-by-sor-juana-ines-de-la-cruz-1691.html.
30. Angelo Morino, *El libro de cocina de Sor Juana Inés de la Cruz* (Bogotá: Norma, 2001), 37.
31. Morino, *El libro de cocina*, 36.
32. Morino, *El libro de cocina*, 43.
33. Josefina Ludmer, "Las tretas del débil," in *La sartén por el mango: encuentro de escritoras latinoamericanas*, ed. Patricia Elena González and Eliana Ortega (Río Piedras, Puerto Rico: El Huracán, 1985), 47–54.
34. Josefina Muriel de González Mariscal, "Presentación," in *Libro de cocina*. (Toluca, Mexico: Instituto Mexiquense de Cultura, 1996), 7.
35. Lavín and Benítez Muro, *Sor Juana en la cocina*, 7.
36. Lavín and Benítez Muro, besides providing an extensive introduction to the history and ingredients of conventual cuisine, have included in their edition of Sor Juana's recipe book modern version of the dishes.
37. Morino, *El libro de cocina*, 53.

38. See Diana Salomé Corona Ortega, *Gastronomía novohispana: un enfoque filológico* (Mexico City: Universidad Nacional Autónoma de México, 2011), 46–79.
39. Lavín and Benítez Muro, *Sor Juana en la cocina*, 73.
40. Lavín and Benítez Muro, *Sor Juana en la cocina*, 73.
41. "Pon una cazuela untada con manteca y luego una capa de gallina y otra de jitomate, cebollas rebanadas, clavo, pimienta, canela, cominos, cilantro, ajos en pedacitos, perejil en lonjitas y azafrán, así continuarás y al último lonjas de jamón y vinagre, y puesto a cocer entre dos fuegos. Después de que está cocido su caldo necesario, chorizones, pasas, almendras, aceitunas, chiles y alcaparrones." Lavín and Benítez Muro, *Sor Juana en la cocina*, 88.
42. "Chiles desvenados y remojados de un día para otro, molidos con ajonjolí tostado, y frito todo en manteca, echaras el agua necesaria, la gallina, rebanadas de plátano, camote, manzana y su sal necesaria." Lavín and Benítez Muro, *Sor Juana en la cocina*, 92.
43. "Hecha pedacitos la piña en conserva, una capa de marquesote y otra de piña, vino, almendras, piñones, canela y la última capa de claras de huevo batidas, y ponle fuego arriba." Lavín and Benítez Muro, *Sor Juana en la cocina*, 106.
44. Morino, *El libro de cocina*, 59.
45. Morino, *El libro de cocina*, 60.
46. Morino, *El libro de cocina*, 62.
47. Morino, *El libro de cocina*, 63.
48. Morino, *El libro de cocina*, 76.
49. Morino, *El libro de cocina*, 89–95.

PART II

A Modernized Table

National Identities, Regionalisms, and Transnational Foodways

CHAPTER 4

Immigrants, Elites, and Identities

Representing Food Cultures in Nineteenth-Century Latin America

LEE SKINNER

The opening to free trade that took place in much of Latin America in the nineteenth century affected the ways in which people ate and thought about what and how they were eating in two significant ways. Immigrants from Europe and elsewhere opened restaurants, and merchants began importing food and beverages, especially wine, from other countries. Advertisements in periodicals targeted at the upper class and the newly developing middle classes drew attention to the French, Spanish, or German menus of fine dining establishments that attracted metropolitan elites and announced the availability of imported wines, liquors, and luxury food items in local stores. In Peru for example, Italian immigrants opened and ran small stores that stocked imported goods, and others found employment as chocolate makers, millers, and pasta makers. The Second Empire in Mexico popularized French food, an influence that lasted long after the departure of the French army. At the same time, food and eating habits were also used as pretexts to comment on and to represent individuals' and nations' relations to modernity, progress, and elite status; people's lifestyles and decisions about food could be shown to represent their relationships to the metropolitan centers of Europe and the United States, which were held up as models for the nascent Latin American nations. This essay examines representations of food and eating in Mexico and Peru, countries which experienced waves of immigration from France, Italy, and China, and argues that such representations were mobilized in order to advance particular agendas about politics and national and group identities while at the same time perpetuating hierarchies of race and class that reinforced social and racial divides.

The eating habits of Latin Americans in the nineteenth century were at once deeply personal and fraught with greater implications and meanings about class, race, and identity. As people looking to better their economic status made new homes in Latin America and as governments of these new nations increasingly relaxed import-export laws and consciously inserted their countries into the global marketplace, patterns of eating developed that demonstrate multiple and multivalent influences from around the world. At the same time, these patterns of eating and habits around food were linked to national conversations about progress, modernization, civilization, and the future, as defined by representations of food and its different modes of consumption in journal articles, cookbooks, and advertisements. To emulate or incorporate European food and modes of eating was frequently presented as desirable for Latin American elites and aspiring elites and was linked to other important conversations about Latin America's relationship with, imitation of, and rejection of European models.

Immigration to Latin America was not uniform; immigrants came in greater numbers from some areas and countries in Europe and Asia rather than others and headed to a few specific places in Latin America en masse, while other Latin American nations experienced a small but culturally significant number of foreign arrivals. Between 1850 and 1900, for example, Uruguay's population grew sevenfold and Argentina's quadrupled, due in large part to immigration mostly from Europe.[1] Immigration itself was disproportionate and most immigrants to Latin America went to Argentina, where in the span of the hundred years from 1830 to 1930 six million foreigners arrived to make their homes. In the 1880s alone Argentina attracted eight hundred and forty thousand immigrants.[2] Brazil and Cuba also experienced large numbers of immigrant arrivals. While a significant portion of these immigrants eventually returned to their countries of origin, their influence on cuisine was important, as they introduced and popularized foods by opening markets and restaurants.

Nonetheless, regardless of the specific numbers of immigrants or size of the foreign community in a given country, Latin American consumers, especially those in large metropolitan areas, emulated European eating habits. While immigrants influenced—often enormously—food and attitudes about food, the prevailing mindset about the superiority and desirability of European culture, intellectual life, political systems, and lifestyles had perhaps even more influence on the ways that Latin Americans thought about food and sent and received signals about their identities based on food, meals, and eating. In addition to the arrival of immigrants and travelers from abroad, elite Latin Americans made their own journeys to Europe and North America and returned having been influenced by their experiences overseas. Writing of Colombia, for example, Aída Martínez Carreño explains, "Through sheer desire, a social class was emerging in the country that, through differences in consumption, maintained a rigid, classist code of values, differentiated quality from quantity and that sought to align itself with the upper classes of powerful countries."[3]

Nineteenth-century Latin American liberals consistently defined their goals for their countries as the achievement of progress and modernity and saw these aspects as emanating above all from the United States, England, France, Germany, and Scandinavia. They rejected the colonial past and traditions tied to it and sought to instill democratic liberalism in their political systems. Industrialization and large-scale agriculture were seen as modernizing the backward economies of their countries and depended on the construction of infrastructure such as railroads, port cities, warehouses, and more. These new industries and commercial ventures also depended on—and led to—the growth of cities, urban planning that created wide boulevards suitable for public transportation, and public buildings and economic enterprises to support the larger populations living in these cities. All these residents, of course, needed to eat, and a growing number now had the financial resources, thanks to their employment in the developing sector of the middle class, to purchase and consume luxury food items, to hire chefs, and to go to cafés and restaurants. Benjamin Orlove and Arnold J. Bauer state succinctly, "The sphere of consumption, and in particular the use of domestic and imported goods, is one of the key contexts in which national identities were stated, contested, and affirmed in postcolonial Latin America."[4] Latin Americans could, in short, literally consume modernity.

Peru principally experienced immigration from Europe and Asia. In 1857, there were more than thirteen thousand Europeans living in Lima, constituting 13 percent of the city's total population; by 1876, there were approximately nineteen thousand Europeans in the country, an increase of almost 50 percent.[5] These European immigrants, who mostly came from Italy, brought with them their desire to consume food and drink from their countries of origin. At the same time, they took advantage of Peru's growing economy and the development of a significant middle class in Lima in particular in order to sell "imported consumer goods. Other immigrants who experienced a rapid economic expansion dedicated themselves to productive activities, such as the chocolatiers, the millers, and the noodle makers."[6] The *Guía de domicilio de Lima para el año de 1864*, which listed the names and addresses of all individuals and their occupations in the city, offers a plethora of information about the foreign residents selling food to Peruvians. Of the twelve chocolatiers listed, for example, ten have surnames indicating French or Italian heritage, such as Bignon, Figari, Lepiani, and Debron.[7] Among the proprietors of casual eateries and cafés we find names such as Alerson y Vennuad, José Bailly, Francisco Bambachi, Tomás Berminzoni, Pedro Boisseau, Augusto Lefrançois, Simeon Pelissier (who had two locations), Juan Roix, and Juan Thiessen.

The preponderance of Italians in Lima can be seen in the fact that in 1887 there were six hundred and fifty small markets (*pulperías*) in Lima, the equivalent to today's convenience store. These markets sold prepared food and liquor to be consumed on the premises or taken away. Almost five hundred of those, or 80 percent, were owned and operated by Italians.[8] In her 1895 novel *Herencia*, Clorinda Matto de Turner describes the bustling, industrializing atmosphere of Lima and the consumption patterns of its residents. Textile workers "counted over their daily wages in order to leave them in the markets whose doors were filling up with locals," and the upper classes favor aristocratic bars where they savor cocktails and *aperitivos* rather than *cachito*, an indigenous corn beer.[9] A central character in the novel is Aquilino Merlo, an Italian immigrant, whose specialty is "green pasta, colored with chard juice, which brought so many customers to 'The Crystal Goblet [his market].'"[10] Stores like Merlo's offered the convenience of prepared foods to their working-class clientele, and they also functioned as social hubs for neighborhoods. As Bonfiglio puts it, they were "places for the neighborhood to congregate and sometimes for social gatherings. The store owner knew his customers personally and had an individualized economic relationship with each."[11] Yet Peruvian elites viewed the Italian shopkeepers with a certain degree of suspicion. The economic opportunities awaiting European immigrants to Peru were entrepreneurial in nature; successful immigrants established businesses across many sectors. Rather than being seen as a boon for Peruvian society, such entrepreneurship was sometimes depicted as taking advantage of vulnerable native-born residents, and entrepreneurialism became equated with foreigners and acquired negative connotations.[12] *Herencia*'s Merlo manifests this ruthless grasping at economic success; unscrupulous and sexually avaricious, he seduces Camila Aguilera, daughter of an elite family, and forces her into marriage in order to climb the social ladder. In the novel's penultimate scene, he beats her in a drunken rage. Matto de Turner portrays him as motivated by a mixture of "carnal passion and greed for money," hardly the representative of modernity and progress that she and other Peruvian intellectuals sought for their nation.[13]

While Merlo's store is fictional, Matto de Turner also names the well-known establishment Broggi Hermanos, which sold candy and confections, imported liquors, ice cream, and sodas. Far from being a *pulpería*, Broggi Hermanos attracted the upper classes and aspiring middle classes, and Matto de Turner specifically marks it as a source of desirable goods—and goods that are good for people to desire, unlike the cheap liquor Merlo distills from potatoes in his storefront. Tram riders journeying down Plateros de San Agustín in the opening pages of *Herencia* stare into the windows of Broggi Hermanos.[14] Indeed, the three Broggi brothers and their ventures provide a telling example of the cultural significance of Italian food and eating customs in Lima through much of the nineteenth century and into the twentieth. The brothers, Martino, Angelo, and Pietro (often called Pedro), immigrated from Italy in 1844 and opened their store on Plateros de San Agustín 15 and 17 the following year. Later they partnered with fellow Italian immigrant Nicolás Dora on the café Broggi y Dora on Espaderos. That street boasted numerous stores founded by Europeans and stocked with European goods. As Luis Alberto Sánchez explains, "Broggi y Dora brought together, depending on the time and the day, politicians, journalists, writers, financiers, high-class prostitutes and bullfighters. Luis Varela y Orbegoso and the staff of *El Comercio* (one of the principal newspapers of Lima) regularly went to the Broggi bar to drink their morning cocktail and their special aperitivo; at night, the delicious chocolate with toast."[15] Both the appearance of the Broggi establishments in novels, memoirs, and magazine articles and their representations as a place to see fellow members of the upper classes socializing, drinking, and eating demonstrate the cultural resonance and impact of Europe as a locus of consumerist desire. Broggi Hermanos and Broggi y Dora offered an experience that Peruvian consumers wanted: the opportunity to live as Europeans did, eating, drinking, and spending time in the same kinds of environments as people did overseas. Moreover, the fact that this consumption took place in public meant that their appropriation of European practices was visible to others, be they peers, the aspiring lower classes looking enviously out the windows of the streetcar, or the upper classes whom Broggi's customers sought to emulate in turn.

Casa Broggi, the Broggis' banquet hall, frequently hosted dinners and parties that were featured in the popular journal *Actualidades*, published in Lima from 1903 to 1908. Magazines and newspapers often included short articles about organizations or clubs and their social activities, as when, in 1907, *Actualidades* described a dinner hosted by and for the Swiss immigrant community.

> Last Sunday, celebrating their national anniversary, the members of the Swiss community here in the capital united over a splendid lunch, served in the elegant dining room of Restaurant Broggi, on Plateros de San Agustín. The Swiss community in Lima is one of the nicest, hardest working, and most honorable of the foreign communities. It constitutes a solid element of advancement and progress in this country, and thus, besides the culture and intelligence that characterize those who comprise it, they are unanimously appreciated by us.[16]

Here, the journalist singles out the Swiss immigrant community as an important contributor to Peru's national progress; the Swiss help make Peru modern through their hard work and virtuous comportment. *Actualidades* invites its readers to participate in the national modernizing project by creating an imagined space in which they, like the enlightened editors of the journal, seek to promote the ideal of modernity by praising the European immigrants whose presence improves Peru. At the same time, *Actualidades* creates an implicit readership of native-born Peruvians versus the Swiss immigrants. The Swiss banquet allows *Actualidades* to foster a shared notion of Peruvian national progress and to lay claim to being modern itself, given that the journal is capable of recognizing the merits of these immigrants and the cultural value of venues like Casa Broggi. Restaurants serving European food and hosting gatherings of businessmen and their associates represent a European lifestyle, and Europe, as we have seen, in turn represents the modern ideal which journals like *Actualidades* promote. When *Actualidades* praises both the physical space of Casa Broggi and the people dining there for their work ethic, culture, and intelligence, the journal demonstrates that it too helps Peru become modern. Through the very act of reading this account, the journal flatteringly implies, the Peruvian audience takes part in advancing national progress and modernization. The assumption is that readers, like the editorial staff of *Actualidades*, can discern the significance of the Swiss community's work and lives in Lima and their connections to Peruvian modernity.

Another group of immigrants with undoubtedly lasting impact on Peruvian culture and cuisine were the Chinese. Between 1849 and 1874 approximately ninety thousand Chinese arrived in Peru on eight-year labor contracts to work on the railroads, in the guano industry, and in agriculture.[17] As the laborers incurred additional debt during their time in Peru, their contracts were often extended, leading to indefinite periods of indentured servitude. However, some Chinese arrived in Peru free of contracts, while others were able to work out their contracts and then make their own way in the country. They imported Chinese food items such as soy sauce, spices, and liquors, and later opened the casual restaurants that would become known as *chifas*.[18] Newly free Chinese often became private chefs, as having a Chinese chef was "synonymous with prestige among the most aristocratic Liman households."[19] As Juan de Arona famously wrote in 1891, "un cocinero chino es el desideratum" (a Chinese cook is the desideratum, or sine qua non); note that Arona's use of a Latin term to describe the desirability of the Chinese cook further underscores his own elite status as well as that of those who hire said Chinese chefs.[20] These chefs were called upon to prepare Peruvian food and the European specialties that their employers used to impress their guests, but they also incorporated Chinese cooking techniques such as stir frying and seasoned the food with the spices with which they were familiar. Likewise, restaurants run by Chinese offered the Peruvian dishes their clientele was familiar with as well as Chinese specialties such as noodles and fried rice to the menu. Between 1869 and 1872, the number of Chinese cafés in Lima went from nineteen to 146, which bespeaks the growing acceptance of, if not the Chinese themselves, their food.[21] Nonetheless, the Peruvian elites by no means aspired to emulate China or Chinese political, economic, or educational systems, as they did with the European role models. Writing in 1897, Clemente Palma ferociously critiqued all aspects of Chinese society and culture, claiming "the Chinese don't represent any active life principle, nothing useful, nothing practical, they don't constitute a force of any kind."[22] In language that evokes social Darwinism and positivism, he criticized their "sick, impure blood. The Chinese carries in his veins the germs of repugnant diseases . . . which, as is well-known, spring from vices in the blood, from racial weakness and degeneration. The moral organism of the Chinese cannot be superior. . . . Chinese intellect is subtle, and we have already noted that intellectual subtlety is a sign of degeneration."[23] Physically, morally, and intellectually, Palma writes, the Chinese are not simply inferior, they are deteriorating and pose a threat to Peruvian society, a formulation which places the Chinese immigrants firmly and permanently into the category of "others," of non-Peruvians, and which does not allow for the possibility of assimilation.

Given the complex attitudes toward the largest immigrant groups, it is perhaps not surprising that middle- and upper-class Peruvians continued to look to an idealized Europe as the standard-bearer for desirable cultural practices including the consumption of food. The imported goods most vaunted in advertising were French and British.

A lengthy advertisement in *Actualidades* for Mumm's champagne on September 21, 1907, compared the consumption in the United States to that in Peru, pointing out that almost all champagne drunk in the United States was Mumm's. The advertisement uses the first-person plural both to include the readers and to create an atmosphere of exclusivity; this "we" has special, firsthand access to knowledge about elaborate and important parties in Europe that is now being shared with Peruvian readers. "In our latest exchanges with Europe we have seen that in all the Parisian parties thrown for the Swedish and Danish king and queen, in British parties for the colonial ministers; in the Hague in the Conference of Peace banquets; all the toasts have been a triumph for the famous Cordon Rouge which we are also appreciating so much."[24] Just like the European dignitaries honoring royalty and marking crucial political events, the Peruvian writers and their readers are drinking Mumm's. The champagne is a symbol of socioeconomic status—just as buying and reading *Actualidades* itself is—and a symbol of access to cultural capital.

In another ad, this one from December 14, 1907, gender and culture intersect as a man compliments a woman on her skin, good health, and temperament, and she replies that all are due to the fact that she drinks Vichy water. Here, fascinatingly, the female consumer understands that using a French product signifies her participation in the modernizing project and educates her male counterpart to that effect. Yet her body remains the object of his gaze as he assesses her physical attributes and familiarly calls her "friend." Despite his (attempted) appropriation of her body, she has sufficient agency to make her own decisions about what to

Illustration in *Actualidades*, artist unknown, September 21, 1907.

Actualidades advertisement by Peruvian illustrator and caricaturist Julio Málaga Grenet, December 14, 1907.

consume and enough cultural power to be represented as better informed and more up-to-date—more modern—than her male friend. The message is, perhaps, that women can be drawn into the modernizing project through an appeal to their concern about their physical appearance; but it may also be that food and drink provide a level playing field for both sexes to experience the cultural consumption that allows them to make visible to others their modern cultural identity. These advertisements, and others like them, linked an aspirational lifestyle to the consumption of imported goods, and made both the lifestyle and the consumer items accessible.

As occurred in Peru, in Mexico immigration coupled with the widespread belief that the United States and Europe were ideal models of modernity and progress helped drive consumer practices. Jeffrey Pilcher and José Luis Juárez López have both written extensively of the connections between Mexican cuisine and Mexican national identity in the nineteenth century. Juárez López posits that differentiated eating habits were used to mark class and racial distinctions and that the idea of a national cuisine, meant to distinguish Mexico as unique, did not take hold.[25] The emulation of European models reached its apogee during the dictatorship of Porfirio Díaz between 1878 and 1910, although, as Pilcher points out, the first published cookbook in Mexico "helped launch [the] penchant for Parisian cuisine as early as 1831."[26] My work here focuses specifically on the explicit and implicit messages about progress and identity that the creators of written and visual texts imparted to their audiences. These creators popularized aspirational consumerism, as I call it—the idea that by literally consuming what Europeans did, Mexican audiences could become the people they wanted to be.

Foreigners had begun influencing Mexican consumer culture well before the *Porfiriato*, however; after Independence in the 1820s, Salvador Novo points out, the arrival of foreigners (other than Spaniards) spurred the construction of elegant lodging that now merited "the new French name of 'hotels,'" instead of the rustic hostelries that were travelers' only option until then. Most importantly for our purposes, these foreign travelers also needed suitable places to eat the food to which they were accustomed, so hotels were constructed to include "dining rooms to immediately host the guests, although they also admit outside customers wishing to taste the hotel's dishes that imitate the foreign delicacies to which we suppose the travelers from France, Germany, or England are accustomed."[27] As elsewhere in Spanish America, consumption patterns were led by external pressures and followed by native-born upper- and middle-class families. Guillermo Prieto remembered a friend in midcentury Guadalajara who served meals in which "tasty beans were stewed and the ultra-famous silver and gold squash were ever-present, life's pleasure and a delight to the palate. Of course all this national richness mixed with finesse and opportunity with the finery of European cuisine."[28] Prieto engages in a complex set of maneuvers involving nostalgia and aspiration. Reminiscing half a century later, he romanticizes traditional, regional food of the region, yet his friend is also marked as somewhat eccentric because he not only eats these dishes himself but also serves them to guests. At the same time, the food is decidedly not traditional because it is served alongside of, and possibly cooked with techniques from, European cuisine. Prieto may seem to elevate Mexican regional cooking, but his rendition of his friend's cuisine instead reveals the implicit attitude that European dishes are superior. Along similar lines, a story in the Porfirian magazine *El Mundo Ilustrado*, "Los dos claveles" (The Two Carnations), included the main character's memories of returning home as a young man after significant time away and being welcomed with a festive Mexican meal. "At that time Mexico didn't yet have the Cordon Bleu American women who cooked mole like the Puebla women of decades past; no young 'miss' sold 'real Mexican tamales,' and no American served in 'The Queen Xochitl' or someplace like it 'the richest pulque in the country' and the privilege of our good, classic dishes depended on a few cooks."[29] This description both mocks the way that American "discoveries" of Mexican specialties make them newly trendy and participates in that by detailing with such specificity the food items as prepared by Americans. The narrator does not describe the food he actually ate at the welcome-home dinner; rather, he evokes the current phenomenon of Americans popularizing for Mexicans their own Mexican food. We only see the food he ate through his representation of the Yankeefied versions currently in vogue. These types of references to Mexican food bespeak an ambivalence about the cultural value of traditional cuisine.

France and England were the principal aspirational models for the Mexican middle and upper class. While the number of immigrants was small in proportion to both the total number of immigrants in the country and to the Mexican population, they helped bring a desire for European goods by modeling their consumption for their Mexican counterparts and, in many cases, by establishing businesses that imported and sold such items.[30] According to Javier Pérez Siller, French immigrants were active in hostelry, restaurants, pharmacies and perfumeries, candy and cake shops, bookstores, presses, lithography and photography studios, designers and hairstylists, and sellers of wine and luxury products.[31] If the habits of the Maurer family, immigrants from Alsace at midcentury, are any indication, French immigrants sought to maintain their culinary traditions in their new home. The Maurer brothers first ran a bakery in Mexico City but then bought a mill and hacienda outside Puebla. When the younger brother married the Mexican-born daughter of French immigrants, she continued purchasing wine and food imported from France.[32] By the 1880s, the *afrancesamiento* (Frenchification) of the *Porfiriato* was in full swing. Mexican elites almost obsessively looked to France for role models in all aspects of their daily lives, from clothing to books, food, and even bicycles. Porfirio Díaz hired a Frenchman, Sylvain Dumont, to take charge of all his official banquets; menus were printed, naturally, in French. A typical meal hosted by Díaz for official purposes was this one in 1910: "Consomé Princesa; Cromesquis a la italiana; Salmón Metternich; Cocteleta de Maintenon; Suprémes de Volairés Talleyrand; Timbal; Gelatinas de faisán dorado; Glass de pistache; Gateaux Assortis y vinos alemanes, oporto, champaña cordón azul de la Viuda de Clicquot" (Princess consommé; Italian cromesquis; Salmon Metternich; Maintenon Shaker; Suprémes de Volairés Talleyrand; Timbale; Golden pheasant in aspic; Pistachio glacé; Gateaux Assortis and German wines, port, Cordon Bleu Champagne from Veuve Clicquot).[33] Not surprisingly, such banquets required hundreds of waiters and scores of chefs and sous chefs, and an invitation was hotly sought after.[34]

In 1901 Adolfo Prantl and José L. Groso published *La ciudad de México: Novísima guía universal de la capital de la República de México*, a guidebook consisting of four sections: information for visitors to Mexico City; a directory of those working in the city in industry, commerce, education, and other professions; a directory of all aspects of the federal government, including biographies of the most notable politicians; and a description of Mexico City's geography and buildings. Their thousand-page tome was well illustrated with photographs and engravings. Clearly a luxury purchase, it was targeted to members of the Mexican elite, whether residing in the capital or not; upper-class readers in cities such as Guadalajara or Veracruz could have used it to plan their trips to the capital and to imagine daily life in the bustling metropolis. Prantl and Groso dedicated an entire chapter to restaurants, cantinas, cafés, and ice cream parlors, which they began by stating firmly, "the principal restaurants being run by foreigners, the cooking is French, Italian, English, or American and sometimes they serve Mexican dishes."[35] The order in which they list the national cuisines goes in descending order of status and culinary excellence from the French to the Mexican, as further borne out in the following affirmation: "There are in Mexico City some first-class restaurants that stand out for their luxury, delicious food and stellar service, such as that of M. Sylvain Dumont, the Hotel Sans . . . [and] the Maison Dorée."[36] Dumont was the only restaurateur with an eponymous establishment, which speaks to his renown among the Porfirian elites, but the other restaurants that Prantl and Groso deemed "important" were also French-run and featured French food.

Upper-class Mexicans did not routinely feast on French delicacies, but a typical menu for upper- and middle-class households would have included several dishes of European origin. *El Mundo Ilustrado* regularly published suggested menus for female readers; the April 1, 1900, lunch menu included beef bourguignon and York ham in aspic, while the dinner menu featured Genevan-style trout, "German salad," and Chantilly meringues. A month later, on April 29, readers could imagine themselves lunching on pickled tuna, lambs' feet cooked in the English style, Chateaubriand steak, and Spanish artichokes. Recipes for several of these suggestions followed, ensuring that the reader—or her cook—could follow through on the magazine's recommendations. As well as including food typical of Europe or the United States, these menu planners notably excluded Mexican or other South American plates. This clearly sent the message that the readers of *El Mundo Ilustrado*, a periodical by and for the Porfirian elite, were meant to grace their tables with European food, not Mexican. Indeed, these readers were not given the option to choose between the two cuisines; European items were the only ones on offer.

El Mundo Ilustrado also instructed readers in the appropriate customs and behaviors related to food. In 1904, an article divided meals into "ordinary" and "luxury" lunches or dinners. While the author assumed that the journal's female readers were familiar with ordinary meals, he or she painstakingly explained the possible variations on the luxury meal, which could mean either the French or Russian style. In French-style service, all hot dishes are placed on the table at once; after the diners have partaken of all the hot foods, the dishes are removed and all the cold dishes are served. However, Russian style is more demanding of the chef's and the housewife's skill in coordinating with one another to avoid lengthy pauses between courses, as each course is served individually.

While these modes of service have offered gourmets, chefs, and arbiters of good taste many hours of robust debate, *El Mundo Ilustrado* provides a happy compromise in which the cold dishes are placed on the table at once, thus delighting the diners' palates and eyes, but the hot dishes are served individually, thus ensuring that diners can enjoy them at the appropriate temperature. Finally, the magazine points out, the diners will not even know if the hostess has chosen the French or Russian style of service; presumably they will assume that she is so familiar with European dining habits that she can successfully combine the two. Embedded in the journal's advice is the implicit norm that its readers are regularly hosting dinners meant to impress their guests not just with the deliciousness of the food, but with the worldliness and sophistication with which it is served. *El Mundo Ilustrado* supposes—even knows—that its readers are deeply concerned with demonstrating their elite status and that they link social standing with the ability to imitate and reproduce European customs at home.

The same 1904 issue featured "Five O'Clock Tea," by "Duchess Laura." The very fact that the title is in English signals the enthusiastic adoption of the British custom of serving tea accompanied by various finger foods. María Susana Victoria Uribe comments that for the Porfirian upper class, "it was more distinguished to go to a *five o'clock* than to the old colonial mid-morning break of hot chocolate and sweet buns," and the description given by the duchess makes it clear that tea is a pretext for exhibiting good taste and elite cultural values: "everyone knows that the day when a lady hosts her friends, she must offer them a refined and delicate collation, that is, an exquisite tea; besides, this is a pretext for displaying an infinity of good taste, from serving utensils to tablecloths and napkins."[37] The hostess who offers her guests tea demonstrates that she is privy to the particular social codes governing hospitality and takes advantage of the opportunity to display her good taste in table linens and china. More important than the food itself are the "beautiful plates and tiny forks" which it graces. Duchess Laura lists the variety of food and drink to be offered, but hastily adds that one can serve tea economically and, while she proffers recipes for tea cakes, pastries, and several exotic drinks such as "Persian drink," reiterates that "if, besides, you decorate your parlor with some flowers and plants, and most of all, if you possess the special art of entertaining your friends with discreet and pleasant conversation, they will not lack for anything and you will have the satisfaction of witnessing their pleasure." The article seems to put into play two different sets of values: one based on conspicuous consumption (the great variety of food and drink, the elaborately decorated table) and one based on the skills of the hostess (her conversational abilities). Yet Duchess Laura's emphasis in much of "Five O'Clock Tea" on the display of consumer items, which occupies multiple paragraphs, in contrast with the total of two sentences assuring readers that serving tea does not necessarily have to be expensive, instead imparts the message that copying upper-class British habits and having numerous other people see that imitation constitutes an important aspect of Porfirian upper-class life. The hostess gains cultural capital through her ability to impress her peers with her refinement, good manners, and perfectly set table, all of which are further inscribed within an environment in which European and British models are privileged.

Peruvian and Mexican elites, like their counterparts throughout Latin America in the nineteenth century, sought to create societies that were modern, progressive, and up-to-date, and looked to the United States, England, and Europe for their models in doing so. While immigration from Italy and China had important and real effects on Peruvian society, Peruvian writers for the most part represented their presence in Peru as negative. Reporting and advertisements in newspapers and magazines instead construed French, English, and US products and behaviors as appropriate objects of consumer desire, as also happened in Mexico. In both countries, this maneuver enabled the elites to reinforce their own social status through their visible consumption of imported goods and through their behaviors, as they reproduced European customs and manners in private and in public. They ascribed higher value to European elements and then, by presenting themselves as successful users of European goods and lifestyles, assigned themselves enhanced cultural status. Such attitudes would inevitably incite a backlash, but not until later in the twentieth century.

Notes

1. Michael Goebel, "Reconceptualizing Diasporas and National Identities in Latin America and the Caribbean, 1850–1950," in *Immigration and National Identities in Latin America*, ed. Nicola Foote and Michael Goebel (Gainesville: University Press of Florida, 2014), 2.
2. Goebel, "Reconceptualizing Diasporas and National Identities," 2.
3. Aída Martínez Carreño, *Mesa y cocina en el siglo XIX: Colombia* (Bogotá: Ministerio de Cultura, 1990), 67. Translations are my own throughout the chapter.

4. Benjamin Orlove and Arnold J. Bauer, "Giving Importance to Imports," in *The Allure of the Foreign: Imported Goods in Postcolonial Latin America* (Ann Arbor: University of Michigan Press, 1997), 8.
5. Giovanni Bonfiglio, *La presencia europea en el Perú* (Lima: Fondo Editorial del Congreso del Perú, 2001), 33.
6. Giovanni Bonfiglio, *Los italianos en la sociedad peruana: una visión histórica*, 2nd. ed. (Lima: Saywa, 1994), 64.
7. Manuel Atanasio Fuentes, *Guía de domicilio de Lima para el año de 1864* (Lima: author's printing, 1863), 359–60.
8. Bonfiglio, *Los Italianos*, 66.
9. Clorinda Matto de Turner, *Herencia (novela peruana)*, ed. Mary Berg (Buenos Aires: Stock Cero, 2006), 7–8.
10. Matto de Turner, *Herencia*, 22.
11. Bonfiglio, *Los Italianos*, 66.
12. Giovanni Bonfiglio, "Migración y empresarialidad en el Perú," http://usmp.edu.pe/idp/wp-content/uploads/2015/11/migracin_y_empresarialidad_para-web.pdf, 17.
13. Matto de Turner, *Herencia*, 69.
14. Matto de Turner, *Herencia*, 9.
15. Luis Alberto Sánchez, *Valdelomar: su tiempo y su obra* (Lima: Inpropesa, 1987), n.p.
16. "El banquete de la colonia suiza," *Actualidades*, September 21, 1907, 763, accessible at https://hdl.handle.net/2027/coo.31924100624653.
17. Sofía Indira Molero Denegri, "La construcción sociocultural de la gastronomía china en Lima: siglo XIX-XXI" (PhD diss., Universidad Nacional Mayor de San Marcos, 2010), 46.
18. Molero Denegri, "La construcción," 49.
19. Molero Denegri, "La construcción," 63.
20. Juan de Arona, *La inmigración en el Perú, monografía histórico-crítica* (Lima: Imprenta del Universo de C. Prince, 1891), 53.
21. Molero Denegri, "La construcción," 66–67.
22. Clemente Palma, "El porvenir de las razas en el Peru" (bachelor's thesis, Universidad Nacional Mayor de San Marcos, 1897), 16.
23. Palma, "El porvenir," 16.
24. *Actualidades*, September 21, 1907.
25. José Luis Juárez López, *Engranaje culinario: La cocina mexicana en el siglo XIX* (Mexico City: Conaculta, 2012), 60–61.
26. Jeffrey Pilcher, *¡Que vivan los tamales! Food and the Making of Mexican Identity* (Albuquerque: University of New Mexico Press, 1998), 63.
27. Salvador Novo, *Cocina mexicana: Historia gastronómica de la ciudad de México* (Mexico City: Porrúa, 2010), 105.
28. Guillermo Prieto, *Memorias de mis tiempos* (Mexico City: Imprenta de la Viuda de Bouret, 1906), 361.
29. "Los dos claveles," *El Mundo Ilustrado*, September 18, 1904.
30. Apparently only a few hundred French migrated to Mexico during the *Porfiriato*. See Henri Bunle, "Migratory Movements Between France and Foreign Lands," *Internal Migrations, Volume II: Interpretations*, ed. Walter F.

Willcox (New York: National Bureau of Economic Research, 1931), 206. http://www.nber.org/chapters/c5110.

31. Javier Pérez Siller, "Inversiones francesas en la modernidad porfirista: mecanismos y actores," in *México Francia: Memoria de una sensibilidad común; siglos XIX–XX*, ed. Javier Pérez Siller and Chantai Cramaussel, vol. 2 (Mexico City: Centro de Estudios Mexicanos y Centroamericanos, 1993).
32. Mariano Enrique Torres Bautista, "Vivir a la francesa en México. La familia Maurer y su establecimiento en el México anterior al Porfiriato," in *Extraños en tierra ajena: migración, alteridad e identidad, siglos XIX, XX y XXI*, ed. Raquel Barceló Quintal (Mexico City: Plaza y Valdés, 2009), 70.
33. María Niembro Gaona and Rodolfo Téllez Cuevas, "Historia y mestizaje de México a través de su gastronomía," *Culinaria* 4 (July–December 2012): 54, http:/web.uaemex.mx/Culinaria/culinaria_historia/cuatro_ne/pdfs/historia_del_mestizaje.pdf.
34. Juárez López, *Engranaje culinario*, 145.
35. Adolfo Prantl and José L. Groso, *La ciudad de México: Novísima guía universal de la capital de la República de México* (Mexico City: J. Buxó y Cia, 1901), 37.
36. Prantl and Groso, *La ciudad de México*, 37.
37. María Susana Victoria Uribe, "La minuta del día: Los tiempos de comida de la elite capitalina a principios del siglo XX," *Historia y Grafía* 34 (January–June 2010), http://www.scielo.org.mx/scielo.php?script=sci_arttext&pid=S1405-09272010000100002.

CHAPTER 5

Native Food and Male Emotions

Alimentary Encounters between White Travelers and Their "Others" in Nineteenth-Century Colombia

MERCEDES LOPEZ RODRIGUEZ

For authors and readers alike, travel literature is a field of intense emotions: the fascination of traveling and exploring, the challenge of writing and portraying amazing landscapes and intriguing customs and people.[1] Behind the scenes and in the margins of the narration, other feelings lurked within white men (European and Latin American) visiting rural Colombia in the nineteenth century. Their accounts are filled with complaints about the taste, smell, and lack of cleanliness of the local cuisine. The act of eating native foods broke the boundaries between white bodies and local ones, creating anxiety about undesirable contact and racial contamination. These alimentary encounters allow us to explore the emotions expressed by white men in their narratives regarding native foods: disgust, fear, discomfort, even frustration. The centrality of food encounters, and the literary performances of the responses that they triggered, are better understood when we read these narratives against the rigid set of emotions permitted to white men. Imagined as the apex of a pyramid of racial and gender constructions, white men presented themselves as the epitome of rationality, emotional moderation, and restraint in contrast to the more emotional displays of nonwhite men and of women.

The intersection between native food and white emotions helps us understand how race assumes materiality in social life even beyond the limits of the human body. The construction of whiteness extends beyond individual features such as skin color and hair; it is also conceived as a moral and intellectual profile that emanates from the non-racialized bodies of Europeans and their American descendants. This article delves into eating practices and representations of food as giving materiality to the racialized link between body and personality, paying attention to the role of emotions as a paramount factor in the depiction of difference between white explorers and local dwellers. It specifically explores the role of disgust toward native food as a method of racial formation that enforced discourses concerning the dangers of contamination to the white male body. Food, as a cluster of cultural practices, provides a privileged space to reflect on the multiple ways that gender and race shape our everyday life. We will also explore what was deemed edible, what practices of eating were acceptable, and how white travelers negotiated their own thoughts toward and relationship with something as intimate as food.

This article seeks to enrich ongoing discussions on coloniality, race, class, and food, by dealing with the materiality of both culture and race and with the embodied, everyday practices that were so instrumental to the implementation of segregation, disenfranchisement, and exclusion. To this extent, it builds on the critical approaches to the intersections of race, emotions, and food advanced by Sara Ahmed and Kyla Wazana Tompkins. Food as a cultural artifact allows the exploration of awkward materialities (sticky, dusty, among many others) and the performance of emotional reactions toward them as a way of exploring fears of racial and class contamination in which the socially excluded "others" enter the white body and transform its emotional profile.

The motif of disgust and aversion to native food and eating practices traverses the narratives of European travelers such as Jean-Baptiste Boussingault and Elisée Reclus and of Latin American authors like Manuel Ancízar and José María Samper, tracing a commonality between food and the racialized bodies of Indians, mixed-race, and Black peasants and workers. Rebecca Earle's work has shown the historical depth of the connection between dietary practices and the creation of cultural and racial identities in context of traveling. Her studies reveal the centrality of the ideas about native foods in the formation of models of physical difference among European explorers and their American descendants.[2]

Race, Emotions, and Food: White Men Losing Their Temper over Native Food

Race is a social construct that links the body of the individual—culturally represented as a repository of a selected set of characteristics (skin color, hair, ancestry)—to a fixed cognitive, psychological, and emotional profile, which emanates from the racialized body. Scholarly understanding of race has privileged the visual component of this definition, paying less attention to the other senses involved in the formation of racial discourses. As the historian Mark Smith argues, "Modern discussion of 'race' and racial identity are hostage to the eye."[3] In an effort to increase our understanding of the subject, and considering white US southerners, he affirms that they "used more than just sight to validate, betray, and affirm racial identity."[4] Indeed, "race" is comprised of feelings and sensorial experiences through which abstract notions acquire materiality in everyday life. This article delves into the emotional makeup of race, exploring the feeling of disgust toward food as a way to create, redefine, and enforce discourses about whiteness as cleanliness and purity. The dirtiness and messiness of the culinary practices of Indians, mixed-race peasants, Black workers, and even local whites was a racialized trope in the narratives of Europeans who often represented nineteenth-century Colombia as a not-white-enough nation. Local white intellectuals such as Manuel Ancízar tried to prove the whiteness of Andean Colombian peasants as part of a discursive process of founding the nation.[5] Nevertheless, they frequently slipped into rhetorical devices, deeply ingrained in travel writing, that equated dirtiness with "Indianness."

Javier Villa Flores and Sonya Lipsett Rivera have argued that emotions are not gender neutral but rather central in maintaining power relationships of gender and race in colonial societies where they are used to mark differences and "to accentuate social divisions."[6] In a postcolonial context, travel literature presents disgust as a natural reaction of white men toward the filthiness of native food, a male emotion that highlights the separation between their bodies and those of indigenous or female cooks of African descent. Ahmed has also called our attention to the fact that emotions are always culturally produced and very often play a fundamental role in the formation of nationalist discourses that attribute negative emotions to certain bodies who are not supposed to be part of the nation.[7] This is the case with indigenous and Black people, who despite forming the greater part of the population were not included in national narratives because they were not considered a desirable section of the nation, but rather an obstacle to it. In this context, "the association between the senses and emotion, between race-thinking and gut feeling"[8]—as articulated by Smith regarding the history of the southern United States—is also a crucial part of the history of race in the Andes. Race and racial contamination constituted through sensorial experiences beyond the realm of sight. Smell, taste, and touch are instrumental in defining the bodily differences that ultimately make up the materiality of race.[9]

Sensing and Feeling Race

In 1885, the Colombian José María Samper, a white writer, politician, entrepreneur, and fervent advocate of racial mixing, summarized his opinions about the subject by enumerating the flaws of pure races. Whites were nervous, imaginative, thoughtful, jealous, charming, too proud, and even boastful. Pure Indians were resistant, patient, passive, mistrustful, and hardworking despite their lack of initiative and imagination.[10] For white Colombians like Samper, a man's race would determine his personality and, even more, his emotions. Feelings are also inscribed in the network of physical and intellectual characteristics socially and culturally codified as race. More important for this article, accounts of racial types always focus on portraying a masculine type.[11] Therefore, masculine emotions are racially defined, but at the same time they present accurate evidence of the individual's racial profile—not a minor consideration in the highly racially mixed Latin American societies where racial anxieties were and still are commonplace. Samper's descriptions provide us with a clear example of the association between race and personality in the minds of nineteenth-century intellectuals, but one element in his portrait of pure Indians refers specifically to their alimentary and culinary practices. According to him, the pure Indian is "frugal in his diet and intemperate in his drinking,"[12] indicating that emotions as well as eating practices and attitudes toward food are racially determined. Indigenous people, mulattoes, and mestizos are unable to control their emotions, but white male individuals can, and therefore can escape from the racial determination that seems so prevalent in the representation of the "other." Samper warns his readers about the seductive personalities of proud mulattoes who like perfume and are very good dancers.[13] Other white travelers around the Andes cautioned their readers against the treacherous behavior of Indians and mestizos. Even white women were often represented as victims of their own sentimentality and emotions.[14]

Of course, nineteenth-century literature offers innumerable examples of white men battling with their feelings. In *María* (1867), Efrain, the protagonist, deals with the sadness and melancholy caused by the loss of his paternal state "El Paraiso" and his beloved María.[15] Don Demóstenes, in the novel *Manuela* (1858), is tempted by the beautiful peasants of the parish to the point that he sometimes forgets the white senorita who waits for his return in Bogotá. White male literary characters experience powerful feelings: love of country, passion for women, rage and anger. But dealing with their feelings is a trait of sophistication and moral distinction, often attributed only to them. I will argue here that emotions are a central element in the process of creating differences between white travelers and indigenous and Black local men. Social conventions and cultural constructions of emotions allow white men to experience and express a limited array of emotions, most of them related to their accepted public roles as leaders.

White women and men are morally capable of the most sublime feelings—love, sacrifice, tenderness. In colonial and postcolonial multiracial societies, decency is part of the moral distinction that separates white women from mulattas, mestizas, and female Indians. In this way, female decency becomes a trope for whiteness.[16] Far away from the private and domestic spaces of the haciendas and the houses of white residents of Bogotá, writers and visual artists represent drunken mestizos and Indians, intoxicated by excessive consumption of maize liquor or *chicha*. Circa 1870, the Bogotano painter Ramon Torres Mendez authored a complete series of street fights involving working-class women and men, portraying once again their inability to control certain emotions: jealousy, wrath, aggressiveness.[17]

Thus, emotions are always involved in the formation of racialized discourses about the "other." The assumption that white people have the capacity to control their emotions is the ultimate trait of moral superiority that justifies the hierarchical order of the nation. To understand how race is produced in everyday life, we need to pay attention to a set of feelings often mentioned in encounters between the white bodies of writers and the colored bodies of peasants: disgust, repugnance, and revulsion toward the sweaty bodies of rowers on the Magdalena River, or the dirty hands of Andean peasants. Traveling throughout the territory of Colombia exacerbated the threat posed by these bodies, normally prevented by distance. This proximity blurs limits and favors contact, while emotions take over the individual. In her analysis of the cultural production of disgust, Ahmed points out the significant role played by food in reducing the distance between white and colored bodies. The skin is the last border of separation between white individuals and the native "others." But this limit disappears when food enters the body of the person, creating emotional responses ranging from satisfaction and pleasure to revulsion and sickness.[18]

White travelers displayed in their texts one particular set of emotions intended to separate them from any other group: disgust. The feeling constitutes the ultimate rejection of the proximity of the racialized, morally inferior body of the "other." Through the emotion of disgust, the white body reclaims its own space, reestablishing its borders. By eating the food of the natives, white bodies become vulnerable because "the act of eating dissolves the boundaries between self and other."[19] However, as Ahmed has argued, the feeling of disgust requires a performative act of enunciation, of utterance. Moreover, this performance requires an audience able to understand and share the emotion. Thus, the performative act is initiated during the contact between white and colored bodies but is only completed during the process of writing. Narrating the experience to a literate, metropolitan audience, able to witness the act of repudiation of contact, becomes a fundamental step in recovering control of the self.[20]

Making Sense of Food

The young French traveler and scientist Jean-Baptiste Boussingault was in his early twenties when he visited the new nations of Venezuela and Colombia and became involved in their struggles for the independence, eventually becoming a colonel in Simón Bolivar's army. Among the many adventures he narrates in his prolific memoirs, his comments about the poor taste and hygiene of Bogotano food and kitchens have a special place:

> I established the distinction between scrambled and fried eggs because of a rather unpleasant accident at the beginning of my stay and to which I got used to. Even in the best houses there were no proper kitchens, it was not necessary to have a kitchen like the ones we are used to having in France. In one room, three large stones were placed at ground level that served as a tripod. And then came what

> Bergman called the filth of the atmosphere, that is, the dust in the air, considering that the broom was a very little-known instrument and the hair abounded in that dirt, since the ladies and their slaves used to comb their hair in the kitchen. On the eggs in a saucepan, the hair retained its flexibility, and by the color, its origin could be guessed. I felt a terrible disgust chewing them. Before eating, I removed as many hairs as possible, just as I would have done with the bones of a fish.[21]

Many elements of this extensive quote merit careful consideration. First of all, the power of the anecdote relies on the simplicity of the food involved. Here, Boussingault's readers are facing an unassuming breakfast of fried eggs, rather than a strange or exotic dish far beyond the European imagination. The uncanny element comes from the undesirable mix between the eggs and the bodies of the women and their slaves, men of color who work and live in the kitchen where the eggs are cooked. In the darkness of the kitchen, their hair cannot be separated from the dirtiness of the ground where they prepare food, and thus the bodies of the Black slaves and women cannot remain distinct from the food that will enter the body of the French scientist. In this context, the only possibility of depuration comes from altering the materiality of both: hair and eggs. Through the process of cooking, the corporal remains of the servants are incorporated into the food. Moreover, they are transformed and become part of the meal. Boussingault begins the narration of this anecdote emphasizing the materiality of the spaces where food is prepared. However, there is also the materiality of the food—hair transformed into fish bones—the decisive element that separates what is edible and what is not. The process of transforming the hairs' consistency makes them edible. Boussingault knows that he is eating the bodies of the servants. But the transformation in the texture serves as a rite of purification. We might even call it a form of cannibalism, tolerated by the young French scientist, who accepts eating the hairs of women and slaves, once they are properly cooked and mixed with the rest of the eggs. The question that arises here is what makes something edible. The intended purpose of Boussingault's story seems to be to produce disgust among his readers, but seasoned with humor. Through the narration, the French scientist is performing his revulsion, and in this way he is reestablishing the separation between his body and the hair of the women and the slaves. The purification thus starts with the process of cooking the eggs covered in hairs and ends in a performance of the experience for an indulgent audience who will share his emotions.

Whatever their food preferences at home, white travelers in the Colombian Andes cannot control their diet with all its attendant flavors, smells, and textures. Travelers, fictional and real, depend on mixed-race, Black, or indigenous people to satisfy their most basic needs. In *Manuela*, the main character—the white, literate, young liberal politician Don Demóstenes—is traveling across the Andean rural parishes in the company of his indigenous personal servant and the local porters hired to carry his heavy trunks of books. After complaining about the precarious lodging conditions in Colombia, he finds accommodation in a dark and unpleasant inn attended by Rosa, a beautiful young peasant and the inn's owner. He asks for a meal, and she responds with surprise and mockery: food is not available for travelers. Out of compassion for Demóstenes, she finally offers him some meat, but when he tries to inquire about its origin, she admonishes his curiosity—"Why do you want to know that?"—implying that sometimes ignorance is a blessing.[22]

The Colombian politician, explorer, and intellectual Manuel Ancízar confirms in his accounts the precarious conditions that travelers faced in Colombia:

> Asking for food would have been like anticipating the future, since cooking is not yet a service in our inns, except what they call ajiaco, a type of stew made of potatoes of which they give a free bowl to poor passers-by as long as they drink and pay for a pint of chicha.[23]

Ancízar (the real traveler) and Don Demóstenes (the fictional one) must confront the lack of separation between themselves and the locals. There are neither special accommodations prepared for them nor special food. They have to share not only the food of the locals, but also their eating practices and conditions, and notions of what is edible. This situation is particularly destabilizing for local elites who previously enjoyed a position of advantage in the socio-racial hierarchy. After spending the night in Rosa's inn, Don Demóstenes wakes up covered in hives, a terrible experience also described by Ancízar when visiting an Andean town:

> The dwellers are all white and tall. The issue with untidiness is not exaggerated, and as proof of this I will say that having lodged us with nothing less than one of the best houses, after a long time of waiting, they served us a meal that we had to eat due to the urgency of hunger but had to close the windows to eat in darkness so that we would not pay attention to the unwelcome substances—abundant in the so-called stew, served in what were once dishes. Truly, this

was compensated with having woke the next day with our bodies covered in hives, caused by animals that you will allow me to leave anonymous.[24]

The two tropes, bad food and insect bites and stings, are interwoven in the narratives because both are attacks on the white body—intolerable penetrations beyond the surface of the skin, intrusions that cause discomfort or pain. White travelers, forced by the need to survive, can no longer control access to their bodies and are compelled to negotiate their positions, regaining control of their sensorial experiences to endure the hardships. Don Demóstenes and Ancízar eat the native food in darkness to avoid seeing and knowing its nature. In both cases, the filthiness of the rooms and the lack of proper and clean spaces to eat create a special challenge. The liberal politician Ancízar, and the conservative writer Eugenio Díaz (author of *Manuela*) were both Colombian authors committed to proving the whiteness of Andean citizens of the nation, despite the accusations of European travelers who saw the local whites as Indians or mixed-race.[25] But their efforts are undermined by their own use of the motif of dirtiness. Andean dwellers have long been racialized in the accounts of colonial functionaries, authorities, and other travelers, making it almost impossible to escape the paradox of trying to prove the whiteness of the peasants while at the same time describing their untidy practices. For this reason, Ancízar's quote about his visit to the town attempts to moderate its racializing effect by beginning with the affirmation that the inhabitants are all visibly white and tall. The constant mention of the white Colombian travelers' feelings of disgust and repugnance reestablishes the separation of their bodies from the native surroundings, but it undermines their efforts to demonstrate the whiteness of the local population.

In contrast to the Colombian white descendants of the colonizers, European and American travelers do not have a local political agenda to support in their narratives. They are free to complain about the food and the dirtiness. They can openly racialize the servants and disparage local ingredients and cooking practices. Isaac Holton, an American traveler, seems in his writings to feel a particular disgust for cumin seeds and achiote, condiments widely used in Colombian cuisine. Following all the tropes about dirtiness, he also abominates the native kitchens. Yet he is even more concerned with the treacherous nature of the ingredients:

Ignacia, an Indian girl of 17 years, and a little over five feet in stature, came into my room and spread a cloth on my table. What else she put on I cannot say, only first there was something that they called sopa, because it resembled soup in being eaten with a spoon. I can offer no conjecture as to the ingredients. Another dish was the ajiaco that we saw at Cuni: it contained potato, fluid a little thickened with something, and traces of meat. Another dish contained what comparative anatomy would call chicken, but the palate would conjecture might be lizard. But is colored yellow. This is one of the inventions of Spanish cookery. It is often done with arnotto, called achiote or bija. It is Bixa Orellana. Sometime afterward I objected to his addition, which only served to prevent the eye from judging of the real condition of things. La Señora named it cover-dirt [*tapa-mugre*], and banished it from her kitchen.[26]

Despite Holton's whining about the materiality of the native food, he is actually not concerned with the dirtiness of the environment, probably because it is a reality that he takes for granted, to the point of dealing with it in just one or two sentences here and there about the "Granadan kitchen."[27] He praises himself for being resistant to the hardships of the local food, only to be defeated by the "abominable" sausages of the town of Cuni: "It was the only thing I found myself absolutely incapable of eating."[28] Holton is a resourceful writer, able to use a rhetorical device to complain about the local food but maintaining his self-image as a man in control of his emotional reactions. Instead of making himself the protagonist, he narrates a story of Stuart, "a New York hatter, just speaking a few words of Spanish, who has been tormented and half-starved by the abominated Granadan cookery and especially persecuted with cumin seed."[29] Holton refers with plenty of detail to the tribulations of Stuart, who pointlessly tries to cook sausages without the native interference of cumin. In his efforts to escape the tyranny of the local ingredients, the New Yorker attempts what no white man has done before—he will cook his own food: "He has seen sausages cooked; nay, he is sure he can cook them."[30] Of course, a reader from the twenty-first century would picture Stuart working in a kitchen, maybe chopping ingredients and stirring them in a pot. But this image could be nothing further from that of a nineteenth-century white man such as Stuart:

By broken Spanish and gesticulation, he superintends operations they [the natives] have never seen before. With the vigilance worthy of a man whose life has been attempted a dozen times with cumin-seed, he watches against the introduction of all heterodox ingredients, and of that in particular.[31]

Stuart never touches the food while cooking; his remarkable efforts in the kitchen rather involve giving orders to the natives while they prepare the white man's nourishment. The experiment ends in disappointment for the New Yorker hatter:

> Eagerly, he sits down to a large table, made of boards, with a full dish before him of sausages cooked as well as any that ever came from his mother's kitchen. The first morsel is now between his teeth, and he discovers—oh, horrors!—that things can be put inside of a sausage! . . . Horror of horrors! My delicious anticipations all vanished with one fell stroke, for it revealed to me the fact that this, too, had been plentifully besprinkled with the always used and never-failing cumin seed!"[32]

Stuart's story is dated ten years before Holton's actual visit to the town of Cuni, but the "horrors" he endured are perpetuated in his writing, directly quoted by Holton. Every time we read the story of the New Yorker hatter's failed attempt to cook sausages in Colombia, the performance of his disgust is newly reenacted. Even more, his rejection of native food is bolstered by the emotional burden of nostalgia for his mother's kitchen, and the inability of the natives to understand him: "Stuart's failure was attributed by the natives to his not knowing the proper way to cook [the sausages]."[33]

White masculinities are performed in relationship to others. These others are always changing in the narratives, but very often their "otherness" is embodied in categories of race and gender: local urban white women of Bogotá in Boussingault's accounts, Indian girls in Holton's, white female peasants in Ancízar's and Díaz's descriptions. Native food becomes an extension of the corporality of these "others." Performing repugnance and disgust restores the distance between them that was temporarily destabilized by the intrusion of native food inside the white body. The centrality of these emotions gives white men permission to whine and complain because this loud expression protects both their whiteness and their masculinity. The omnipresent trope of disgust for native food is more than evidence of racism, it actually ensures and reinforces the colonial order based in the moral superiority of white men. Even the most sympathetic travelers cannot elude it because it is part of the emotional structure that supports and sustains their identities.

In 1855, the French geographer Elisée Reclus embarked on a journey to the Sierra Nevada de Santa Marta with the purpose of establishing an agricultural colony. In the preface of his account he humbly refers to the enterprise's failure, but still has words of admiration for the country and the people.[34] Yet despite his positive emotions toward Colombia, he makes no effort to hide his repugnance for the food of the mixed-race rowers:

> In that swamp, where a fiery and stinking atmosphere hung in the air, the zambos stopped for lunch. They took out of a rucksack some yuccas roasted in ashes, some leftovers of fish, and a bottle of chicha [maize liquor]. Sharing everything, they generously invited me to participate in their frugal meal. I accepted the invitation, but I must confess that my appetite suddenly left me when I saw one of my hosts stirring with the handle of his handgrip the large number of dead fish that floated in the wake. He discarded with disdain those whose heads were already stained with yellow lines, fishing out the others using a small harpoon and carefully saving them for dinner.[35]

The whole episode brings back the fundamental reasoning that sustained the entire colonial order. Reclus's travel account greatly differs from the others analyzed here. He uses words like "generosity" to show his appreciation for the moral character of the zambos. But he also agrees with the Colombian Samper in representing the personality of the colored populations through their attitude toward food, evident in the story and in the use of words such as "disdain." Because it is an extension of their racialized bodies, the native food always confirms the moral superiority of the white travelers, even if some whining and complaining is required to protect their whiteness and masculinity.

Notes

1. I would like to express my gratitude to Fritz Culp for his help with the translation of passages cited in this article.
2. Rebecca Earle, *The Body of the Conquistador: Food, Race, and the Colonial Experience in Spanish America, 1492–1700* (Cambridge: Cambridge University Press, 2014). For more on white Latin American elites experiencing others' food, see Vanesa Miseres's chapter in this same volume.
3. Mark Smith, *How Race Is Made: Slavery, Segregation, and the Senses* (Chapel Hill: University of Carolina Press, 2006), 2.
4. Smith, *How Race Is Made*, 4.
5. Mercedes Lopez Rodriguez, *Blancura y otras ficciones raciales en los Andes Colombianos del siglo XIX* (Madrid: Iberoamericana Veurvert, 2019).

6. Javier Villa Flores and Sonya Lipsett Rivera, *Emotions and Daily Life in Colonial Mexico* (Albuquerque: University of New Mexico Press, 2014), 12.
7. Sara Ahmed, *The Cultural Politics of Emotion* (Edinburgh: Edinburgh University Press, 2014), 49.
8. Smith, *How Race Is Made*, 4.
9. Smith, *How Race Is Made*, 2–4.
10. José María Samper, *Filosofía en cartera: colección de pensamientos sobre religión, moral, filosofía, ciencias sociales, historia, literatura, poesía, bellas artes, caracteres, viajes, etc. en prosa y en verso* (Bogotá: Imprenta de La Luz, 1887), 56.
11. See Nancy Appelbaum, *Mapping the Country of Regions: The Chorographic Commission of Nineteenth-Century Colombia* (Chapel Hill: University of North Carolina Press, 2016), 61–66.
12. Samper, *Filosofía en cartera*, 56.
13. Samper, *Filosofía en cartera*, 56.
14. Following the theoretical insights of Monica Greco, Ana Peluffo discusses the hierarchization of the language regarding emotions that confines them to a feminine devaluated sentimentalism, while using the word "affection" to talk about the more abstract and masculine notion. Ana Peluffo, *En clave emocional. Cultura y afecto en América Latina* (Buenos Aires: Prometeo Libros, 2016), 22.
15. Jorge Isaács, *María* (1866; repr., Madrid: Sociedad General Española de Librería, 1983).
16. Eileen J. Suárez Findlay, *Imposing Decency: The Politics of Sexuality and Race in Puerto Rico, 1870–1920* (Durham, NC: Duke University Press, 1999).
17. Efraín Sánchez, *Ramón Torres Méndez, pintor de la Nueva Granada* (Bogotá: Fondo Cultural Cafetero, 1987).
18. Ahmed, *The Cultural Politics of Emotion*, 85–86.
19. Kyla Wazana Tompkins, *Racial Indigestion: Eating Bodies in the 19th Century* (New York: New York University Press, 2012), 4.
20. Ahmed, *The Cultural Politics of Emotion*, 95.
21. Jean-Baptiste Boussingault, *Memorias del explorador francés Jean-Baptiste Boussingault, que describe los momentos más relevantes de su vida y hace mención de sus logros como explorador y científico* (Bogotá: Banco de la República, 1985), 237.
22. Eugenio Díaz, *Manuela* (Paris: Librería Española de Garnier Hermanos, 1889), 2–4.
23. Manuel Ancízar, *Peregrinación de Alpha por las provincias del Norte* (Bogotá: Imprenta de Echeverria Hermanos, 1853), 140.
24. Ancízar, *Peregrinación de Alpha*, 140.
25. See Lopez Rodriguez, *Blancura y otras ficciones*, chapters 1 and 2.
26. Isaac Holton, *New Granada: Twenty Months in the Andes* (New York: Harper & Brothers, 1857), 141. New Granada was one of many names for Colombia during the nineteenth century.
27. Holton, *New Granada*, 120–143.
28. Holton, *New Granada*, 120.
29. Holton, *New Granada*, 120.
30. Holton, *New Granada*, 120.

31. Holton, *New Granada*, 120.
32. Holton, *New Granada*, 120.
33. Holton, *New Granada*, 120.
34. Elisée Reclus, *Viaje a la Sierra Nevada de Santa Marta* (Bogotá: Biblioteca Popular de la Cultura, 1992), 5.
35. Reclus, *Viaje a la Sierra Nevada*, 35.

CHAPTER 6

A Matter of Taste

Aesthetics, Manners, and Food in Eduarda Mansilla's Experience in New York

VANESA MISERES

In *Recuerdos de viaje* (Memories of Travel, 1882), the renowned Argentine author Eduarda Mansilla (1834–1892) narrates her travels in the United States during the second half of the nineteenth century. Mansilla was a writer of great visibility within the Argentine high society and the city's cultural sphere. She was not only the niece of the former governor of Buenos Aires, Juan Manuel de Rosas, but also the sister of Lucio V. Mansilla, one of the most important figures of the intellectual group known as the Generation of 1880—with which Eduarda Mansilla shared a proclivity for European mannerism. But more importantly, her works are now studied as fundamental representations of and contributions to the literary production of nineteenth-century Argentina. Eduarda Mansilla gained considerable notoriety in the press of her time, writing for *La Ondina del Plata* (1875–79), *El Nacional* (1852–93), *La Nación* (1862–), and *La Gaceta Musical* (1874–87), among other newspapers and magazines circulating at that time in Buenos Aires. In addition, some of her literary texts, such as the novels *El médico de San Luis* (1860), *Pablo o la vida en las pampas* (1869, originally written in French), and *Cuentos* (1880)—a collection of short stories for children—were widely disseminated in Argentina and in Europe, where the writer maintained strong links with celebrated literary circles.[1]

Despite her familiarity with and affinity for Europe, particularly the language and cultural environment of France, Mansilla changes geographic destination when it comes to her foray into travel literature.

Eduarda Mansilla in New York. Photograph taken by notable Civil War–era photographer Frederick F. Gutekunst in 1861. *From the private collection of Manuel Rafael García-Mansilla.*

Recuerdos de Viaje narrates the writer's arrival in and travels throughout the United States. This text brings together Mansilla's two residencies in the United States: one in 1861, when her husband, diplomat Manuel Rafael García, traveled to study the functioning of the judicial system while intellectual Domingo Faustino Sarmiento served as Argentina's ambassador in Washington.[2] Her second stay in the United States was between 1868 and 1873, when García was appointed plenipotentiary minister of his country.[3] During her travels, Mansilla visited different places such as New York, Washington, DC, Philadelphia, Niagara Falls, Boston, and part of Canada. The subjects and attitudes found in Mansilla's work maintain the care and sense of decorum that a woman of her position and class was expected to keep; she also delves into a number of interesting aspects of American society's ethnography, history, and politics.[4] *Recuerdos de viaje* includes reflections on issues as varied as the status of women in the United States, their domination of the domestic sphere, and the positive impact of their introduction to the labor force; the geography, architecture, politics, and history of the country; the war between the North and South, slavery, and government treatment of indigenous populations.

In this chapter, I analyze an element omitted from my previous work on Mansilla and absent from the existing literature on Mansilla's travel writing, namely her relationship with and observations about American food and manners. As the previous chapter exemplifies, food imagery was a predominate feature in nineteenth-century travelogues. The act of eating local foods and writing about it, affirms Mercedes Lopez Rodriguez, helps travelers establish boundaries between the self and the other in racial and/or cultural terms that will usually function as a performance of the traveler's superiority over the locals. Here, I will focus on Mansilla's reflections on the subject during her travels through New York. In the mid-nineteenth century, New York and its foodways underwent remarkable changes. Industrialization resulted not only in an increase in the city's population, but also in the development of a much more complex food system that included, among other things, a large amount of processed foodstuffs from all over the country and abroad to satisfy the equally compound patterns in new consumers' daily life. As Cindy R. Lobel explains, New York served "as an index to the potentials, contrasts, and inequities of the United States as the city developed into a world power and the seat of industrial capitalism."[5]

In her ethnographic observations, impregnated by a strong perspective on gender, Mansilla makes multiple references to this transformation of the city. She describes the manners, customs, and eating habits of Americans and judges them negatively, from a position of moral, educational, and spiritual superiority. The words of Cuban poet José Martí in his celebrated chronicle "Coney Island" aptly expresses her sentiment: "Those people eat quantity; we, quality."[6] Mansilla enunciates herself as an ambassador of quality and "good taste"—a criterion formed by her belonging to the Europeanized aristocracy of Buenos Aires and by her long stays in the Old Continent—and uses food to elaborate on a larger argument against the politics and culture of the United States.

My analysis reveals that Eduarda Mansilla finds in food and manners (or in the lack thereof) a mark of North American Anglo-Saxon heritage. Through eating and the practices around it, the author catches a glimpse of the nation's modernity, which she links to an aggressive expansionist, materialist, and utilitarian essence. Such attributes will be broached time and again by Latin American intellectuals in the nineteenth and twentieth centuries to describe the role of the United States in the continent. Resonating with the views of José Martí, Rubén Darío, or José Enrique Rodó, among others, Mansilla's reflections on the present and future of North America responds to the imminent threat that Latin America will be *devoured* by United States expansionism. Through a discourse that praises the elevated spirituality and sense of aesthetic of the Latin origins of her culture, the traveler confronts the *gluttony* of North American political intentions toward the region.

Life Aboard and the "Tasteless" Anglo-Saxon Culinary Traditions

Recuerdos de viaje begins with a section titled "Preliminaries" in which Mansilla details the moments prior to her arrival in the United States and describes life aboard the English steamboat by which she traveled. From the onset of her narration, the author establishes the aesthetic-cultural opposition between Anglo-Saxon and Latin cultures, at this point referring to the differences between English and French travel companies. For Mansilla, while the French Line is distinguished by its cosmopolitan crew and the fact that among the French "one eats admirably," the English steamboats can be characterized, according to her, by the fact that "one eats badly, that is, à la English; everything there is tasteless, exempt from the appeal of form and substance, that so greatly enhances French food."[7] This opposition has a long history, as Stephen Mennell has shown in *All Manners of Food* (1987). Mennell addresses the naturalized belief of French food as superior to British to assert that this contrast in the culinary cultures of the two countries "is not in any 'innate' differences in the 'taste' of English and French people."[8] Rather, the association that Mansilla establishes between rustic English food and a sophisticated French table relies in the ways each nation has related historically with the city and the country. While French haute cuisine had its origins in courtly cookery—courts being urban institutions—England granted a greater prestige to the way of life associated with living in the country, also reflected in its cookery.[9]

Ideas on good and bad taste are also formed in this contrast between rural and urban styles preserved in a country's tradition. For Mansilla this has a particular relevance. First of all, distinguishing "good" from "bad" taste—Mansilla does precisely that in her travelogue—is an act based, according to Pierre Bourdieu, on a socially constructed condition or hierarchy that considers education and the cultural and economic context to which a subject belongs; therefore, it is always arbitrary, historical, and contingent.[10] In this way, both in the quoted passage and when she later affirms that "Paris is more tempting" than the United States or concludes that she prefers "even to shipwreck" with the French, Mansilla's explicit association of good taste with French civilization is not simply a demonstration of the author's individual and arbitrary choices.[11] It is the result of the training or *habitus* (from Bourdieu) she received, which shaped her attitudes since childhood.

One must not forget that during this period, European culture permeated Argentine politics and society, not only because of a strong foreign presence in the country, but also because many Argentine intellectuals and members of high society traveled to Europe and kept up with European literatures, fashions, philosophies, arts, and manners.[12] Moreover, Europe provided a model to follow the continent's path toward a more civilized and modernized society. In his groundbreaking essay *Facundo* (1845), Domingo Faustino Sarmiento proposed that Argentina's political and social matrix is best understood as an opposition between civilization and barbarism. He and future generations of intellectuals and politicians linked civilization with the spread of a European model for South American cities; barbarism, on the other hand, was associated with the lifestyle of the gauchos, the inhabitants of the countryside.[13]

In terms of food, fin de siècle liberal oligarchs—the group to which Mansilla belonged—consumed French haute cuisine as part of the same pursuit of Western modernization. Although both Argentina and the United States equally sought in Europe a model for trends in culinary arts and etiquette, the tension between the global and the local in Argentina's national identity, as Jeffrey Pilcher has shown, was most formative.[14] While Argentine culinary traditions included African, indigenous, and mestizo influences, Mansilla seems to reject such diversity with a performance of an urban French taste as national.[15] The author adopts an attitude similar to that of the European travelers analyzed by Lopez Rodriguez in this volume to represent the United States as her "other." Putting into action the manners and habits *à la Françoise*—at the core of her elite education—allows her to reposition herself and the culture she represents as superior with respect to aesthetics and taste before the United States. Declaring her preference for French food while visiting an unknown country in which she does not enjoy any privilege (on many occasions, she makes reference to the democratic character of the United States), Mansilla intelligently carries out a rhetorical maneuver that grants her authority both in her traveling and in her writing.

Although David Viñas connects Mansilla's travelogue with the context at the time of realization of her trip (not of writing and publication as I do here), he also points out that Mansilla's preference for the French indirectly represents the local political environment and the author's privileges within it:

> It alludes to what happens in Argentina after the Battle of Pavón in 1861 or in Paraguay as a result of so-called free trade. Apparent and unconnected details. But they are fashioned, allusively, as reproductions of the conflict between the mercantile and industrialist culture in the prepotent advance of the North, to the detriment of the more archaic—and presumably more benevolent—forms that in the South remain linked to patriarchal relations and the production of agrarian rhythms.[16]

Viñas's analysis turns to the 1860s, at which time Mansilla was in the United States and the liberal project of a free-market nation-state began, to consolidate by the time of *Recuerdos de viaje*'s publication. The Battle of Pavón meant the near-total collapse of the federal forces based in the countryside and the end of the Argentine Confederation that Mansilla's family represented. Not coincidentally, the author is sympathetic to the southern United States, identifying not only with the politics of the South, but also with the region's "[monopoly on] elegance and refinement."[17] Put

Cunard Line.

R.M.S. "Campania."

MONDAY, FEB. 26th, 1900,

MENU.

Hors d'œuvres, various

Crème Hollandaise   Consomme à la Russe

Crimped Codfish—Brown Oyster Sauce

Rissoles à la Montglas

Turtle Filets à l'Indienne

Compote de Pigeon à la Macedoine

Roast Sirloin and Ribs of Beef—Yorkshire Pudding

Braised Duckling—Green Peas

Roast Haunch English Mutton—Red Currant Jelly

Boiled Turkey—Celery Sauce

Baked Cumberland Ham—Madeira Sauce

Fresh Mushrooms   Carrots   Piquante Sauce

Brussel Sprouts   Potatoes Maitre d'Hotel   Boiled Rice

Boiled Bermuda Potatoes   Mashed Potatoes

Roast Quail Demi Glace

Lettuce and Celery

Tarte aux Abricot   Gelee au Champagne   Savoy Roll

Choux à la Crème   Petits Fanchonettes

Tapioca Pudding   Diplomate Pudding—Wine Sauce

Fondu au Fromage   Canape d'Anchois

Glaces Neapolitaine aux Wafers

Dessert

Cheese   Tea   Coffee

Copy of a 1900 menu aboard the Cunard Line, the English steamship company by which Eduarda Mansilla traveled to the United States. *Public domain, New York Public Library Digital Collections.*

in this context, *Recuerdos de viaje* responds to a nostalgic look at a past that preceded the new policies responsible for changing the world scene and her personal fear of seeing her value system declining.

The Arrival and Discovery of a Rustic Modernity

Norbert Elias establishes that the appropriation of the models of behavior at the dinner table or on the street—among other social circuits on which the famed and widespread manuals of urbanity and good manners were focused—are counted among the most important individual movements of the general process of civilization. That is to say that in the details of what and how to eat, the modes of thinking and speaking are also modeled and realize a wider transformation in the conduct of a society. Contrary to the world of French etiquette and unlike what Mansilla performs as a perfect assimilation of those customs among Argentine high society, the experience of the author arriving the United States is very different. Her disembarkation in New York is narrated as a moment of confusion and chaos during which the author is unable to understand local codes. According to Mansilla, port personnel are "unceremonious," and port workers and hotel staff are "rude, ugly," and "quite unkempt."[18] In subsequent passages, Mansilla insists on these faults to perhaps indicate, returning to Elias, that the civilizing process, marked by an effective imitation of the European model, has not ended in the United States: "Trying to do things with the precision with which such things are done in France, in England, or in Italy, is an insoluble problem."[19]

Although studies on women travelers have insisted on the predominance of private spaces in the works of female authors who elaborate on these spaces through ethnographic and descriptive notes (what Mary Louise Pratt calls "feminotopias"),[20] Mansilla privileges public spaces when she refers to the customs of New Yorkers: first, the ship and the port, then the hotels, the restaurants, and the streets. On Broadway, Mansilla highlights the decadent quality of the area and the absence of entertainment for travelers, who find no attractions to delight his or her nocturnal strolls. Food reappears as a criterion for measuring the experience. Mansilla says that a visitor can "die of boredom" consuming ice cream or sherry cobblers.[21] The choice of these elements is not accidental in the text. During the second half of the nineteenth century, sherry cobbler was the drink that symbolized the democratic success of the United States. Its popularity was related to the landmarks of North American modernity:

imports (in this case, sherry wine from Spain and England), refrigeration systems (the drink is served on ice), and expansionist policies (the highest consumption and local production of sugar with the annexation of the state of Florida).[22] For Mansilla, these signs of progress, which are praised and imitated by other travelers like her compatriot Sarmiento, are presented as insipid practices, lacking in good taste and unattractive to a person trained, as she was, in the European tradition.

Associating with boredom an element created within American urban society, on the other hand, suggests an implicit criticism of all those elements that make the nation a unique and powerful presence on the continent. Mansilla attacks, in much the same way, the North American tradition in other chapters dedicated to the politics of the country; she condemns, for example, the lack of knowledge among citizens of the United States about their nation's Latin American neighbors. In one passage Mansilla discusses the meaning of the word "America," particularly the different meanings with which it is charged in North versus South.[23] The author reflects on the political and ideological burden of this concept as she explains:

> The North American is the vainest being I have dealt with, and his patriotism consists of greater vanity than love.
>
> To him, American means: citizen of North America; he knows no other America than that of the Union: the rest [of the continent] is not taken into account; the learned disdain it, the ignorant ignore it. They know something about Mexico, if only because, day after day, they have appropriated some piece of the old empire of Moctezuma. We already know what California has represented all along to the Yankees. They know the road to Central America. But, of South America, which to them usually means Brazil, oh! how little they know! I shall even go so far as to say that nothing matters to them.[24]

Mansilla suggests that Americans' vanity, that blasé sense of superiority that forms the basis of American power, arises from people's lack of knowledge of and interest in other cultural models and referents. The ignorance of the United States lies, moreover, in the privilege that this nation gives to a type of empirical and utilitarian knowledge, which is limited to the satisfaction of an immediate need (they only know Mexico because it is a contiguous territory from which they can benefit). Classical education, bookish knowledge, and universal culture have no place within this project.

But the most interesting note in the association of culinary

SHERRY COBBLER. 47

97. THE COBBLER.

Like the julep, this delicious potation is an American invention, although it is now a favorite in all warm climates. The "cobbler" does not require much skill in compounding, but to make it acceptable to the eye, as well as to the palate, it is necessary to display some taste in ornamenting the glass after the beverage is made. We give an illustration showing how a cobbler should look when made to suit an epicure.

98. Sherry Cobbler.

(Use large bar glass.)

2 wine-glasses of sherry.
1 table-spoonful of sugar.
2 or 3 slices of orange.

Fill a tumbler with shaved ice, shake well, and ornament with berries in season. Place a straw as represented in the wood-cut.

Sherry Cobbler recipe from *The Bar-Tender's Guide* (1862) by Jerry Thomas. *Public domain, Exposition Universelle des Vins et Spiritueux, Vintage Cocktail Books Free Digital Library.*

criteria with the politics and idiosyncrasies of the country can be found in Mansilla's references to the general consumption of oysters in the city:

> Incredible is the number of oysters consumed in the United States. Oysters is the word, the cry that catches the attention of travelers arriving in the autumn. "Oysters, oysters," you can hear the boys repeating in all manner, in the railroad stations, alternating with vendors and sweet [candy] stands—awful and not so sweet to a palate such as ours. How delicious are those fried oysters, wrapped in striped biscuit, placed in layers superimposed on cardboard boxes, which, warm and appetizing, come to leave pleasant contentment in the memory and the stomach of the famished traveler.[25]

As Mansilla observes, oysters were in the nineteenth century a staple food for Americans throughout the country. There was no need to live on the coast to consume them: since 1830 a company in Baltimore was engaged in sending oysters to the whole country by rail. Originally, they were sent canned in vinegar, and soon the canned oysters industry arose, reaching more regions as the railway system improved.[26] Most were consumed raw, but the United States had also inherited the English taste (the one disdained by Mansilla) for fried oysters, as mentioned by the author. There is no recipe book in the first half of the nineteenth century that does not include various dishes with oysters: soups, pies, schnitzels, among others.[27] In New York, by 1860, around twelve million oysters were sold in markets. Rich and poor alike consumed them equally (prepared in different ways and to various degrees of sophistication) in saloons, street stalls, restaurants, cafés, and homes.[28]

In her reference to this gastronomic phenomenon, Mansilla notes that oysters are "the basic food of the people," which is sold and consumed without rituals of etiquette or set mealtimes. Striking is the linguistic distance established with the author's decision of naming the foodstuff in English ("oyster") in her Spanish text, as though she were trying to detach from the described culinary experience. Moreover, the word "oyster" is transformed into a cry voiced by vendors, a rustic clamor, an irregular and inarticulate noise that comes, metonymically, to account for the entire act that envelops the sale and consumption of this food. It is no coincidence that the author makes the comparison, just paragraphs later, with the vendors of *mazamorra* in Argentina, a white hominy pudding rooted in the very indigenous traditions at the origins of the country's cultural history that Mansilla does not wish to represent. Thus, oysters

Oyster Stands in Fulton Market (1870), illustration by Alfred R. Waud. *Public domain, New York Public Library Digital Collections.*

indicate a complex foodscape that combines the rusticity of New Yorkers' eating habits with the modernity of the city's food industry (canning, refrigeration, and shipping) and its economic and social structures in general.

Mansilla devotes a larger section to the manners and preferences of North Americans at the time of eating:

> Brillat Savarin has said: Tell me what you eat, and I will tell you who you are. Grounded in this axiom, I am studying the American people in some detail, even their nutrition. . . . I will never forget my astonishment at my first meal, in the New York hotel, as I observed an elegant eighteen-year-old girl eating half a lobster, even sucking the antennae with delight, with an eloquent expression, her beautiful face transparent. . . . These women who seem to walk on air, like our orchids from Paraná, eat and drink like the heroes of Homer.[29]

The traveler quotes one of the most famous aphorisms of French lawyer, gourmet, and epicurean Jean Anthelme Brillat-Savarin (1755–1826). In *The Physiology of Taste* (1825), a pioneering book on the history and philosophy of food in Western culture, he establishes a direct relationship between the character of individuals, their way of being, and what they eat. Brillat-Savarin argues that food is a defining element of a nation and offers, therefore, a transcendental view of everything that involves eating as a social and physiological act: manners, protocol, flavors, types of dishes, history of food, and presence of food in classical literature, as well as numerous aspects related to digestion, diseases, and disorders associated with nutrition. He condemns all types of excessive eating as lowly acts of physiological satiety, the exact opposite of what Mansilla presents in her account. The grotesque Yankee appears in the image of the young woman not eating or savoring a dish, but devouring a lobster, sucking at its antennae, with a voracity typical of the classical heroes and far from both the standards of Argentine ladies referred to, in the comparison, as a local flower and the elegance expected from women in Brillat-Savarin's account and other popular books on manners of the period.[30]

Mansilla depicts a group of women who, having cast aside their table manners, devour insatiably and mechanically chunks of meat, slurping liquids and feasting in a way that "only the realism of [Émile] Zola,"[31] the naturalist French novelist whose work documents the lowly behavior in society, can reproduce. The passage embodies a paradox: the freedom that the author celebrates in the professional lives of the women of the United States is rejected when speaking of their manners. The traveler cannot accept that eating can be another space for the expression of freedom and pleasure. There is a discomfort with that sensual dimension of food, which for Mansilla must be controlled by standards of etiquette. On the contrary, American women, in the scene presented, seem to enjoy food and apparently have disavowed the social codes surrounding its consumption.

The women Mansilla sees in the streets and busy restaurants of New York are not the same ones she meets in the embassy salons. The former are probably middle-class women to whom the experience of eating out represented more an act of urban socialization than the refined ritual that it was for the Argentine aristocrat.[32] Despite the negativity expressed toward their behavior, when connecting gender and eating one can find an aspect of Mansilla's ethnographic view of food rather empowering. As a traveler, she did not set her sights on the women who cook; rather, she focused on urban women who eat. Food is presented in relation to the American woman outside of what Warren Belasco calls the "bedroom-kitchen orbit"—that is, without restricting the association of food with women to a domestic framework.[33] The latter also speaks to the writer herself and her place of speech: Mansilla did not enter the kitchen as a fellow female observing procedures and recipes, as her colleague Juana Manuela Gorriti does in *Cocina ecléctica* (1890). Rather, Mansilla set food in an urban, social, and collective framework, which serves to explain other phenomena of a political nature.[34] The kitchen, as for many women who wrote on the subject, works in *Recuerdos de viaje* as a vehicle that permits a departure from its confines.[35]

The following examination of the generalized habit of eating while standing is perhaps the moment at which the relationship between food and politics is best insinuated:

> Time is money, and the bar room in which, without ever sitting down, one finds at hand food and drink is preferable to everything, when precious time is scarce and economized. Those bad, indigestible meals, made this way, thinking of ungrateful and even sometimes cruel things, produce later atrocious stomachache or dyspepsia.[36]

Mansilla analyzes here another facet of urban eating in New York: worker's food. She notes that without class distinction, lawyers, stockbrokers, businessmen, and poor store clerks share the taste for fast food such as the aforementioned oysters or fish sandwiches so that they can quickly return to work after lunchtime.[37] Unlike the multi-course meals Mansilla prefers for herself, in the blue-collar restaurants of New York, "food was secondary to other factors—speed, convenience, and cheapness."[38] For Mansilla, the brisk dining habits of New York's working classes reflected the rushed pace and materialist nature of the commercial metropolis. Periodicals and magazines from the city such as *Harper's* or *The New York Herald* also reflected on the transformation of restaurants from a place for sociability to one of expediency, "akin to today's fast-food restaurant."[39] Additionally, Mansilla assumes here a doctor's role, basing her thinking on the hygienist theories in vogue in the late nineteenth century, which were particularly popular in Argentina, in order to link food to manners of consumption—Mansilla reformulates Brillat-Savarin's adage as such: tell me *how* you eat, and I'll tell you *who* you are. For her, the ways in which a meal is prepared and eaten have immediate effects on the human body. Considering this comment as a social metaphor, the traveler points out that the excessive consumerism of the United States will be responsible for an irreparable cultural evil inflicted on the body of the nation. In the words of Charlotte Biltekoff, Mansilla's comment is aligned with a "scientific moralization" of the American diet that finds a historical connection between excessive consumption of food and the formation of citizenship in the United States.[40]

Mansilla's perspective takes us directly to what only a year later Martí would express in his aforementioned chronicle "Coney Island" about the opposition between quantity and quality to highlight the particularities of the North and the South of the continent. Both authors find a dimension not only social, but also moral in the American way of eating. Martí builds his thoughts on the continental identity "as a geocultural fear of being devoured," that is, the fear of the rest of the American continent of being consumed and appropriated by the United States.[41] Likewise, the devouring, sucking, and gorging in Mansilla maintain a close relationship with the judgments of her contemporaries about the "cannibalistic" spirit of the United States, its economic materialism, and even its aforesaid expansionist policies (devouring territories in the same excessive manner in which its citizens eat).

The constant and varied references to the United States as a modern nation that, nevertheless, comes across as brutish in its functional character and bad taste illustrates Mansilla's intellectual capacity to enter fully into one of the most heated discussions of the turn of the century: the rescue of spiritualism and Latin cultural values as the roots of South America to confront the threat of the continental North's Anglo-Saxon materialism. The aesthetic and culinary parameters that Mansilla uses to construct a barbaric image of the United States are of vital importance to analyze the ways in which a woman, with class privileges but without full access to political life, enrolls in the tradition of representing the United States under a monstrous image that intellectuals like Martí have not yet fully formulated and that the Uruguayan José Enrique Rodó would express almost two decades later in his seminal essay *Ariel* (1900).[42] After traveling to the United States and venturing into the very "bowels of the monster," Mansilla uses the tools available to her as a woman—who despite her distinguished origins faced restrictions both in her education and her experiences—to build her own perceptions of her Latin American identity as standing in stark opposition to the United States' character.[43] If Priscilla Parkhurst Ferguson affirms that collective identities are created, among other things, through the formalization of everyday cooking practices into stable patterns, Mansilla creates an Argentine and Latin American identity through a discursive performance—a gastronarrative—of the consumption of quality and "good taste" versus the negative effects of consuming quantity.[44]

Notes

1. For more details about the literary and journalistic work of Eduarda Mansilla and her trip to the United States, see María Rosa Lojo, Introduction to *Recuerdos de viaje* by Eduarda Mansilla, Colección Las Antiguas (Córdoba, Argentina: Buena Vista, 2011), 11–37; Vanesa Miseres, *Mujeres en tránsito: Viaje, identidad y escritura en Sudamérica (1830–1910)* (Chapel Hill: North Carolina Studies in the Romance Languages and Literatures, 2017); Stella Maris Scatena Franco, *Peregrinas de outrora. Viajantes latino-americanas no século XIX* (Florianópolis, Brazil: Editora Mulheres, 2008); Juan Pablo Spicer-Escalante, Introduction to *Recuerdos de viaje* by Eduarda Mansilla (Buenos Aires: Stockcero, 2006), vii–xxiii; and Mónica Szurmuk, *Women in Argentina: Early Travel Narratives* (Gainesville: University Press of Florida, 2000).
2. Domingo Faustino Sarmiento (1811–1888) was a self-educated Argentine who would become president of his country and who traveled to the United States in 1846 with the express purpose of studying educational institutions. His travel letters express his interest in proposing the American personality as a role model for his native Argentina. He admired Yankee industry and democracy and presents a counterpoint to what Mansilla will observe later in her visit. For a connection between Sarmiento and Mansilla, see Francine Masiello, "Lost in Translation: Eduarda Mansilla de García on Politics, Gender, and War," in *Representing the Spanish American Essay: Women Writers of the 19th and 20th Centuries*, ed. Doris Meyer (Austin: University of Texas Press, 1995), 68–79, and Eva-Lynn Jagoe, "Familial Triangles: Eduarda Mansilla, Domingo Sarmiento, and Lucio Mansilla," *Revista Canadiense de Estudios Hispánicos* 29, no. 3 (Spring 2005): 507–24.
3. Lojo, "Introduction to *Recuerdos de viaje*," 11.
4. Lojo, "Introduction to *Recuerdos de viaje*," 15.
5. Cindy R. Lobel, *Urban Appetites: Food and Culture in Nineteenth-Century New York* (Chicago: University of Chicago Press, 2014), 1.
6. José Martí, "Coney Island," in *En los Estados Unidos. Escenas norteamericanas* (Alicante, Spain: Biblioteca Virtual Miguel de Cervantes), accessible at http://www.cervantesvirtual.com/obra-visor/en-los-estados-unidos-escenas-norteamericanas--0/html/. Translations are by Omar Hamal.
7. Eduarda Mansilla, *Recuerdos de viaje* (Buenos Aires: Stockcero, 2006), 2.
8. Stephen Mennell, *All Manners of Food: Eating and Taste in England and France from the Middle Ages to the Present* (Oxford: Basil Blackwell, 1987), 133.
9. Mennell, *All Manners of Food*, 134.
10. Pierre Bourdieu, *La distinción: criterios y bases sociales del gusto* (Barcelona: Taurus, 1998), 15–26.

11. Mansilla, *Recuerdos de viaje*, 4.
12. Jagoe, "Familial Triangles," 508.
13. Jeffrey M. Pilcher, "Eating à la Criolla: Global and Local Foods in Argentina, Cuba, and Mexico," *IdeAs* 3 (2012), 6.
14. Pilcher, "Eating à la Criolla," 6.
15. For Argentine culinary traditions see Aníbal Arcondo, *Historia de la alimentación en Argentina. Desde los orígenes hasta 1920* (Córdoba, Argentina: Ferreyra Editor, 2002), and Margarita Elichondo, *La comida criolla: memorias y recetas* (Buenos Aires: Ediciones del Sol, 2008).
16. David Viñas, *De Sarmiento a Dios. Viajeros argentinos a USA* (Buenos Aires: Sudamericana, 1998), 63.
17. Mansilla, *Recuerdos de viaje*, 122.
18. Mansilla, *Recuerdos de viaje*, 9–10.
19. Mansilla, *Recuerdos de viaje*, 22.
20. Mary Louise Pratt, *Imperial Eyes: Travel Writing and Transculturation* (London: Routledge, 2017), 166–68.
21. Mansilla, *Recuerdos de viaje*, 20.
22. Jordan Stein, "How an Old Sherry Drink Defined an Era of American History," *Saveur*, December 29, 2015, https://www.saveur.com/sherry-cobbler-drink-of-an-era.
23. Beatriz Urraca, "'Quien a Yankeeland se encamina . . .': The United States and Nineteenth-Century Argentine Imagination," *Ciberletras* 1, no. 2 (2008), http://www.lehman.cuny.edu/ciberletras/v01n02/Urraca.htm.
24. Mansilla, *Recuerdos de viaje*, 45–46.
25. Mansilla, *Recuerdos de viaje*, 23.
26. See Charles Perry, "As American As Roasted Oysters," *Los Angeles Times*, December 26, 2011, http://articles.latimes.com/2001/dec/26/food/fo-oyster26; Jan Longone, "From the Kitchen," *The American Magazine and Historical Chronicle* (1987): 3–4, 34–43.
27. Longone, "From the Kitchen," 35.
28. Elizabeth Royte, "The Mollusk That Made Manhattan," March 5, 2006, *The New York Times*, https://www.nytimes.com/2006/03/05/books/review/the-mollusk-that-made-manhattan.html.
29. Mansilla, *Recuerdos de viaje*, 23–24.
30. On the importance of etiquette manuals in Latin America see Beatriz González Stephan, "Modernización y disciplinamiento. La formación del ciudadano: del espacio público y privado," in *Esplendores y miserias del siglo XIX: Cultura y sociedad en América Latina*, ed. Beatriz González Stephan (Caracas: Monte Ávila, 1994): 431–56, and Ana Peluffo, *En clave emocional: cultura y afecto en América Latina* (Buenos Aires: Prometeo, 2016).
31. Mansilla, *Recuerdos de viaje*, 24.
32. Contrary to Mansilla's statement, Lobel affirms that public behavior and manners, although new to the lower classes, were a concern for both New York women and restaurants, which tried to educate their customers in appropriate table manners for eating in semi-public spaces. Lobel, *Urban Appetites*, 129.
33. Warren Belasco, *Food: The Key Concepts* (Oxford: Berg Publishers, 2008), 46.
34. Argentine writer Juana Manuela Gorriti (1816–1892) compiled a cookbook

titled *Cocina ecléctica*. The project consisted in inviting women from all around Latin America to send in their recipes. The contributors included upper- and middle-class women as well as their cooks, women of different racial backgrounds. For more, see Elisabeth Austin, "Reading and Writing Juana Manuela Gorriti's *Cocina Ecléctica*: Modeling Multiplicity in Nineteenth-Century Domestic Narrative," *Arizona Journal of Hispanic Cultural Studies* 12, no. 1 (2007): 31–44.

35. Belasco, *Food*, 46.
36. Mansilla, *Recuerdos de viaje*, 25.
37. Mansilla, *Recuerdos de viaje*, 25.
38. Lobel, *Urban Appetites*, 114.
39. Lobel, *Urban Appetites*, 114.
40. Charlotte Biltekoff, *Eating Right in America: The Cultural Politics of Food and Health* (Durham, NC: Duke University Press, 2013), 13–44.
41. Carlos Jáuregui, *Canibalia: Canibalismo, calibanismo, antropofagia cultural y consumo en América Latina* (Madrid: Iberoamericana, 2008), 313.
42. Beatriz Colombi, *Viaje Intelectual: Migraciones y desplazamientos en América Latina, 1880–1915* (Rosario, Argentina: Beatriz Viterbo, 2004), 99. In *Ariel*, Rodó explores the problems of Latin American civilization and argues that its future depends on the evolution of spiritually, aesthetically, and morally enlightened citizens. The text takes the form of a lecture being delivered by an elder professor to his young students. Employing the characters of Ariel and Caliban from Shakespeare's *The Tempest* (1610–11) as symbols, the lecture explains the differences between Latin America and the United States. Ariel is beautiful, graceful, and noble, while Caliban is coarse and barbaric. Just like Mansilla's work, *Ariel* considers the negative effects of the United States' utilitarianism and advises Latin Americans to pursue a different path. By pursuing a "spiritual idealism," Latin America should distinguish itself from the United States by fostering spirituality, morality, reflection, art, science, and other forms of high culture found by the author to be lacking in the United States.
43. José Martí, "Letter to Manuel Mercado, May 18th, 1895," in *Obras Completas* (Havana: Editorial Nacional de Cuba, 1965) 8:182.
44. Quoted in Pilcher, "Eating à la Criolla," 3.

PART III

Gender and Food

Consumerism, Desire, and Women's Agency

CHAPTER 7

Homemaking in 1950s Mexico

Women, Class, and Race through the Kitchen Window

SANDRA AGUILAR-RODRÍGUEZ

> *All the industrial effort to perfect and simplify domestic chores has one basic reason: no civilized being lives happily, is healthy and ready to carry out his daily activities if he lives in an unkempt home.*
>
> —*Almanaque Dulce*[1]

In the 1950s a tidy and well-organized home was a sign of civilization. A civilized family, according to the *Almanaque Dulce* (Sweet Almanac), had achieved happiness, healthiness, and productivity with the help of industrial developments. As the homemakers, women were in charge of purchasing domestic appliances to keep their homes tidy and thus bringing civilization to their family's daily life and to the nation. Cookbooks and brochures like the almanac included information about nutritional science, the use of domestic appliances, and generally the right way to run a household. Modernity and civilization were identified with home economics, the use of domestic technology, and processed food—in other words with the material culture and practices of the United States. Although this way of life was only possible for middle- and upper-class households, the aspiring working class browsed these magazines and imitated the practices they could afford, perhaps buying secondhand appliances as they could. Their reality was very different from the one portrayed in the publications: households in which the husband was the sole breadwinner so the wife could remain at home. The *Almanaque Dulce*'s narrative reinforced not only patriarchy, but also racial perceptions by presenting the ideal woman or family as white. Blond or light-skinned characters with European features dominated print media, with indigenous representations associated primarily with ignorance, poverty, and lack of sanitation.

This chapter explores representations of women, class, and race by looking at three publications of 1950s Mexico: *Almanaque Dulce*, *Mujeres de Hogar* (Housewives), and *Cómo cocinar en los aparatos modernos* (How to Cook Using Modern Appliances). The analysis will reveal how gastronarratives, particularly in publications centered on cooking and homemaking, reinforced gender, race, and class roles in 1950s Mexico. Recipes, cooking advice, and publicity were presented as part of a rhetoric promoting traditional gender roles as well as Westernized and middle-class values. Gastronarratives reproduced a discourse that cast European and US material culture and practices as superior. Most of these publications emphasized that a woman's place was at home and that self-denial and sacrifice were cherished characteristics of Mexican women. Class and race were deeply connected, as an analysis of texts and images from these articles will demonstrate. In the ideal Mexican household women worked hard to imitate the practices of the *gente decente* ("decent people," or middle class), even if they did not have the money. The aspiring middle class was expected to leave behind their indigenous and rural backgrounds by changing their daily habits, particularly through cooking, cleaning, and consumption.

This essay is divided into three sections. The first provides a historical context in regard to racial ideology and education. The second addresses how motherhood and housewifery were presented as the aspirational roles for women despite their increasing participation in the money economy; the mass media portrayed the life of a middle-class woman as the ideal or even the expectation, but this was an unattainable reality for most Mexican women. The last section explores how the discourse of *mestizaje* intertwined with representations of class and race in the media, strengthening beliefs in white and Western superiority.

Improving the Race

The process of *mestizaje* that took place in the twentieth century implied that indigenous people could be part of the nation and thus become mestizos once they had embraced European culture and adopted middle-class manners and morals. The mestizo had "a racial and cultural ascription of being civilized, modern, Western, progressive, evolved and superior."[2] Mexico was constructed as a nation formed by indigenous people and Spaniards, but in this mix Western culture had to dominate. Although this rhetoric could be traced back to the colonial era, it was revamped during Porfirio Díaz's government.[3] The *Porfiriato*, as his regime was called, was heavily influenced by positivist ideas claiming that scientific knowledge was the solution to all human problems. In terms of race, Porfirian intellectuals and politicians followed the path of thinkers such as Herbert Spencer who, inspired by Charles Darwin's theory of biological evolution, presented human history as the outcome of the survival of the fittest.[4] To Spencer's mind, Caucasians were clearly superior, as they had been able to conquer the world and develop a material civilization unlike any other. Moreover, the Anglo-Saxons represented the pinnacle of that evolution.[5]

Discussions about race and evolution gave rise to eugenics, a field created by Sir Francis Galton, to improve human beings by studying the hereditary transmission of phenotypes and family history.[6] Eugenicists divided the population into distinct and unequal races asserting differences and creating boundaries. The main point of discussion was whether those differences were fixed and natural (biological) or whether these characteristics could be modified and if so, how to do it. While in the *Porfiriato* the biological perspective dominated, after the Revolution most eugenicists considered that social improvement was possible and could be achieved through education and sanitation rather than genetic inheritance and race strictly. "Backward" populations could improve themselves through learning the "right way of living." This approach aligned with Lamarckian notions, which proposed the inheritance of acquired characteristics and argued that external influences could alter individual life as well as future generations. In opposition, the Mendelian concept of genetics that dominated the United States, Great Britain, and Germany during this time highlighted that successful individuals and groups were genetically and innately superior, with the poor and unsuccessful being viewed as products of poor heredity. Ancestry rather than social life was seen as the determinate factor in defining the success or failure of different groups.[7]

After the Revolution (1910–21), Mexican intellectuals argued that the poor were poor not because they were lazy or inferior, but as a result of living in ignorance and unhygienic conditions, which could be modified.[8] José Vasconcelos, minister of education between 1921 and 1924, solidified the *mestizaje* narrative in his book *La raza cósmica* (The Cosmic Race) published in 1925, but more importantly by incorporating this discourse into education policy. During his time in office he created the Cultural Missions, an education program aimed at decreasing the illiteracy rate, then at 80 percent. On top of teaching how to read and write, these missions instilled Western values and culture among the peasantry and indigenous people. Vasconcelos's program taught Spanish and the Greek classics as well as inculcating middle-class morals and daily practices. Rafael Ramírez, director of rural education under Vasconcelos, demanded "that children not only learn the Spanish language, but also acquire our customs and lifestyles, which are unquestionably superior to theirs. They must know that Indians call us the gente de razón [people of reason] not only because we speak Spanish, but because we dress and eat differently."[9] For Ramírez, indigenous communities had hope as long as they assimilated and left their own culture behind.

Eugenics ideals influenced education through home economics and child-rearing. According to Ellen Richards, a founding figure of home economics, scientific research had to supply women with the knowledge to create an ideal environment at home so they would be efficient with healthy, happy, and productive families.[10] Reformers and policymakers were very concerned about women working in factories and mingling freely with men. Not only was morality seen to be at risk in these spaces, but also women were seen as neglecting their families by earning a living. After the 1920s public policy was enacted to enable conditions for women to remain at home. The rhetoric of motherhood and family life gained strength, most likely in response to the increasing number of women entering the workforce. Gastronarratives reinforced the ideal of the middle-class lifestyle, in which mothers were educated in home economics and stayed at home to look after the family. Cookbooks, magazines, and brochures argued that education was not the most important factor in improving the race; rather, consumption was central to becoming mestizos. Katharine French-Fuller notes: "Technological change linked notions of cleanliness, respectability, class, and gender with concepts of modernity and progress."[11] Thus women played a key role in demanding and introducing new technologies, foodstuffs, and cooking practices deemed appropriate for modern Mexico.

Women's Place Is at Home

Post-revolutionary educators tried to develop a petit-bourgeois patriarchal family model among the working class to stabilize and depoliticize the country. According to Mary Kay Vaughan, in the 1920s women's vocational schooling was designed to remove women from factories and return them to the home.[12] Women's education focused on teaching pupils to be efficient mothers, maintain certain hygiene standards, raise healthy children, practice frugality, and develop a work ethic. In doing so, the revolutionary government intervened in the private sphere by trying to "gain control over it in the name of national development."[13] The Ministry of Education did not consider that women might *want* to work outside their homes. For reformers, women remained the educational and moral force in the family, and the ministry expected to reach the entire family through educating women.[14] Vaughan argues that "this morally motivated trend suggested an attempt to strengthen woman's primary role in the home as a replacer of labor power while marginalizing her participation in the labor force."[15] All female education privileged housework and family life, but while middle-class women had access to clerical training poor women were expected to learn cottage industries.[16]

President Álvaro Obregón (1921–24) considered education a top priority. His minister of education, José Vasconcelos, increased the number of schools and teachers. The governments of Plutarco Elías Calles (1924–28) and Lázaro Cárdenas (1934–40) took an anticlerical stance to strengthen the state's influence on education. Cárdenas's policies insisted on coeducation rather than the consignment of young women to the home or to segregated classrooms. And yet although public education sought to transfer loyalty from the Church to the nation-state, it still promoted values identified with Catholicism such as restraint, submission, obedience, and modesty.

Women's education in both public and Catholic institutions reinforced gender divisions of labor and underscored that a woman's place was at home. But despite an educational policy that enshrined the middle-class family as the model that the working class was supposed to strive for, poor women could not afford to stay at home even if they wanted to. According to official figures, in 1930 women constituted 6.7 percent of the economically active population; in 1940 they represented 7.38 percent; while in 1950 they had reached 13.62 percent.[17] The real numbers were certainly higher as many women engaged in paid work at home or worked as domestic servants.

Between 1920 and 1960 industrialization accelerated, fostering urbanization and migration, particularly to Mexico City. The transition from subsistence agriculture to a consumerist society was a complex process. Most people changed their practices once they had money and migrated to urban areas, but some preserved their rural lifestyles even in the city. This transformation of peasants into workers was a challenge that reformers sought to address, but without questioning social hierarchies and gender roles. State institutions sought to "domesticate" rural migrants by teaching them how to live and organize their households. Drawing from the home economics movement, women's magazines, cookbooks, and advertisements, they promoted women's access to science and technology in their efforts to achieve social transformation. Homemaking became a body of knowledge that required training, which in turn discredited female traditional knowledge. As Megan Elias has showed, in the case of the United States the rhetoric of home economics entailed a paradoxical reaffirmation of women's role as housewives.[18] Home economists implied, however, that the ability to do housework was not a "natural" female characteristic. A healthy and productive family was, in this view, the result of an informed housewife who knew how to manage her household while an ignorant mother sowed disease and vice as a result of unhygienic conditions and poor diet. Moreover, women were encouraged to use technology at home just as men were operating machines in factories.[19] Home economics sought to professionalize housework to mirror the world of men, but without transgressing gender roles or social hierarchies.

Domestic appliances were presented as instruments to facilitate women's daily chores and save time. However, this time had to be spent cooking more elaborate meals, embellishing the home, and keeping the husband happy.[20] An interesting example of this is *Mujeres de Hogar*, which launched in November 1949 and was published by Industria Eléctrica de México (Mexican Electric Industry or IEM). IEM had been founded the previous year as the result of a new policy of import substitution industrialization, which encouraged foreign companies to establish plants in Mexico.[21] The idea was to attract investment, industrialize the nation, and create jobs, with the end goal of increasing self-sufficiency and promoting nationalism. The goods manufactured by these companies were described as "Made in Mexico" despite the fact that most of the companies were owned by foreign capital, imported parts from other countries, and often retained their foreign names.[22] This was the case of IEM, which was a subsidiary of White-Westinghouse. It produced and sold a wide range of products like refrigerators, freezers, washing machines, dryers, irons, toasters, and stoves, using parts and technical knowledge from the United States. *Mujeres de Hogar* included several advertisements promoting domestic appliances alongside articles, interviews, short stories, advice columns, recipes, fashion photography, and exercise routines. It was distributed for free mainly among families who had acquired its products. The magazine had a very conservative tone in regard to gender roles, as evidenced in an editorial published in August 1951:

> Our Mexican women, who are the pride of Latin America, are very different from women of other latitudes because they have very deep feelings of self-denial and nobleness. They could never relinquish these values and join "feminist" movements. . . . [Mexican women's] actions are not guided by any doctrine but her firm and natural condition of being a woman, born to be a mother and to live happily at home.[23]

Mexican women were described as unique in Latin America and also very different from their counterparts in other parts of the Western world in their indifference to feminism and politics. By nature, women were devoted to their husbands and children and happy to remain at home. A Mexican woman's character was frequently described in terms of self-abnegation, with her only goal being to love her family and look after them. This rhetoric echoed state policies regarding female education by reinforcing the idea that a woman's place was at home. Interestingly, this editorial was published at a pivotal moment in the fight for women's suffrage. In 1947 President Miguel Alemán granted women the right to vote in municipal elections. While women's suffrage at a national level was not decreed until 1953 by President Adolfo Ruíz Cortines, we can see a growing concern about the politization of women.[24] The magazine's conservative tone insisted that despite the historical moment, women lacked interest in participating in the public sphere. It seems that they were trying to remind their readers that decent women should not participate in politics nor fight for women's equality. Doing so went against nature and betrayed the ideal of Mexican motherhood.

The magazine portrayed a society in which adult women were married, apolitical, and had enough economic means to avoid paid jobs and buy domestic appliances. In August 1950 it published a text in which a woman supposedly shares a personal story of an encounter with a very elegant lady at a big hotel located on Juárez Avenue, one of the main streets in Mexico City. The elegant lady is defined as a career woman from the United States, while the narrator is a Mexican housewife. They chat in the ladies' room about their lives while the Mexican woman assists the elegant lady by mending her torn skirt. The housewife shares her deep and secret desire to be a career woman, to travel and have adventures, to which the career woman confesses that her life is full of solitude. She has neither children nor a husband "like those in Latin America who you understand little by little, to whom you end up loving with a motherly love, like another child."[25]

Interestingly, this story reveals that some Mexican women aspired to have a different life, to have a career and material success. But such dreams and desires, this story claims, only ever end in loneliness. Family life and motherhood are presented as the only path to happiness. Moreover women, not men, must understand their partners, adapt to them, and love them in the same way they love their children. This implies that wives were expected to adopt the role of mother not only with their children but also with their husbands. Presenting men as children and their wives as their mothers could also be construed as an erasure of women's sexuality. Women were not to be partners or persons with dreams and aspirations beyond motherhood and family life.

The section ends up stating that "career women are all alone and without love. They act like lions to avoid being devoured. They are weak because they do not have a husband, children, and a stable home. Mrs. Housewife, you possess everything . . . that can only be paid with an authentic women's heart."[26] Career women are portrayed as strong yet weak—they behave like men in order to compete with them, but they are betraying their femininity and that is why they suffer. In this juxtaposition, women from the United States and elsewhere in the Western world are perceived as the opposite of those from Mexico. The former are engaged in politics, have professional lives, and may choose not to marry or have children, whereas Mexican women do not follow their personal ambition, do not engage in the public sphere, and are devoted to their family.

The moral of the story is that women who decide to work outside their home have access to money and material goods, but this comes at the price of happiness. A housewife may not have the jewels, fine clothing, or the fame of a career woman, but she has the love and company of a husband and children. Women should be happy with what they have and stop dreaming about a life beyond their traditional role because that cannot bring good to them or to society. In the 1950s, women were encouraged to embrace technological advances, but new gender roles were not welcome.[27]

Despite presenting a narrative in which women were not supposed to work, in June 1951 *Mujeres de Hogar* included an article highlighting female workers in their Tlalnepantla plant. These women "have feelings, they think and have dreams, but they also have a great enthusiasm for the job they perform."[28] The article presents female employees as typical women who dream of getting married, but also as workers who love their jobs; they are not working out of necessity, but because they enjoy it. The magazine showcases a particular woman, Socorro Hernández Reyes, who is described as "young and full of life, she seems to be a girl of school age," implying that she is too young to marry and thus once she finds a husband she may stop working.[29] The article ends by stating that "women's hands are working at IEM and contributing to a better world."[30] This suggests that several women work at IEM despite the fact that men dominate the photographs of both blue-collar workers and higher-rank employees. A picture of IEM's workers published a month later (August 1951) includes only two women among a group of thirty-six men.

IEM claimed that they were contributing to a better world, but whose world was actually improving? The world of the middle class was getting better and becoming more comfortable as they could afford to buy the company's appliances. There was a major difference between the women who had to work to support their families and those who could afford to stay home. Most of the latter had domestic servants and enough money to buy household appliances. Domestic technology was seen as a way to facilitate women's work in case their domestic servants left and as a tool to keep servants happy as well. The cooking section of the August 1950 issue states that the featured recipes are so simple, even women without any kitchen experience can prepare them "when the cook is away and the mistress is alone."[31]

Although *Mujeres de Hogar* did not include images of domestic servants, they were portrayed in a few advertisements published elsewhere. These images reveal how class and race were clearly interconnected at this place and time. Mistresses are middle- and upper-class women with light skin and European features, while their employees are poor indigenous women. A blender advertisement published in *Madame* in 1950 portrays a light-skinned and stylish woman posting a sign that says, "Looking for a domestic servant." A servant, featured as a short, dark-skinned woman with indigenous features, black hair, and squinted eyes, replies "Everything is very nice, the room, the radio, the holidays . . . but you do not have a Waring blender. I also need some help and a Waring makes sauces, purée, baby food and all sorts of dishes. So they bought her a Waring blender."[32]

Modern appliances would help women retain their domestic servants, and thus reinforced their social status. Domestic technology was seen as a way to transform the nation. Consumption of such goods would foster industrialization, economic growth, and Western practices at home, but the items were also status symbols. Working-class women familiarized themselves with appliances by working as domestic servants and later incorporating these items into their homes if possible. Advertisements tried to establish a strong bond between homemaking and nation building. Mexicans would transform their country and themselves through consumption. Acquiring goods and Western practices would uplift the Mexican family, particularly those who migrated from the countryside and had indigenous backgrounds. Consumption was a key element of *mestizaje*, as it became a way to entice people to move away from subsistence agriculture and into the money economy. Women were at the center of this process, particularly at home, where they decided and negotiated what appliances to buy and how to use them.

Domestic Appliances as a Door to *Mestizaje*

Mestizaje, as discussed above, was defined as a mix of European and indigenous cultures but in practice it referred to assimilation.[33] A mestizo was a Mexican of an indigenous or rural background, likely with dark skin, who had adopted Western culture and practices. This transformation was accomplished at school, but family life was as important as formal education. Cookbooks, brochures, and magazines targeted women in their effort to modernize daily life and increase consumption. The use of domestic technology came to signify efficiency and hygiene. Women could now wash their clothes in a washing machine rather than by hand and thereby save several hours per week. They could also cook in less

Illustration from *Cómo cocinar en los aparatos modernos* (1950) by Josefina Velázquez de León. *Courtesy of Biblioteca Nacional, Mexico City.*

time if they had a gas stove, a pressure cooker, or a blender. Moreover, as these appliances implied reduced physical contact with food, they were deemed more hygienic. In 1950 Josefina Velázquez de León, the most prolific cookbook writer of the twentieth century, published *Cómo cocinar en los aparatos modernos*.[34] In the first volume she claims that the book is a response to questions from several women about how to use kitchen appliances. She describes the use of pressure cookers, ovens, mixers, and blenders. This book tends to portray indigenous culture in a negative way by identifying peasant women with a lack of sanitation.

A case in point, the image above shows an old, fat, and untidy woman using one hand to mix ingredients and scratching her head with the other, while a well-groomed cook pushes a button without touching the mixture at all. It reveals social and racial differences: the old woman appears to be shorter and dressed in the simple clothing of an indigenous peasant, while the professional cook towers over her and looks happy and well-rested. Lack of sanitation was associated with the poor and uneducated, who usually had indigenous and/or rural backgrounds, whereas those who used modern appliances practiced good hygiene and had money to buy new technologies. Using electrical appliances, according to this cookbook, facilitates cooking such that women are less tired and can prepare more sophisticated meals, do more housework, and yet be more refreshed and ready to welcome their husbands and guests.

Mujeres de Hogar tended to portray light-skinned or blonde women enjoying the benefits of modern technology as the image below shows.

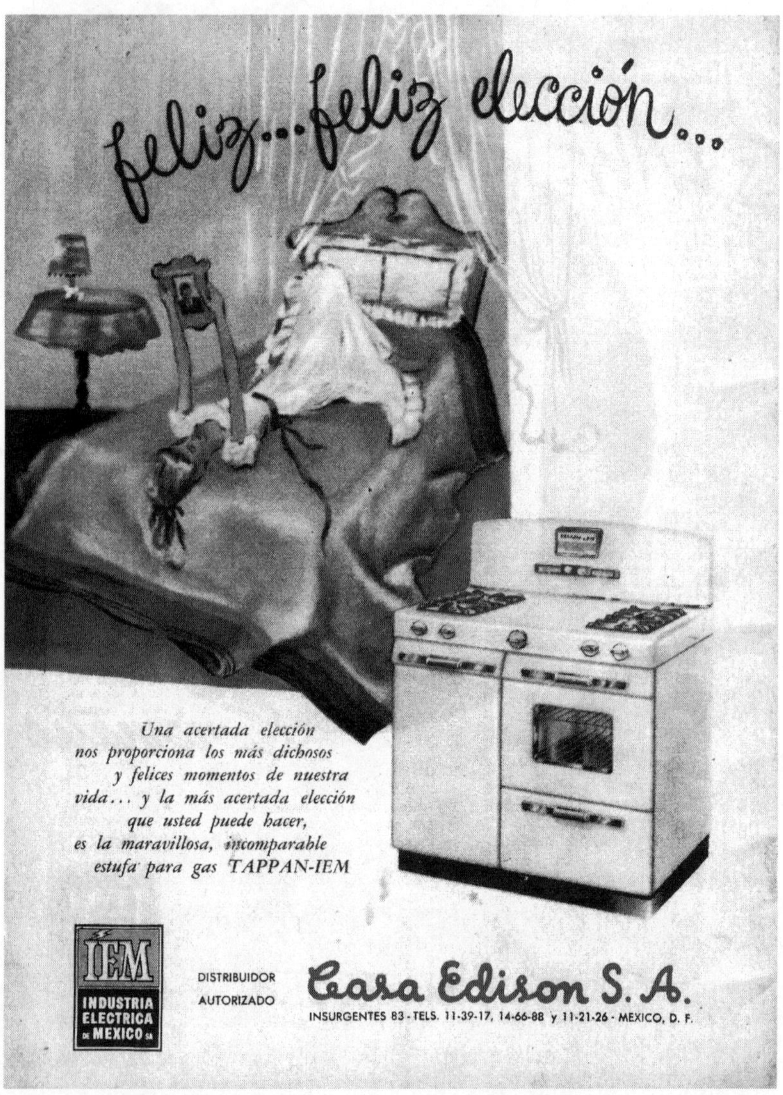

"A happy . . . happy choice . . . ," IEM advertisement in *Mujeres de Hogar*, August 1951. *Courtesy of Biblioteca Nacional, Mexico City.*

This advertisement states, "The right choice will provide us with happiness and joy. The best choice you can make is the wonderful and unrivaled TAPPAN-IEM gas stove."[35] Elements of gender, class, and race come together: a young blonde woman reclines in her bed while looking at an image of a young man, implying that she is thinking about marriage. The advertisement points out that this decision is very important, and if done correctly will bring happiness to the young lady. Therefore, her happiness is dependent upon men and consumption. Choosing a husband is more or less like selecting a gas stove; if a woman makes the right choice and marries a man with enough economic means, he will be able to purchase a gas stove for her and thus make her daily chores less burdensome. Again here: domestic technologies allowed women to be better caregivers and have healthier and cleaner families, and therefore participate in the modernizing project required to improve the Mexican race.

Race was a central element of these images, but they were also tied to class and gender. Poor and working-class women were portrayed as having dark skin and not adhering to Western standards of beauty and cleanliness. Meanwhile, middle-class women were depicted as slender, light skinned, well dressed, and often blonde. Although most Mexican women did not have that phenotype, they could whiten themselves through consumption. Acquiring domestic appliances such as gas stoves allowed families to become respectable and distance themselves from their peasant or indigenous backgrounds. Cooking in a gas stove instead of a paraffin range or charcoal brazier meant a cleaner kitchen, and gas stoves saved women time: they did not have to do as much cleaning, and gas was delivered to the home while charcoal or paraffin had to be bought at specific shops. Women could spend that time trying to achieve the middle-class ideal by cooking more elaborate meals and keeping the house nice and tidy.

Conclusions

The analysis of gastronarratives present in 1950s cookbooks, brochures, and advertisements reveals that the process of *mestizaje* implied the adoption of Western culture and capitalist values without transgressing gender roles. Housewives were instructed through formal education, cookbooks, and print media how to imitate a lifestyle that was portrayed as superior to their own. The indigenous or peasant lifestyle had to be replaced by the material culture and practices of civilized nations. Mexicans needed to live and consume like their US counterparts if they wanted to be like them. However, this transformation did not in any way seek to disrupt traditional gender roles. The rhetoric of *mestizaje* did not bring racism to an end, just as modernity did not challenge patriarchy. Mexican women had to preserve their values and sacrifice themselves for their families. Domestic appliances were not intended to free women to have careers; they were supposed to improve women's performance as homemakers and fulfill middle-class ideals. In sum, 1950s gastronarratives reproduced racial prejudices by assuming that rural culture and women's traditional knowledge did not have any value and therefore had no place in modern Mexico. These narratives reinforced patriarchy by claiming that a woman's place was at home. Women were expected to transform the nation from home by consuming these appliances and thus achieving *mestizaje*.

Notes

1. Anita Anaya, "Por una humanidad feliz," in *Almanaque Dulce* (Mexico City: Unión Nacional de Productores de Azúcar, 1952), 6. Translations are my own throughout the chapter.
2. Alicia Castellanos Guerrero, Jorge Gómez Izquierdo, and Francisco Pineda, "Racist Discourse in Mexico," in *Racism and Discourse in Latin America*, ed. Teun A. Van Dijk (Plymouth, MA: Lexington Books, 2009), 233.
3. Porfirio Díaz rose to power in 1876 under an anti-re-electionist banner, but he remained in power until the Mexican Revolution erupted in 1910. His motto, "order and progress," justified his authoritarian and repressive government.
4. Herbert Spencer, *The Principles of Biology*, 2 vols. (London: Williams and Norgate, 1864).
5. See Hannah Arendt, "Race-Thinking before Racism," *Review of Politics* 6, no. 1 (1944); Nancy Leys Stepan, *The Hour of Eugenics: Race, Gender, and Nation in Latin America* (Ithaca, NY: Cornell University Press, 1991).
6. Laura Luz Suárez and López Guazo, *Eugenesia y racismo en México* (Mexico City: Universidad Nacional Autónoma de México, 2005).
7. Stepan, *The Hour of Eugenics*, 27; Alexandra Minna Stern, "From Mestizophilia to Biotypology: Racialization and Science in Mexico 1920–1960," in *Race and Nation in Modern Latin America*, ed. Nancy P. Appelbaum, Anne S. Macpherson, and Karin Alejandra Rosemblatt (Chapel Hill: University of North Carolina Press, 2003).
8. The Mexican Revolution exploded after Francisco I. Madero won the first democratic elections of the twentieth century. The Revolution brought Porfirio Díaz's dictatorship to an end, opening the path for middle-class reformers and victorious generals. Stepan, *The Hour of Eugenics*, 37.
9. Quoted in Jeffrey M. Pilcher, *¡Que vivan los tamales! Food and the Making of Mexican Identity* (Albuquerque: University of New Mexico Press, 1998), 91.
10. Megan Elias, *Stir It Up: Home Economics in American Culture* (Philadelphia: University of Pennsylvania Press, 2010), 11.

11. Katharine French-Fuller, "Gendered Invisibility, Respectable Cleanliness: The Impact of the Washing Machine on Daily Living in Post-1950 Santiago, Chile," *Journal of Women's History* 18, no. 4 (2006): 80.
12. Mary Kay Vaughan, *The State, Education, and Social Classes in Mexico, 1880–1928* (DeKalb: Northern Illinois University Press, 1982), 191.
13. Mary Kay Vaughan, "Modernizing Patriarchy: State Policies, Rural Households, and Women in Mexico 1930–1940," in *Hidden Histories of Gender and the State in Latin America*, ed. Maxine Molyneux and Elizabeth Dore (Durham, NC: Duke University Press, 2000), 196.
14. Patience A. Schell, *Church and State Education in Revolutionary Mexico City* (Tucson: University of Arizona Press, 2003), 47–52.
15. Mary Kay Vaughan, "Women, Class, and Education in Mexico, 1880–1928," *Latin American Perspectives* 4, nos. 1–2 (1977), 146.
16. Sandra Aguilar-Rodríguez, "Industrias del hogar: mujeres, raza y moral en el México posrevolucionario," *Revista de Historia Iberoamericana* 9, no. 1 (2016).
17. Sarah A. Buck, "The Meaning of the Women's Vote in Mexico 1917–1953," in *The Women's Revolution in Mexico, 1910–1953*, ed. Stephanie Mitchell and Patience A. Schell (Lanham, MD: Rowman & Littlefield, 2007).
18. Elias, *Stir It Up*, 11.
19. Harmke Kamminga and Andrew Cunningham, *The Science and Culture of Nutrition, 1840–1940*, Clio Medica 32 (Amsterdam: Rodopi, 1995).
20. Ruth Schwartz Cowan, *More Work for Mother: The Ironies of Household from the Open Hearth to the Microwave* (New York: Basic Books, 1983).
21. Lorenzo Meyer, "La encrucijada," in *Historia general de México*, ed. Daniel Cosío Villegas (Mexico City: Colegio de México, 1998), 1280.
22. On the Mexicanization of US brands and companies, see Julio Moreno, *Yankee Don't Go Home! Mexican Nationalism, American Business Culture, and the Shaping of Modern Mexico, 1920–1950* (Chapel Hill: University of North Carolina Press, 2003).
23. "Editorial," *Mujeres de Hogar*, August 1951, n.p.
24. Julia Tuñón Pablos, *Women in Mexico: A Past Unveiled* (Austin: University of Texas Press, 1999), 105–6.
25. "Entre nosotras y en voz baja," *Mujeres de Hogar*, August 1950, 4.
26. "Entre nosotras," 4.
27. Elias, *Stir It Up*, 2.
28. "Que sabe usted de IEM," *Mujeres de Hogar*, June 1951, 8–9.
29. "Que sabe usted," 8–9.
30. "Que sabe usted," 8–9.
31. Kiki, "Recetario práctico de cocina," *Mujeres de Hogar*, August 1950, n.p.
32. *Madame* 1, no. 1 (September 1950).
33. Federico Navarrete, *Las relaciones inter-étnicas en México* (Mexico City: Universidad Nacional Autónoma de México, 2004), 121.
34. Velázquez de León published more than 150 cookbooks between 1930 and 1968. Jeffrey M. Pilcher, "Josefina Velázquez de León: Apostle of the Enchilada," in *The Human Tradition in Mexico*, ed. Jeffrey M. Pilcher, Human Tradition around the World (Wilmington, DE: SR Books, 2003), 200.
35. *Mujeres de Hogar*, August 1951.

CHAPTER 8

Sense of Place and Gender in Rosario Castellanos's "Cooking Lesson"

ELIZABETH MONTES GARCÉS

Family Album, a collection of stories published in 1971 by the Mexican writer Rosario Castellanos, includes "Cooking Lesson," a meditation on the lot of the traditional Mexican housewife of the 1960s.[1] In *Space, Place and Gender* (1994), Doreen Massey proposes the concept of "sense of place" to refer to the hybridity of social, economic, and power relations that are established within a particular space and that assign specific roles to individuals within any given society.[2] In "Cooking Lesson," Castellanos's protagonist finds her sense of place in the two domestic spaces where the story unfolds: the kitchen and the bedroom. The present article will utilize some concepts brought forth by several literary scholars (Eileen Zeitz, Bernardita Llanos Madrones, Kemy Oyarzún, and Evelyn Fishburn).[3] However, Castellanos's short story will be analyzed from a unique perspective, as we will study how the author challenges the cartography of space associated with gender in Mexican society during the 1960s. By shining a spotlight on the woman's role in the private domain, the "natural" environment assigned to her through tradition and societal norms, the author proposes that the space created through critical reading, writing, and literary creation are indeed effective mediums that ultimately allow her a degree of liberation from the established societal paradigms.

"Cooking Lesson" is the story of a woman who, upon getting married, is forced to give up a career as a university professor and professional writer in order to become a full-time housewife. The kitchen is the setting for the entire short story; she has been charged with preparing a steak dinner for the very first time in her life. This episode triggers an interior monologue whereby the protagonist reflects on the disadvantages of marriage for an intellectual woman in 1960s Mexico. The use of imagery and irony with respect to the instructions provided by the cookbooks, as well as the protagonist's lack of culinary skills, highlights an incongruity in the traditionally organic relationship between a woman, a kitchen, and the culinary arts. In addition, the focalization on the protagonist establishes links between the defrosting, bleeding, cooking, and carbonizing of the meat and the pain she endures during sexual intercourse on her wedding night.[4]

The récit begins with the protagonist's return from her honeymoon, and a description of the kitchen.[5] The representation of this space as "shining white" suggests a metonymical effect upon the audience; the kitchen is maintained in a state of immaculateness, and therefore, by extension, the protagonist must remain as pure and clean as the space she will occupy for the majority of her life.[6] This imagery is directly linked to the Marian tradition typical of Mexican society in the 1960s, in which the woman must remain chaste at all times and her actions should reflect the values historically espoused by the Virgin Mary. In Octavio Paz's *The Labyrinth of Solitude: Life and Thought in Mexico* (1960), the Nobel Prize winner remarks: "Mexican Catholicism is centered about the cult of the Virgin of Guadalupe."[7] Paz elaborates that the Catholic Virgin of Guadalupe is a passive figure, very distant from Tonantzin, the Aztec goddess of fertility. The socially accepted mores regarding a woman's virginity and passivity are paramount, and the typical Mexican woman of the 1960s should aspire to be as ideal as the Virgin of Guadalupe.

In "Cooking Lesson," both expectation of maintaining a clean kitchen and the societal emphasis on female passivity inherent in Mexican tradition terrify the new wife. She senses that this will lead to a state of atrophy of her intellectual aspirations, a type of death in life due to the fact that her husband won't allow her to pursue a career outside the home. In the kitchen she imagines how its cleanliness relates to the general state of asepsis common in a hospital: "Looking closely, this spotlessness, this pulchritude lacks the glaring excess that causes chills in hospitals."[8] Her description evokes the feelings of rejection the space inspires within her, notably when she states that its extreme cleanliness showcased by the kitchen ironically resembles the aseptic state one may encounter within a psychiatric institution.[9] The connection between the kitchen and the hospital goes beyond the notion of cleanliness. In both places, cooks or surgeons must follow specific and repetitive procedures to either cook wholesome meals or cure patients of injuries and diseases. The protagonist in "Cooking Lesson" does not want to be secluded in the kitchen, performing routine domestic procedures, because the kitchen itself is a deathbed for her true passion of intellectual thought and creation. Furthermore, the narrator indicates that, paradoxically, preparing a meal in this immaculate kitchen would most likely leave the space dirty: "It's a shame to have to get it dirty."[10] Although Castellanos utilizes the verb "mancillar"—to get dirty—in reference to the kitchen, there is a clear connection between the domestic space and the housewife herself since both must remain pure.[11]

In *BodySpace*, Nancy Duncan proposes that the conflict between public and private spaces is dominated by a discourse rooted in philosophy, political science, law, and pop culture. The private domain is associated with the domestic, the natural, and the corporeal, and themes that generally relate to passion, sexuality, and family. The public domain occupies itself with themes related to the incorporeal, the abstract, and the rational, such as civil society, production, law and order, government, and the state.[12] In "Cooking Lesson" the narrator freely admits that: "I wandered astray through classrooms, streets, offices, cafes, wasting my time on skills that now I must forget in order to acquire others."[13] In addition to the fact that she previously chose to deviate from the path generally reserved for women by attending university, patronizing coffee shops, and frequenting offices, the statement exhibits the protagonist's belief that the Mexican homemaker belongs at home, or at least has been conditioned to think that way, since society has prepared her male counterpart to negotiate the public sphere. Curiously, she concedes that her fingertips are "not very sensible due to prolonged contact with typewriter keys,"[14] which in turn leads us to deduce that she had previously dedicated herself to writing and activities associated with intellectual pursuits.[15]

In traditional Mexican society, a woman's sense of place is defined by her endeavors in the kitchen. Castellanos's short story reinforces—and in turn challenges—this paradigm through a cunning use of irony and rhetorical questions. The newlywed wife wishes to prepare an evening meal, a task that requires her to consult cookbooks containing instructions and advice from expert homemakers. These mistresses of culinary knowledge appear metaphorically in the kitchen via the protagonist's rhetorical questions: "What can you suggest to me for today's meal, O experienced housewife, inspiration of mothers here and gone, voice of tradition, clamoring secret of the supermarkets?"[16] They are the "voice of tradition," bearers of knowledge that only they can successfully impart upon a novice.[17] Their wealth of culinary knowledge traditionally passes from mother to daughter in the form of an oral tradition, making them an "inspiration of mothers here and gone."[18] The use of "you" in the formal register in Spanish reflects a sense of respect for this tradition. But it is also possible to interpret the question as one loaded with irony.

For Margaret Rose, irony entails the use of a code that allows for the communication of two different ideas at once. According to Rose: "The term irony generally describes a statement of an ambiguous character, which includes a code containing at least two messages, one of which is the concealed message of the ironist to an 'initiated' audience, and the other the more readily perceived but 'ironically meant' message of the code."[19] Following Rose's train of thought, the reference to "the voice of tradition" in Castellanos's short story communicates another possible message.[20] The protagonist does not feel any respect for said voice. On the contrary, she rejects the idea that women are naturally inclined toward the culinary arts and that every newlywed woman wants to become a cook and remain in the kitchen forever. As a free-spirited woman, she wants to have the choice to devote her life to other professions that do not necessarily tie her to the household.

As Simone de Beauvoir affirms, housewives dedicate their lives to a profession that, while necessary, is generally considered unimportant: "Dwelling place and food are useful for life but give it no significance: the immediate goals of the housekeeper are only means, not true ends."[21] The fruits of their labors disappear virtually the moment they are placed on the table. For this reason, the protagonist of "Cooking Lesson" uses irony to highlight the fact that she does not identify with the culinary labor of the proper housewife. She does not wish to dedicate her life to projects without a future, nor live within the confines of "one sterile routine."[22]

However, those authors who have managed to achieve culinary perfection publish cookbooks that have in fact become part of library catalogues as well as kitchen shelves. The narrator refers to them as "those acclaimed jugglers that reconcile those irreducible contradictions among the pages of their recipe books: slimness and gluttony, pleasing appearance and economy, speed and succulence."[23] In other words, one could surmise that she greatly admires these women for writing recipes that call for quality and wholesome yet inexpensive ingredients, while at the same time rejecting them by comparing them to circus performers who skillfully manage a tightrope balance to achieve incredible dishes. To that end it is quite difficult to imagine a dish being high in calories yet unlikely to cause weight gain.

Their eagerness to share their culinary knowledge leads the authors to use a vocabulary that is incomprehensible to the average Mexican woman. The narrator asks: "Well, just who do you think you are talking to? If I knew what tarragon and ananas were, I wouldn't be consulting this book, because I'd know a lot of other things, too."[24] The lack of understanding between the cookbook's author and her reader, in her emphasis that she feels completely out of place, highlights the protagonist's unwillingness to become familiar with the kitchen space and her refusal to identify as the "the angel in the house."[25] She does not characterize herself as a simple housewife. Rather, she considers herself an intellectual woman and a voracious reader of literature, as evidenced by the fact that the same bookshelf that holds her cooking manuals also holds copies of Miguel de Cervantes's *Don Quixote* (1615) and Ludwig Pfandl's critical analysis of Sor Juana Inés de la Cruz's poetic works. Quite possibly because of this the protagonist asks the cookbooks' authors to "write a dictionary of technical terms, edit a few prolegomena, invent a propaedeutic to make the difficult culinary art accessible to the lay person" so that she may decipher and understand the recipes.[26] Even though Castellanos never explicitly states what the protagonist's profession is, her use of academic vocabulary—with terms such as "prolegomena"—allows us to deduce that she is well-read and that she may have worked at a college or university, a public space completely unrelated to the domestic environment. There her place is defined in terms of her relationship with literature and not her role in the kitchen; therefore she asserts to the authors: "I . . . solemnly declare that I am not, and never have been, in on either this or any other secret you share."[27] She uses the popular saying "no estar en el ajo" in order to reaffirm the fact that she does not belong to the community of housewives who share a common knowledge of the culinary arts. The expression "no estar en el ajo" is a playful double entendre. While it conveys the idea of exclusion or lack of acceptance, the meaning is essentially transmitted by referring to garlic, and the excluded individual is that one clove that does not coexist with the rest of the bulb.

If the protagonist's search for a meaningful space bears meager results within the kitchen, she is even less successful in the bedroom. The use of imagery and a focalization centered on the protagonist encourage a connection between what happens in the kitchen and events in the bedroom. In spite of all the challenges she faces with the cookbooks, she decides to prepare a steak. She retrieves a package of frozen meat from the refrigerator, which upon thawing allows her to see its true color: "Red, as if it were just about to start bleeding."[28] Through an internal focalization the protagonist associates the redness of the meat with the sunburn she got while relaxing on the beaches of Acapulco. In other words, the raw meat not only sparks a flashback to her honeymoon, but also establishes a metaphorical relationship between the meat and the female body. Both the meat that is used for cooking and the recently wed girl are "as if it were just about to start bleeding," and in fact do bleed: when the beef is placed on the kitchen grill and when the girl is deflowered by her husband.

Michel Foucault has pointed out that the act of deflowering in a female represents a moment of crisis in a woman's life. In "Of Other Spaces" (1986) he coined the term "heterotopia" to designate "real places—places that do exist and that are formed in the very founding of society—which are something like counter-sites. . . . All the other real sites that can be found within the culture, are simultaneously represented, contested, and inverted."[29] In the 1960s it was traditional for newlywed Mexican couples to honeymoon in Acapulco, and thus for Foucault, such a place represents a heterotopia of crisis: "The young woman's deflowering could take place 'nowhere' and, at the moment of its occurrence the train or honeymoon hotel was indeed the place of the nowhere, this heterotopia without geographical markers."[30] In this regard, the deflowering may occur "nowhere," much like in "Cooking Lesson," where the protagonist surrenders her maidenhead in a random Acapulco hotel, leaving her feeling disconnected from her surroundings in a sort of "exile."[31] This illustrates her complete disconnection from both the rite of passage of surrendering her virginity to her husband and the site where it occurs.

The whiteness of her nightgown on her wedding night contrasts with the descriptions of both the grilled meat and the deflowered woman. On one hand, "the whiteness of my clothes" is a metaphor that emphasizes the woman's virginity, while on the other we observe a comparison between the transparent nightgown and the thin layer of frost on the wrap used to store the meat she retrieves from the refrigerator.[32] The moment of sexual penetration injures the protagonist. The couple consummates their marriage in the missionary position, with the husband on top, at which point, as she herself expresses: "I moaned, from the tearing."[33] Her cries resemble the sound of "the oil [that] is starting to get hot" that "spits and spatters" when she places the raw meat on the grill.[34] The parallelism becomes evident when the narrator identifies with the meat she is roasting: "The meat under the sprinkling of salt has toned down, some of its offensive redness and now it seems more tolerable, more familiar to me."[35] The salt used to season the meat is an obvious allusion to the male seed.

After making love, the protagonist feels diminished, much like the meat she is prepares, which coincidentally ends up burned. Through a focalization centered on the protagonist's thoughts and feelings, the reader realizes that she is conscious of the fact that she feels powerless given her husband's sexual dominance: "When you throw your body on top of mine I feel as though a gravestone were covering me, full of inscriptions, strange names, memorable dates."[36] Both the image of the gravestone falling on the protagonist—with its obvious mortal connotations—and the declaration "I bear an owner's brand" remit the protagonist to Foucault's "nowhere," without a sense of place and where her only legitimate option is living as her husband's property.[37] She is but a mere blank page, who has been inscribed or written on by her husband.

In her essay "Las tretas del débil" (1984), Josefina Ludmer points out that female authors tend to write about spaces that have been the locus of their subjugation in order to distance themselves from them, to create a different sense of place, that allows them to accomplish their goals. According to Ludmer, the strategy "consists of changing not only the individual's sense of place but also the place itself and everything else that is placed there, from the assigned and accepted vantage point."[38] Applying this concept to an analysis of "Cooking Lesson" reveals that the use of various literary techniques such as internal focalization, irony, and rhetorical questions, shows the process that the protagonist utilizes to undermine the sense of place that has been imposed upon her through marriage. She is forced to exist within the confines of the domestic space, under her husband's control, ready to satisfy his every desire, yet in Castellanos's story, the kitchen is also a space of reading, reflection, and literary creation. In that regard, Kemy Oyarzún has pointed out that "the kitchen is no longer seen as the invisible, unproductive domestic sphere. It becomes aesthetically and ethically productive."[39] In fact, the use of culinary metaphors allows Castellanos to repurpose both the kitchen and the Mexican woman's sense of place. Recall that Massey proposed that sense of place is not a fixed notion, but changes over time and according to external influences and identity negotiations operative in the social and cultural spheres.[40] This allows Castellanos to use literature to introduce a change in our understanding of women's sense of place.

Castellanos's short story does not present an actual cooking lesson, but rather an analysis of the Mexican cultural context and the construction of femininity in several texts. This analysis, a destabilizing force to be sure, invokes texts from popular culture (cookbooks, fairy tales, women's magazines, letters to Dear Abby, and movies) as well as various global literary classics (*Romeo and Juliet*, *Don Quixote*, *One Thousand and One Nights*). The protagonist alludes to Shakespeare's plays and Jacob and Wilhelm Grimm's fairy tale "Rapunzel" (1790) when describing her own routine as a dutiful wife:

> Is it a lark? Or is it a nightingale? No, our schedule won't be ruled by such winged creatures as those that announced the coming dawn to Romeo and Juliet but by a noisy and unerring alarm clock. And you will not descend today by the stairway of my tresses but rather on the steps of detailed complaints: you've lost a button off your jacket; the toast is burned; the coffee is cold.[41]

The irony evident in this fragment indicates that, unlike in *Romeo and Juliet*, in "Cooking Lesson" the birds are not what awakens the protagonist each morning, but a mundane alarm clock. The newlywed wife does not sit around idle, pondering life within the confines of her castle, because her husband "will not descend today by the stairway of [her] tresses" like Rapunzel's prince. Rather, he insists she dedicate her daily routine to domestic activities—sewing, baking, preparing coffee. For the protagonist marriage is not the equivalent of the happy ending in a fairy-tale romance, but rather the beginning of a dull life as a housewife, subjected to the norms established through tradition and reinforced through patriarchal practices.

Castellanos's protagonist also relies on another important cultural discourse: film. The cinematic arts present the female role as one based on a dynamic between an active male and a passive female, providing a go-to formula for on-screen happiness. While addressing her husband, the narrator ironically asserts: "And one day you and I will become a pair of perfect lovers and then, right in the middle of an embrace, we'll disappear, and the words, 'The End,' will appear on the screen."[42] This description of an ideal marriage is reminiscent of Doris Day's bedroom comedies of the 1950s. In the Mexican context, the woman's role was that of an innocent beauty, evocative of Ismael Rodríguez's Celia in *Nosotros los pobres* (1948).[43] In that film, Celia is Pepe el Toro's girlfriend; praised for her virginity, she will be the perfect wife for Pepe given her willingness to move into his house, prepare all his favorite dishes, and please all his desires. Without a doubt Castellanos's short story establishes an ironic contrast between the ideal image of femininity in film and the difficult rite of passage her protagonist must endure.

In her analysis regarding the relationship between masculine desire and the construction of the female subject in film, Laura Mulvey affirms: "In a world ordered by sexual imbalance, pleasure in looking has been split between active/male and passive/female. The determining male gaze projects its phantasy on to the female figure which is styled accordingly."[44] Mulvey and Castellanos share a similar mindset, given the Mexican author's need to distort the active male / passive female dynamic with respect to sexual desire. Let us remember the excruciating pain—and the lack of pleasure—Castellanos's protagonist experiences while engaging in sexual intercourse with her husband: "But I, self-sacrificing Little Mexican wife, born like a dove to the nest, smiled."[45] Her smile is in fact identical to the grins and smirks required of film actresses, who find themselves defined as sexual objects for the lustful male viewer's gaze. In other words, the protagonist's ironic comments regarding contemporary cinema indicate that change is indeed possible and that the patriarchal norms established by society can evolve for the better.

A further reading of Castellanos's short story also reveals an interesting use of the verb "comerse." Within the Latin American context, "comerse" is associated with "having sexual intercourse, in particular with a virgin."[46] In Castellanos's short story, the deflowered virgin is likened to meat roasting on a grill. In other words, society has quite literally turned her into a food object, not only to be admired but also to be eaten (deflowered) by her husband. The newlywed girl at one point states that she cannot go out in the street because there she is susceptible to unwanted advances from strangers, men in the street that declare: "You are a temptation for any passerby."[47] The use of the word "viandante" also characterizes the woman as a meal ready to be devoured.[48] The focalization makes the reader realize that the protagonist is consumed by her husband, forced to exist in a place that does not exist—Foucault's "nowhere"—and despite the fact that she is now a married woman, she remains a prisoner of male erotic desire. This implies that she is denied the ability to fully participate in the public sphere.

However, the possibility of becoming the object of male desire, as if she were virtually a piece of meat to be eaten by her husband, awakens in the protagonist her creative agency. She no longer wants to play the role of the newlywed woman. She imagines herself starring in a new film, so she proposes a new script and a new sense of place for women in motion pictures when she states: "In my next movie, I'd like them to give me a different part."[49] This particular role is for a "famous woman (a fashion designer or something like that), rich and independent, who lives in an apartment in New York, Paris or London. Her occasional affairs entertain her but do not change her."[50] In drastic contrast to the passive woman that her husband wants her to be, financially dependent and obliging his every sexual desire, the woman who now appears in the narrator's script is active, financially independent, lives in her own apartment, and exercises agency over her own life and sexual desires. Men serve merely to please her, since she does not allow her emotions to overwhelm or guide her. Her sense of place is defined by her career as a fashion designer in the public sphere, and as such, she is not imprisoned within the confines of the domestic sphere as the protagonist is in "Cooking Lesson."

In her play *The Eternal Feminine* (1975), Castellanos asserts that "it's not good enough to imitate the models proposed for us that are answers to circumstances other than our own. It isn't even enough to discover who we are. We have to invent ourselves."[51] As we have observed, "Cooking Lesson" is a lesson not only in learning to read cultural patterns, but also in making us aware of—and wanting to undermine—patriarchal practices present in culture and in canonical texts that relegate women to the private sphere and effectively negate their humanity. The short story is also a lesson in a woman redefining her sense of place through writing. Strategies such as the use of images, focalization, and irony have allowed us to demonstrate that while the newlywed girl is portrayed as passive and willing to accommodate masculine desire in the private sphere, the new woman proposed by Castellanos's text is independent, active, and willing to satisfy her own desires in both the private and the public spheres. Only by redefining the cartography of gender spaces—and taking up a pen—will she encounter her true sense of place.

Notes

1. Rosario Castellanos, "Lección de cocina," in *Álbum de familia* (Mexico City: Joaquín Mortiz, 1971), 7–22, later published in English as "Cooking Lesson," in *A Rosario Castellanos Reader: Anthology of Her Poetry, Short Fiction, Essays, and Drama*, ed. and trans. Maureen Ahern (Austin: University of Texas Press, 1988), 207–15.

2. Doreen Massey, *Space, Place and Gender* (Cambridge, UK: Polity Press, 1994), 5–11.
3. Eileen Zeitz cites the narrative techniques in Castellanos's "Cooking Lesson" (first-person narrator, interior monologue, and flashbacks) as key elements signaling a new direction in Latin American narrative after the Cuban Revolution. Evelyn Fishburn analyzes metaphors such as cooking raw meat on the stove and the woman's deflowering as a narrative strategy to emphasize women's subjugation to a patriarchal system. See Evelyn Fishburn, "'Dios anda en los pucheros': Feminist Openings in Some Late Stories by Rosario Castellanos," *Bulletin of Hispanic Studies* 72, no. 1 (January 1995): 97–110.
4. The term "focalization" was first coined by Gérard Genette to indicate the perspective and angle of vision of the narrative voice, which may or may not coincide with the perspective of the narrator. According to Genette, focalization includes a given character's thoughts and feelings. See Gérard Genette, *Narrative Discourse: An Essay in Method*, trans. Jane E. Lewis (Ithaca, NY: Cornell University Press, 1980), 189–210.
5. The term "récit" (narrative) was coined by Genette in reference to a written work's discourse or the text itself, as opposed to "histoire" (plot), which refers to a written work's narrative content.
6. Castellanos, "Cooking Lesson," 207.
7. Octavio Paz, *The Labyrinth of Solitude: Life and Thought in Mexico* (New York: Grove Press, 1961), 84.
8. Castellanos, "Cooking Lesson," 207.
9. This is a reference to a common practice in the nineteenth century whereby women who were deemed to have deviated from established patriarchal norms were forced into mental institutions, a practice thoroughly documented in Elaine Showalter, *The Female Malady: Women, Madness and English Culture, 1830–1980* (London: Virago, 1987), 97.
10. Castellanos, "Cooking Lesson," 207.
11. The Spanish word "mancillar" is generally translated as "to tarnish," but in Hispanic cultures it also connotates slandering an otherwise good reputation. It is also related to the traditional belief that a woman's behavior can impact her husband's honor and standing. Researcher Julian Pitt-Rivers states that "while masculine honor is a matter of precedence in the first place and the man of honor strives to establish his name in the forefront of his group, the honor of women is rather a matter of virtue and sexual purity." Julian Pitt-Rivers, "Postscript: The Place of Grace in Anthropology," in *In Honor and Grace in Anthropology*, ed. J. G. Peristiany and Julian Pitt-Rivers (Cambridge: Cambridge University Press, 1992), 215–46.
12. Nancy Duncan, *BodySpace: Destabilising Geographies of Gender and Sexuality* (New York, Routledge, 1996), 127–28.
13. Castellanos, "Cooking Lesson," 207.
14. Castellanos, "Cooking Lesson," 208.
15. Susie Porter has studied the history of women who worked for the Mexican federal government outside the home. Despite the fact that she has thoroughly documented how women entered into the public sphere as office workers as early as 1895 and became an important part of the labor force, women

constituted only 4.4 percent of the workforce in the 1950s. Porter also analyzes how in literature and film the portrayal of women workers was not a positive one: "Film portrayals of women celebrated motherhood within marriage and the home," Susie Porter, *From Angel to Office Worker: 1890–1950* (Lincoln: University of Nebraska Press, 2018), 200. Porter further claims that office work was seen as a path to prostitution. Thus, real-life female contributions to the public sector did not radically alter the ideals of domesticity and virginity that Mexican society expected of women.

16. Castellanos, "Cooking Lesson," 207.
17. Castellanos, "Cooking Lesson," 207.
18. Castellanos, "Cooking Lesson," 207.
19. Margaret Rose, *Parody: Ancient, Modern and Postmodern* (Cambridge: Cambridge University Press, 1993), 87.
20. Castellanos, "Cooking Lesson," 207.
21. Simone de Beauvoir, *The Second Sex*, trans. H. M. Parshley (New York: Vintage Books, 1989), 454.
22. Castellanos, "Cooking Lesson," 207.
23. Castellanos, "Cooking Lesson," 207.
24. Castellanos, "Cooking Lesson," 207.
25. "The angel in the house" refers to the ideal wife of the Victorian era. Sandra M. Gilbert and Susan Gubar have written about this characterization of women in nineteenth-century British novels such as Charlotte Bronte's *Jane Eyre* (1847), in which Jane is depicted as the submissive, selfless, devoted angel in the house. Sandra M. Gilbert and Susan Gubar, *The Madwoman in the Attic: The Woman Writer and the Nineteenth Century Imagination* (New Haven, CT: Yale University Press, 2000) 22.
26. Castellanos, "Cooking Lesson," 207.
27. Castellanos, "Cooking Lesson," 208.
28. Castellanos, "Cooking Lesson," 208.
29. Michel Foucault, "Of Other Spaces," trans. Jay Miskowiec, *Diacritics* 16, no. 1 (Spring 1986): 24.
30. Foucault, "Of Other Spaces," 24.
31. Castellanos, "Cooking Lesson," 208.
32. Castellanos, "Cooking Lesson," 208.
33. Castellanos, "Cooking Lesson," 208.
34. Castellanos, "Cooking Lesson," 212.
35. Castellanos, "Cooking Lesson," 209.
36. Castellanos, "Cooking Lesson," 211.
37. Castellanos, "Cooking Lesson," 211.
38. Josefina Ludmer, "Tretas del débil," in *La sartén por el mango: encuentro de escritoras latinoamericanas*, ed. Patricia Elena González and Eliana Ortega (Río Piedras, Puerto Rico: Ediciones Huracán, 1984), 53. My translation.
39. Kemy Oyarzún, "Beyond Histeria: 'Haute Cuisine' and 'Cooking Lesson' Writing as Production," in *Splintering Darkness: Latin American Women Writers in Search of Themselves*, ed. Lucía Guerra Cunningham (Pittsburgh: Latin American Literary Review Press, 1990), 88.
40. Massey, *Space, Place and Gender*, 192.

41. Castellanos, "Cooking Lesson," 211.
42. Castellanos, "Cooking Lesson," 212.
43. Ismael Rodríguez's *Nosotros los pobres* presents the story of Pepe el Toro (Pedro Infante), a simple carpenter who raises his niece Chachita (Evita Muñoz) as if she were his own biological daughter. The movie clearly displays Mexico's Marianist traditions by juxtaposing the image of the virgin—Pepe's girlfriend Celia (Blanca Estela Pavón)—with the image of the whore—Pepe's sister Yolanda, la Tísica (Carmen Montejo).
44. Laura Mulvey, "Visual Pleasure and Narrative Cinema," in *Media and Cultural Studies*, ed. Meenakshi Gigi Durham and Douglas M. Kellner (Malden, MA: Blackwell Publishing, 2006), 346.
45. Castellanos, "Cooking Lesson," 208.
46. *Diccionario de americanismos. Real Academia Española DRAE* (2018), s.v. "comerse."
47. Castellanos, "Cooking Lesson," 213.
48. Castellanos, "Cooking Lesson," 212.
49. Castellanos, "Cooking Lesson," 212.
50. Castellanos, "Cooking Lesson," 213.
51. Rosario Castellanos, "El eterno femenino," trans. Diane E. Marting and Betty Tyree Osiek, in *A Rosario Castellanos Reader: An Anthology of Her Poetry, Short Fiction, Essays, and Drama* (Austin: University of Texas Press, 1988), 356.

CHAPTER 9

Lemons, Oregano, Satisfaction, and Hopeless Melancholy

Agency, Subversion, and Identity in Mayra Santos Febres's "Marina y su olor"

NINA B. NAMASTE

In the hands of fiction writers, smell is open to diverse possibilities not usually associated with human sensorial control. Contemporary Latin American women writers use domestic spaces, culinary imagery, and the "lesser" senses, such as smell, as a means to criticize patriarchal norms that perpetuate multilayered levels of oppression, as María Claudia André and Renée Scott, among others, have duly noted. Traditionally devalued as lowly, smell has often been used as a means to delineate and debase the "out" group, be it women, Black people, foreigners, homosexuals, or any other marginalized group.[1] "Marina y su olor" (Marina's Fragrance) in Mayra Santos Febres's first collection of stories—*Pez de vidrio* (Glass Fish, 1994), winner of the 1996 Juan Rulfo Prize—tells the story of a poor, young Black girl who eventually becomes an independent and financially secure mature woman thanks in great part to the fantastic smells she emits from her body. The story purposefully and "simultaneously appropriates and subverts a cluster of stereotypes that associate Blackness, femaleness, and lower classes with foul odors, moral contamination, and 'animalness.'"[2] Furthermore, smell functions as a source of racial, gendered, and sexual agency; through her ability to control smells, the story questions the social constructs of race, class, sexuality, and gender in Puerto Rico. In order to contest and rewrite the negative stereotypes surrounding Black women and provide a model of an exceptional, independent, active, liberated Puerto Rican woman of color satisfied with life, Santos Febres purposefully appropriates senses, language, and spaces. Subverting stereotypes and highlighting the malleability of race, class, and gender categorizations directly contests structures of dominance and power and the rigidity of social categorizations.

The smells released move from passively emitted to actively manipulated and produced and the transformations in Marina's ability to exude and produce smells corresponds to her advancing age, growing self-awareness, and path toward independence. From age eight to thirteen, Marina issues "spicy, salty and sweet aromas" and people come from miles around to inhale the "smell of the day." After moving to the Velázquezes' house at age thirteen to work as a domestic, she discovers her "prodigious ability to harbor smells" and that she smells of the ocean, fulfilling the meaning of her name.[3] One day she is surprised to note her body smelling of the menu she is planning—"her elbows [smell] of the fresh cilantro and sweet pepper base [to dishes], her underarms of garlic, onion, and red chili peppers, her forearms of grilled sweet potato with butter, in between her budding breasts [it smells] of marinated sirloin covered in onions, and further down of white, fluffy rice, exactly how she makes it."[4] From that day on she prompts her body to emit remembered smells, marjoram and mint being her favorites. Once she is confident in her ability to produce concrete smells, she then experiments with abstract, emotional smells such as sadness and loneliness.

When she is almost fifteen she notices men for the first time and falls madly in love with the scent of Eladio Salamán; she gifts him her smell of "scared bromelias and burning saliva."[5] At fifteen Marina becomes more and more indignant at the verbal insults and lack of freedom imposed upon her in the Velázquez household. When she no longer tolerates the unsolicited sexual advances and blackmail from the Velázquezes' son, Hipólito, she becomes so angry she loses control of her ability to produce smells at will: "From each and every pore in her body came a rusty smell mixed with the stink of burnt oil and acid turbine cleaner."[6] Unwilling to tolerate Hipólito's constant harassment, she quits her job and returns home to revive her family's dying restaurant. Though we don't know what happens to Marina after the age of fifteen, at forty-nine she "more often than not smelled of pure satisfaction."[7] The pattern of passively emitting delightful odors when she is young, to consciously evoking difficult, mature, comingled smells of emotions when she comes of age parallels

Marina's burgeoning awareness of the fact that she doesn't need to accept ill treatment.

Marina's smells closely portray her own state of emotion and reaction to life events, constantly propelling her toward a greater sense of self-discovery, self-fulfillment, and liberation. When she is most satisfied with life and her experiences, such as when she is running the family restaurant, she entrances others with her pleasing scents and imbues them with happiness. In contrast, negative life experiences produce emotionally draining, sickening, and metallic scents or disrupt her olfactory abilities entirely. When she is away from her family and loved ones, she experiments with and recreates the smells of melancholy and desolation. She envisions, repugnantly, being with Hipólito after one of his advances; accordingly her body smells of rotten fish to such a foul degree that she makes herself nauseous. When she cannot be with her lover, Eladio, she works hard to reproduce his smell but she becomes so distracted and forgetful in the process that she mixes up the smells and flavors of the dishes she is cooking. For instance, she makes everyone vomit when she serves a potato and meat lasagna smelling of oats and sweet mold, the smell of Hipólito's underwear. Moreover, when she is barred from seeing Eladio, she cannot remember smells at all and serves bland food that tastes like "empty closets."[8] On the brink of desperation, she decides to "send" for Eladio by letting her personal scent be carried by the wind, and when Hipólito harasses her yet again she deliberately and meticulously fumigates the Velázquezes' house with the smell of "desperate melancholy," "memories of dead dreams," and "disjointed, disconnected aromas."[9] When she is once again satisfied with life as the center of the family restaurant, her body "exhales" organic scents such as oregano and lemons and she smells of "pure satisfaction."[10] The maturation and sophistication of the smells she produces parallel her own emotional growth, consciousness, and path toward liberation.

Marina's ability to generate smells relies on her ability to recall memories, which is in turn intimately connected to her personal liberty. Social scientists have confirmed that people effectively remember smells, which provoke powerful memories, which then provoke equally strong emotional responses.[11] As Sigmund Freud put it, "Memory stinks just as an actual object may stink."[12] Marina remembers smells and uses them to reproduce others of her own creative volition. For instance, to create the scent of sadness—"morning mangrove and the heat of sheets somewhere between rancid and almost sweet"—she thinks of the day her mother dropped her off at the Velázquez house and of her father sitting in his chair imagining what could have become of his life if he had become a famous clarinetist.[13] Yet the process of producing such sentimental smells is so physically taxing that she decides to "collect" smells from others, including her bosses, neighbors, and fellow servants. When she reaches her limit and infuses the house with hopeless melancholy, the text states she "picked" up the smell from her alcoholic father's body. Metaphorically, Marina's sensorial ability, just like her liberation, relies on others' experiences and how she experiences them in turn as she transforms them into her own. Others may be the source of her inspiration, but only she dictates and decides her path toward olfactory production and freedom.

Marina's ability to remember and craft smells is intimately connected to having the metaphoric space and freedom to create. Thinking about someone or a particular object fosters her ability to produce and emit aromas from her body, while a lack of freedom erases her "olfactory memory" altogether. For instance, when she is placed on house arrest and barred from seeing Eladio, Marina cannot evoke or control her sensorial abilities. When she is most physically, emotionally, and psychologically oppressed by others, her creative and productive capacities are devastated. Thus, the entwined trio of memory, olfactory skill, and freedom demonstrate the crippling effects of oppression and subjugation. Nevertheless, the injustice of domination spurs Marina into action and toward an ultimately liberating space, the family restaurant El Pinchimoja.

Douglas Porteous coined the term "smellscape" to describe particular smells as a function of a particular person, place, time, or memory, and Santos Febres constructs her own uniquely Puerto Rican smellscape.[14] Smells are not usually a central component of identity formation, yet Santos Febres challenges this by creating a particularly positive, emotive smellscape through Marina. "Marina y su olor" displays an array of aromas specific to Puerto Rican cuisine, specifically primary ingredients such as the aforementioned garlic, onions, chili peppers, sweet potatoes, rice, mint, marjoram, etcetera. In addition, the descriptions of emotion-smells are intimately tied to the island. Most of Marina's scents related to emotions (other than sheer anger, which produces a metallic, grimy, rusty, caustic odor) involve organic matter—mangroves in the morning, the earth in a rainforest, frightened bromelia plants, mint covered in dew—all native to Puerto Rico. The story connects smells that are defined as pleasant and good in a wider Western sociocultural context to everything that is Puerto Rican. Moreover, the fact that the Puerto Rican smellscape comes from Marina's body, a young, Black, oppressed-then-liberated, independent Puerto Rican woman, could, metaphorically, represent a positive Puerto Rican identity based in the racialized feminine and the sensorial. The affirmative identity hinges on appropriation and subversion of negative stereotypes—Black women as too emotional, too sensitive, too base, too natural, too sexual—all of which are converted into positive, affirming, powerful characteristics in the hands of Santos Febres using smells rooted in Puerto Rican flora and fauna.[15]

For Marina, smell serves as a source of self-protection and vindication, as well as a means to gain independence. Marina's body smells of rotten fish when she imagines Hipólito touching her, which functions as a means to gird herself to reject his sexual advances and, one imagines, to repel Hipólito himself. Refusing Hipólito is an important act of defiance, considering the historical legacy of *derecho de pernada* or "right of the first night."[16] In a clear act of rebellion and vengeance, Marina fumigates the Velázquez house so that no one will ever set foot in the place. Her ability to produce smells is the source of her future independence. Economically she has a secure future by reviving El Pinchimoja, not just with her fabulous cooking but with her alluring aromas that draw in clients and keep the restaurant bustling with business. No longer will she need to be a servant, subjugated to other people's whims and control; she will serve herself as an owner-operator. Economic independence means she no longer is subjugated to the will of a wealthy mistress or a predatory man, but now decides and rules her own future, body, and personhood.

The smell of "pure satisfaction" that Marina exudes at forty-nine can also be read as sexual satisfaction, a part of her corporeal identity. With her smells she leaves men stupefied, "searching for a way to lick her to see if her body tasted like they smelled"—a phenomenon she didn't fully understand at thirteen but that she is now fully conscious of.[17] Her first love and sexual awakening parallels her growing ability to produce sophisticated odors. When she comes back from seeing Eladio she makes a dinner that was "the tastiest [meal] ever eaten in the Velázquez dining room and in the town's history because it smelled of love and Eladio Salamán's sweet body," implying that her intimacy led to the most delicious cooking ever.[18] In a clear pattern, Santos Febres takes the aspects of Black womanhood that are most denigrated, such as their sexuality and their body, and converts them into an affirming, essential part of the process toward emancipation and a celebrated contribution to her community. As Dorothy Mosby states, "Marina presents a redemptive quality that subverts the notion of the sexually dangerous, pathological, and predatory Afro-descent woman."[19] Her power stems from the knowledge of her ability, her practiced control of it, and the use of her olfactory skills for reasons she deems necessary and worthy. In the end, Marina is happy with who she is and her life as an economically, sensually, and corporeally independent Black woman who is valued and appreciated by others based on her actions and deeds, not her status.

Additionally, Santos Febres appropriates and subverts traditional, patriarchal language as a means to display other, equally valid modes of communication, refute the stereotype of inarticulacy, demonstrate iniquity and prejudice within verbal interactions, as well as voice Marina's resistance and liberation. For example, Marina uses her ability to produce and emit smells as a means of eloquent expression and communication. She seeks out Eladio and finds him by following his scent all around town. When Marina is with Eladio she tells him to memorize the scent she is giving him, her personal scent of frightened bromelia plants and passionate, burning saliva, and he "drinks" it so that it becomes glued to his skin like a tattoo. On the brink of despair at being sequestered, constantly monitored, and insulted by the Velazquezes, Marina "perfumes the town" so that Eladio will come to her. He recognizes her "scent message" and immediately seeks her out. Thus, smell in Santos Febres's story functions as an active, effective, and expressive mode of communication, particularly between lovers, that does not rely on codified, verbal language.[20]

Just as Marina's skill develops into true artistry, so does Santos Febres's in creating a unique language unto itself to describe the aromas Marina formulates, thus creating a sensibility and vocalization of what is usually considered inarticulate. The sense of smell has often been scorned and undervalued because of humans' inability to analytically describe what an odor smells like, yet Santos Febres responds to these challenges by using explicit vocabulary not usually associated with smell.[21] For instance, "earth from the rain forest, mint covered in dew, brand new basin, saltpeter in the morning" describe Eladio's smell—condition, matter, and time mixed together.[22] The aged and graceful Doña Marina París smells of enchanting oregano, the male species of mahogany, and little lemons used to scorch swallows—in this example affect, sex, and function are comingled.[23] The smells of emotions constitute other descriptions not usually associated with smell: sadness smells like mangroves in the morning and the heat of a sheet, something in between sour and a bit sweet.[24]

The synesthesia, or blurring of two or more senses via language, adds a distinctiveness and expressiveness to the narration and to the protagonist's makeup that is eloquent and subversive. Doubly layered is the fact that the author is Black, paralleling Santos Febres and Marina's refutations of inarticulateness.

The few spoken phrases in the entire short story expose the inflammatory rhetoric connected to inequitable power structures, while also giving voice to the emerging liberation so central to Marina's being. There are only five spoken lines: in chronological order, two are Doña Georgina Velázquez's insults ("Bad, indecent, stinky, stinky black woman!"), one where Marina tells Eladio to remember her scent ("This is my scent. Affix it to your memory"), one when Hipólito blackmails her ("That way you can keep your job and avoid mom's insults"), and the last, as Marina leaves the Velázquez house never to return ("So that they can say that blacks stink!").[25] The phrases by Doña Georgina and Hipólito demonstrate dominance, power, racism, and classism, with the clear intent to keep Marina in an inferior position. They also show the problematic relationships between women of differing socioeconomic classes and races, specifically how shallow, caustic verbal abuse is deployed to maintain such hierarchies. Marina's final phrase uses a false stereotype as her weapon and tool for liberation. Contrastingly, the phrase she tells Eladio is of love and bequest. While in a traditional narrative women are objects of desire and pleasure for men, which supports unequal power dynamics, Marina's giving of her scent demonstrates her position as agent or subject. In sum, Santos Febres uses language, just like the sense of smell, to contest the stereotypes that debase Black women. She inverts negative stereotypes into reappropriated and positive sources of power, identity, and liberation.

Critics such as María Claudia André and Renée Scott affirm that the kitchen, in works by Latin American women authors, is a site for resistance and appropriation.[26] While Marina is in a disadvantaged position as a Black servant in a white household, the kitchen acts as a core site for the discovery and practice of her culinary and olfactory talents. The kitchen is not a place for her disadvantage, but rather one of self-empowerment and, when she is back at the family restaurant, economic independence. Also, Marina converts the kitchen from a space of hiding, where Black grandmothers were relegated to hide a family's ancestry, into a source of self-definition and confrontation.[27] Just as Marina appropriates the stereotype of a "stinky black woman," so, too, does she appropriate the kitchen as a site of resistance, discovery, empowerment, and liberation.

Due to Marina's various appropriations, smell is a subversive force, a means to contest stereotypes. Not only does Santos Febres appropriate and invert the senses, language, and spaces of the dominant white patriarchal culture, but she also appropriates the process of othering. W. E. B. Du Bois argued that one way to effectively counter racism is to rewrite negative stereotypes, and Santos Febres does this through Marina.[28] Furthermore, Santos Febres methodically undermines racist, classist, and sexist categorizations via Marina's talents and actions. Marina is not a lesser "other" by how those in power define and limit her, but rather a confident "other" based on how she stakes out her individual, unique, valued sense of self. In addition, Santos Febres questions imposed, strict categorizations, thus subverting the assumed stability of race, class, and gender categories. Ultimately, the author demonstrates the constructed, fabricated nature of stratifications that reinforce inequitable power structures.

The senses have often been used as a distinguishing marker to highlight difference, and the concomitant inferiority imposed by the difference. For instance, historically marginalized groups considered "other" were (and often still are) described as malodorous by the dominant group. Jim Drobnick, editor of *Smell Culture Reader* (2006), states:

> Avoidance behaviors, prejudicial comments and stereotypical characterizations are rationalized by the supposed presence of a repugnant odor, which, in the end, turns out to be projected upon the other rather than actually perceived. Malodors thus function rhetorically and arbitrarily, for they can be attributed to any designated population segment, and in fact operate as a technique for in-group identification.[29]

Specifically connected to race, Mark Smith documents how a rhetoric surrounding the senses was used to impose and maintain strict boundaries between racial categories of white and Black.[30] Since increased miscegenation makes it difficult to visually categorize a person's race, the other senses were used to justify forcing people into such categories. In particular, Blacks' supposed stink was thought to be a tell, even if the person looked white: "Blackness was not just seen—it could be smelled, heard, and felt."[31] At times of mixing across social classes, or when strict hierarchies could not be maintained purely on visual distinctions, the senses (particularly smell) became an essential tool to uncover and highlight the "other" and their inferiority.[32]

Some of the most impactful scenes and interactions highlighting the process of othering are between Marina and Doña Georgina Velázquez. Hipólito sees Marina and Eladio in town holding hands and tells his mother, with obvious embellishments, to which Doña Georgina responds by insulting Marina with "bad, indecent stinky, stinky black woman!" Though Doña Georgina does not to fire her, she reduces Marina's salary and doesn't allow Marina to go anywhere unaccompanied, even to the market, which along with the insults is another means to further shame her. Doña Georgina pummels Marina with insults of "smug, from the dregs, stinky [woman]!" when her cooking is tasteless and insipid as a result of her confinement.[33] Doña Georgina exhibits the exact behaviors Drobnick describes—she makes prejudicial comments and stereotypical characterizations regarding Marina's smell and her supposed sexual laxity. Though she smells so pleasing to others, to Doña Georgina she reeks because Marina is under her "domain" as a Black female servant. Doña Georgina uses language and financial and physical confinement to denigrate Marina. Yet just as she does with the senses, language, and space, Santos Febres inverts the negative process of othering to create a positive identity for Marina.

Marina uses her body's ability to create smells as a protective mechanism from further abuse, as a weapon and as a means to affirm her emancipation, thus reversing the othering process. Though in no instance does she speak directly to Doña Georgina or Hipólito in the story, Marina's final phrase "speaks" to or responds to Doña Georgina's verbal abuse. The thing supposedly repugnant in Marina, smell, becomes precisely what others will find repugnant about the Velázquez house. In effect, Marina inverts Doña Georgina's disparagement. As Alan West-Durán comments, "If previously Georgina had made Marina into the 'other' (racially, socially, sexually), it is now Georgina who will be the 'other' (shunned by her community)."[34] In another inversion, those who construct, vocalize, and implement such malevolent prejudice end up destroyed.[35] In true poetic justice fashion, the one being oppressed, Marina, finds her path toward freedom while those oppressing, Doña Georgina and Hipólito, end their days isolated and socially demoted. Additionally, the "disjointed, disconnected aromas" that she produces when she is prohibited from seeing Eladio are the same smells that signal her departure and liberation from oppression. The only difference is who is in control; on house arrest Marina is not in control of her body, abilities, or life, whereas at the end it is she who controls her being, skills, and future. Marina takes what she is blamed for by her oppressors, her scent, and converts it into the precise tool necessary to her liberation. Marina doesn't simply reverse the power structures and become the one to dominate her former tyrants, but rather uses smell as a mechanism to reclaim her right to be valued as an individual and self-regulate her own body.

Just as the status of the "other" is socially constructed so too is that of class, thus making its value malleable. Santos Febres subversively reverses the assumed good/upper-class/white social value by pointing out the discrepancy between social status and deeds. The Velázquezes are supposed to be the "better" family due to their upper-class wealth, their valued whiteness, and their high social standing. Yet Doña Georgina and Hipólito are characterized by their racist, egotistical, predatory, and haughty actions. Hipólito, in particular, sexually harasses Marina, embellishes the truth to get Marina into trouble and possibly lose her job after she rejects his sexual advances, and attempts to blackmail her. Doña Georgina also abuses her position and repeatedly insults and controls Marina's movements even though she is supposedly a beata, or exemplary Christian woman. Their high social standing doesn't make for respectful or honorable actions, but rather the contrary. Furthermore, the smell of mold when Marina describes Hipólito can function as a metaphor for his decomposing, "rotten" self—Hipólito doesn't just smell rotten, he is morally rotten and behaves repulsively.[36] In a total inversion, Marina, of supposed low status because of her race, class, and gender acts in redeeming ways. Unlike Doña Georgina, who inherited her title based on class privilege and whose actions prove such a title undeserved, Marina as the forty-nine-year-old owner and matriarch of the restaurant El Pinchimoja is conferred the title of Doña Marina París by her restaurant patrons precisely for her integrity. Thus, the imposed, lesser categorizations of Black/lower-class/bad, as well as the fervently protected, greater categorizations of good/upper-class/white, are far from the reality when one takes into account personal character and actions. As a result, the fixed category of class becomes less stable and more open to questioning, and with it, the social construction that is race.

As a former slave-holding and slave-dependent colony, Puerto Rico's legacy of strict racial hierarchies is still evident today, yet Santos Febres undermines the rigidity and inevitability of such hierarchies.[37] In addition, she points out the persistence of structures of oppression based on race. For instance, Doña Georgina, because she is white and upper-class, feels at liberty to control Marina's actions and sexuality as well as verbally assault her and dock her pay. Hipólito, the son, treats his socioeconomic status as an excuse to sexually harass and blackmail Marina. These characters never reflect on their abuses of power, but rather act as if it were their prerogative and right to command others' bodies and actions, which is a legacy of colonialism in Puerto Rico. Puerto Ricans often deny that racial hierarchies exist and prefer to say "we are all Puerto Ricans" in an attempt to downplay racial hierarchies and maintain a view of their society as non-racist.[38] Nevertheless, in Puerto Rico, "the significant fact is that there is a social, aesthetic, and even moral value hierarchy corresponding to skin colour (and other phenotypical features such as hair texture, shape of the nose, shape and size of the lips), regardless of the fact that some—relatively few—individuals of dark skin, wooly hair, flat noses and full lips may have achieved middle-level social status."[39] Furthermore, historians have documented the progressive "whitening" of Puerto Rico over the years; so much so that in the 2000 census 80 percent of the population considered itself white.[40] Despite the multiple, lasting legacies of slavery, many in Puerto Rico deny the devaluation of Black culture and the structures that perpetuate such evisceration. Santos Febres highlights the continued othering and denigration that occurs based on race, as well as what happens when one person refuses to accept those confines.

Santos Febres contests the construction of race and the myth of "we are all Puerto Ricans" with its accompanying implication that race doesn't matter there. In particular, what makes Marina "Black" are her antecedents and social interactions with others, which point out the social construction of race and the falsity of clearly defined, visually based racial categories. For instance, Marina's great-grandmother was a white Spanish shopkeeper who married a Black man when she came to the island, which makes Marina's heritage mixed blood. Yet the fact of Marina being sent to work at Doña Georgina's house as a servant, and the way she is treated as inferior and insulted with racial slurs, categorizes her as Black. The story points out that while miscegenation is the historical norm in Puerto Rico, colonial-era relationships of tyranny still prevail. Santos Febres mocks the obsession with the "pure" white Spanish bloodline through Doña Georgina's famed passion for a typically Black dish, shrimp with cassava. The author shows that contrary to public opinion, race in Puerto Rico does indeed still matter since racial hierarchies and values are a social construct based on relationships of domination that preserve the status quo and malign anyone who is not white and upper class.

Part of Santos Febres's attempt to destabilize fixed categories of race manifests in the fact that Marina's phenotypical characteristics are rarely mentioned. Only once does she refer to kinky curls (and these are hidden in braids or under handkerchiefs) and just twice mentions high cheekbones and darkness, supposedly Black characteristics. Otherwise Marina is described primarily with regard to her remarkable ability to produce smells. As Arleen Chiclana y González states, Santos Febres "condemns the incongruous Western paradigms of subjectivity that are relentlessly fixated on the visual."[41] Since, for Marina, racial categorization is an imposed condition, it is not until she removes herself from relationships of racial domination (with Doña Georgina and Hipólito) that she is freed. Also, since Marina is described by her abilities and journey toward liberation rather than her phenotypical traits, the racial categories based on physical appearance are undermined. Her value is based on individual agency rather than solely external social forces or categorizations.

Santos Febres points out that just because everyone is of mixed heritage doesn't mean that racism is any less of a problem, and that just as race is a social construction, so too is racism. Doña Georgina is obviously racist given the insults she pummels Marina with, but racism isn't just a white-versus-Black problem. Marina's mother, Edovina, insists that the young Marina watch over the restaurant cook, María, to make sure she doesn't use coconut oil because such usage would make them look like "a group of surly, unpolished, rough blacks."[42] Edovina also thinks that Blacks lack culinary sophistication, and that Marina is in danger because of Black men's excess sexuality, which can lead to taboo sexual practices such as incest.[43] Thus, racial categorizations based on supposed inferiority are culturally constructed in society, rather than an innate characteristic. Santos Febres highlights the need to recognize the Black *and* white (not Black *or* white) heritage, as well as shine a light on the entrenched prejudice that favors white upper classes.

Class markers are readily present throughout the text, although, again, the story inverts the positive value associated with high socioeconomic status to destabilize fixed notions of class. Edovina is specifically described as the granddaughter of a Spanish shopkeeper, thus implying social status based on origin and class, yet the shopkeeper in question was a failed one. Doña Georgina is described as a "white, supposedly model Christian, rich woman," yet she acts horrifically toward others. Every night Hipólito goes to town looking for mulattas and very dark-skinned women with whom to have sex, whether they be prostitutes or women he takes advantage of via his social position, but he certainly never contemplates marrying any of them. Moreover, Hipólito is enraged by Marina's refusal of him in favor of what he calls "the Black sugarcane worker," Eladio (in contrast, Marina refers to Eladio's skin as the reddish color of mahogany, his body tight and fibrous like the heart of a sugarcane).[44] The implication is that Hipólito sees himself as superior in all ways to Eladio, and definitely to Marina, and thus uses his position to fabricate a story about Marina's sexual laxity that will get her into trouble and enable him to control her. Within the context of this story, such actions are considered predatory and base, the precise stereotypes inflicted on the lower classes. Power and wealth, and the insistence on maintaining a high level of both, are at the crux of why others are maligned.

Santos Febres's comingled discussion of postcolonialism, race, class, and gender highlights the unnatural construction of oppression and of the strict categories that ingrain and perpetuate such oppression. In an interview, she states, "Sexual oppression is always linked to race, to class, to ethnicity, to sexual preference, to migratory status, to so many things. To pinpoint gender as such a central element would be an error. My understanding of womanhood is organically intertwined with my experiences of other oppressions, of colonialism."[45] The multilayered and blurred categories related to race, class, and gender in "Marina y su olor" provide the mechanism to contest these fixed notions. The malleability and variation within such categories destabilize the perceived notions of the "other." Therefore, through Marina's path of discovery and liberation, Santos Febres provides a model of Du Bois's "rewriting stereotypes."

Marina's extraordinary abilities, in addition to her liberation, blur and defy discrete, facile categorizations. Though Marina's body is never described, the smells that she controls and emits come from her body, making it the site for her identity construction, but not in any traditional genderic sense. She is neither defined nor limited by phallocentric concepts of the female body, beauty, or attractiveness, but rather empowered by her prodigious ability to produce smells. Her physicality and body, while positively excessive and fantastic for its abilities, are at the same time unimportant in visual terms. If Luisa Valenzuela and Hélène Cixous speak of "writing with the body" as liberating and as a means of resistance, it stands to reason that writing with the body's other senses, such as smell, would be equally subversive.[46] Also, as Carmen Rivera Villegas contends, the Black female slave body was the site of confrontation between the dominant culture and the subaltern.[47] Marina's Black female body is also the site for confrontation precisely because, as Santos Febres states, "The body is the site of perception, the filter, and the page on which life writes itself. The body reflects the way in which history touches a person."[48] Thus, Marina "writes" with her aromas and odors in order to stake out physical, linguistic, sensorial, and personal space for herself.

Through Marina's body-centered ability to emit aromas, Santos Febres "gives voice to her colonial identity and to her body while simultaneously disrupting the social constraints that gender roles oblige."[49] Strict categories of race, class, gender, and the consequent stereotypes created based on those categories, erase both individuality and individuals. Marina's ability to "write/produce smells with her body" allows her to reclaim her individuality, uniqueness, independence, and sense of self while also subverting the stereotypes that attempt to confine her within a strict parameter of acceptable behaviors. Santos Febres affirms, "I believe the way to go is to stress difference as one erases it through writing," and her character does precisely that.[50] Elba Birmingham-Pokorny elaborates, "Santos Febres calls for the recognition and retrieval of the Black body from erasure in order to write and inscribe a multi-layered identity in the still undefined space of the Puerto Rican social landscape. . . . These identities exceed all categories and defy the prevailing belief in a fixed, essentialist female identity and a homogenous national culture in Puerto Rico."[51] Through her unique ability Marina finds a source upon which to build her identity based on difference, while at the same time she erases the differences, and supposed inferiority, imposed on her by others.

While in the majority of cases Santos Febres challenges notions of racial and gender stereotypes, some still prevail. For instance, Marina's mother has a baby every year, her father is a hopeless drunkard, and Marina's ability to send "scent messages" could be considered animalistic. Moreover, the connection between women, the kitchen, and food is a historically fraught one, and the story's framing of domesticity as a source of agency has a problematic aspect that is never addressed. Almost in an idealized notion of woman, Marina, like Mother Earth, feeds people via foods and smells, and more importantly, the emotions the two evoke. Santos Febres doesn't challenge the association between women and food that translates into comfort and contentment for others. Marina never ventures beyond the realm of what is considered acceptable for a woman in the sense that she remains a cook (not a chef) and a nourisher who serves others. Marina escapes someone else imposing those confines and roles on her, yet her "freedom" still operates squarely within the prescribed realm of the feminine.

Santos Febres likewise never challenges the larger Western concepts of good and bad smells. Rachel Herz and other social scientists have documented the cultural specificity of reactions to smells. While animals are born with an instinctual awareness of scent that includes a biologically programmed flight response to the smell of predators, humans are not genetically predisposed to react to smells. Only at around three or four years old do they learn which ones are culturally acceptable versus unacceptable (and to perform the appropriate reactions).[52] In fact, scientists assert that there is no one universally offensive smell.[53] In "Marina y su olor," positive emotions evoke positive smells, while negative emotions provoke negative smells. Anger produces a metallic, grimy, rusty, caustic odor while happiness and satisfaction are connected to foods considered delectable by cultural consensus—such as lemons, oregano, mint, and fluffy rice. In particular, good smells are connected to organic matter indigenous to Puerto Rico, so the "in group" of Puerto Rican smells is unquestionably positive and valued. Thus, while blurring the lines of race, class, gender, and other socially constructed categories, the author never questions the standard notions of good versus bad smells, nor the profound connection of femininity to domesticity. Noting such problems in the text highlights the complicated and comingled notions of power, race, class, gender, sexuality, and the senses.

To conclude, during different time periods and in different countries, hierarchies of the senses have served to delineate, legitimize, and justify divisive social stratification and hierarchies. Mayra Santos Febres's short story "Marina y su olor" demonstrates an outright refusal to accept such a stratification and othering. The protagonist, Marina, uses smell as a means to affirm her identity, release herself from oppression, and secure her economic independence, social position, and community standing. Marina sees through the supposed superiority of the Velázquez household and finds integrity in how one acts, not in one's socioeconomic class, status, or racial background. She uses the very stereotypes that limit her to emancipate herself from the Velázquezes' control and all that they represent. Since odor has no boundaries, the use of smell as Marina's identifying marker is essential to challenging constructed and imposed race, class, and gender limitations.[54] Marina blurs categorical boundaries with her remarkable ability to produce aromas and emotive fragrances from her body and defies any attempt to place her into a clearly delineated category or stereotype that can erase individual identity. Therefore, while oppression based on race, class, and gender difference is very real indeed, Santos Febres, via Marina's gift, questions the durability and fixedness of such categories used to limit others. Ultimately, race, class, and gender structures that maintain social inequity are culturally constructed and restrict people's behavior and opportunities, yet are malleable and can be blurred and contested. Santos Febres proposes that a change in the power structures is, indeed, accessible and possible via open resistance to oppression and a strong, independent construction of one's identity based on one's talents, as seen through Marina.

Notes

1. Alain Corbin, *The Foul and the Fragrant* (Cambridge, MA: Harvard University Press), 142–51; Constance Classen, "The Witch's Senses: Sensory Ideologies and Transgressive Femininities from the Renaissance to Modernity," in *Empire of the Senses*, ed. David Howes (New York: Berg, 2005), 72.
2. Dorothy Mosby, "'The Erotic as Power': Sexual Agency and the Erotic in the Work of Luz Argentina Chiriboga and Mayra Santos Febres," *Cincinnati Romance Review* 30 (2011): 95–96.
3. Marina means "olor a mar" (smell of the sea) or "mujer del mar" (woman of the sea) as noted in Carmen Pérez, "'Marina y su olor' y 'Hebra rota': Lo maravilloso y lo mítico," *Exégesis* 15, no. 43 (2002): 64.
4. Mayra Santos Febres, "Marina y su olor," in *Pez de vidrio* (Río Piedras, Puerto Rico: Huracán, 1996), 46. Translations of the story's text are all mine.
5. Santos Febres, "Marina y su olor," 49.
6. Santos Febres, "Marina y su olor," 50.
7. Santos Febres, "Marina y su olor," 43.
8. Santos Febres, "Marina y su olor," 49.
9. Santos Febres, "Marina y su olor," 50.
10. Santos Febres, "Marina y su olor," 43.
11. Lyall Watson, *Jacobson's Organ and the Remarkable Nature of Smell* (New York: Plume, 2001), 180.
12. Quoted in Carol Mavor, "Odor di Femina: Though You May Not See Her, You Can Certainly Smell Her," in *The Smell Culture Reader*, ed. Jim Drobnick (New York: Berg, 2006), 282.
13. Santos Febres, "Marina y su olor," 46.
14. Douglas J. Porteous, "Smellscape," in *The Smell Culture Reader*, 89.
15. Mavor, "Odor di Femina," 282; Constance Classen, *Aroma* (London: Routledge, 1994), 70; Mark Smith, *How Race Is Made: Slavery, Segregation, and the Senses* (Chapel Hill: University of North Carolina Press, 2006), 9.
16. Mosby, "'The Erotic as Power,'" 94. The "noche de pernada" or "derecho de primera noche" was a medieval European practice in which the feudal lords, on wedding nights, had sex with serf women. These women gave their virginity, literally and figuratively, to the feudal lord instead of their newly wedded husbands.
17. Santos Febres, "Marina y su olor," 43.
18. Santos Febres, "Marina y su olor," 48.

19. Mosby, "'The Erotic as Power,'" 96.

20. María Inés Ortiz has noted this similarity with regard to food for Tita in Laura Esquivel's *Como agua para chocolate* [Like water for chocolate, 1989]. María Inés Ortiz, "La gastronomía como metáfora de la identidad en la literatura puertorriqueña del siglo XX" (PhD diss., University of Cincinnati, 2007), 162.

21. Watson, *Jacobson's Organ*, 81–82.

22. Santos Febres, "Marina y su olor," 47.

23. Santos Febres, "Marina y su olor," 43.

24. Santos Febres, "Marina y su olor," 46.

25. Santos Febres, "Marina y su olor," 48–50.

26. María Claudia André, *Chicanas and Latin American Women Writers Exploring the Realm of the Kitchen as a Self-Empowering Site* (Lewiston, NY: Edwin Mellon Press, 2001); Renée Scott, *What Is Eating Latin American Women Writers? Food, Weight, and Eating Disorders* (Amherst, NY: Cambria Press, 2009).

27. Carmen Rivera Villegas, "La celebración de la identidad negra en 'Marina y su olor' de Mayra Santos Febres," *Espéculo* 27 (2004), accessible at http://www.ucm.es/info/especulo/numero27/marina.html.

28. Quoted in Smith, *How Race Is Made*, 9.

29. Jim Drobnick, preface in *The Smell Culture Reader*, 15.

30. Smith, *How Race Is Made*, 9.

31. Smith, *How Race Is Made*, 47.

32. Corbin, *The Foul and the Fragrant*, 129.

33. Santos Febres, "Marina y su olor," 49.

34. Alan West-Durán, "Puerto Rico: The Pleasures and Traumas of Race," *Centro Journal* 17, no. 1 (2005): 66.

35. Rivera Villegas, "La celebración," n.p.

36. Ortiz, "La gastronomía como metáfora," 167.

37. West-Durán, "Puerto Rico," 60.

38. Mervyn Alleyne, *The Construction and Representation of Race and Ethnicity in the Caribbean and the World* (Kingston, Jamaica: University of West Indies Press, 2002), 135.

39. Alleyne, *The Construction and Representation*, 136.

40. West-Durán, "Puerto Rico," 60; Ortiz, "La gastronomía como metáfora," 165; *Puerto Rico 2000: Resumen de características de la población y vivienda* (Washington, DC: US Census Bureau, 2002), 52.

41. Arleen Chiclana y González, "The Body of Evidence: Body-Writing, the Text and Mayra Santos Febres' Illicit Bodies," in *Unveiling the Body in Hispanic Women's Literature*, ed. Renée Scott and Arleen Chiclana y González (Lewiston, UK: Edwin Mellen Press, 2006), 64.

42. Santos Febres, "Marina y su olor," 44.

43. Rivera Villegas, "La celebración," n.p.

44. Santos Febres, "Marina y su olor," 48.

45. Elba Birmingham-Pokorny, "'The Page on Which Life Writes Itself': A Conversation with Mayra Santos Febres," in *Daughters of the Diaspora: Afra-Hispanic Writers*, ed. Miriam DeCosta-Willis (Kingston, Jamaica: Ian Randle, 2003), 458.

46. Dianna Niebylski, *Humoring Resistance: Laughter and the Excessive Body in*

Latin American Women's Fiction (Albany: State University of New York Press, 2004), 7.

47. Rivera Villegas, "La celebración," n.p.
48. Birmingham-Pokorny, "'The Page on Which Life Writes Itself,'" 457.
49. Chiclana y González, "The Body of Evidence," 164.
50. Birmingham-Pokorny, "'The Page on Which Life Writes Itself,'" 455.
51. Elba Birmingham-Pokorny, "Reclaiming the Female Body, Culture, and Identity in Mayra Santos Febres' 'Broken Strand,'" in *Daughters of the Diaspora: Afra-Hispanic Writers*, 468.
52. Rachel Herz, "I Know What I Like: Understanding Odor Preferences," in *The Smell Culture Reader*, 195.
53. Herz, "I Know What I Like," 197.
54. Here I reference Watson, *Jacobson's Organ*, 168.

CHAPTER 10

Exquisite Paradise

Taste and Consumption in Hebe Uhart's "El budín esponjoso"

KARINA ELIZABETH VÁZQUEZ

Hebe Uhart was born into a middle-class family in Buenos Aires, Argentina, in 1936 and died in October 2018. She studied philosophy and became a prolific writer, served as a rural teacher, and taught literature at high schools and universities. Uhart maintained a very low profile despite great admiration from her peers and being an ardent participant in writers' conferences, workshops, and presentations. After a long career in narrative and short fiction, it was only with the 2010 publication of *Relatos reunidos*, for which she received the Fundación El Libro Award for the Best Argentine Book of Literary Creation, that she gained widespread recognition. She became particularly renown for short fiction by the time of her death and has left behind a large body of work—primarily short stories as well as some chronicles and novellas, all with small publishing houses. Her famous short story collection, *El budín esponjoso* (1977), was followed by others, including *La luz de un nuevo día* (1983), *Memorias de un pigmeo* (1992), *Guiando la hiedra* (1997), *Del cielo a casa* (2003), *Turistas* (2008), and *Un día cualquiera (mapa de las lenguas)* (2015). Her novels include *Leonor* (1986), *Camilo asciende* (1987), *Mudanzas* (1995), and *Señorita* (1995). An animal lover and avid traveler, she published the travel chronicles *Viajera crónica* (2011), *Visto y oído* (2012), *De la Patagonia a México* (2015), *De aquí para allá* (2017), and *Animales* (2018).

One of the most distinct characteristics of Uhart's fictional universe are the everyday situations, spaces, objects, and characters, conspicuous in their simplicity and plain language, that become radiators of hidden truths. Her short stories lead readers not to contemplate the existence of other realities, but to realize the inherent complexity locked within the small and the simple. As Graciela Speranza has pointed out, Uhart's stories offer "simple and enigmatic truths that are hidden in the universe of the everyday . . . [which] reveal a more abstract and essential order."[1] The house, the classroom, the neighborhood, the spaces of the everyday are the loci for philosophical reflections. The small stories of domestic life reveal a full spectrum of nuances that make visible the singularity and importance of every simple gesture. The orality of her narrators and characters transposes the social dynamic that organizes and rules an individual's experience. Through phrases uttered instinctively and "just like that," the author exposes the minutiae, the "micro physics" of the ordinary world.[2] Her stories do not illuminate what the characters think, but rather expose what they do by inviting the reader to explore the singularity of the real. In this sense, Uhart creates fictions that propose a "philosophy of the domestic."[3] Family conflicts, feminine domesticity, the imaginary of middle-class upward mobility, devoted teachers within a wasted educational system, suffering of impoverished students, and ruptures between mothers and daughters are present in her stories as the ingredients of the daily concoction of power, one that is ingested through a transcendence of the smallness. Bedrooms, balconies, living rooms, local shops, classrooms, and kitchens are settings for philosophical explorations of perception, experience, and thought.

"El budín esponjoso" is one of the author's most famous short stories. Set in no specific historical period, it is narrated in the first person by a girl who embarks on a culinary experience: baking a spongy loaf cake (*budín*), similar in consistency to the famous Italian cake named Torta Paradiso (Paradise Cake), using a cake mix. The narration textually reproduces the girl's conversations and negotiations with her mother, and her exchanges with a friend who accompanies her in this task. As the description of the baking adventure progresses, it becomes clear that despite following all the steps in the recipe something strange and unavoidable starts to happen, rarifying the whole situation. Within the girl's simple language Uhart weaves the nuances of daily life—an individual's subjectivity, actions, and perceptions—into a broader invisible reality impregnated with modern consumption imperatives. After a series of stumbles and due to her uncontrollable curiosity, as well as her mother's lack of interest in guiding her, the culinary exploration ends in a disaster: the cake is an inedible burned mass. The culinary failure reveals tensions between the symbolic system that feeds the girl's desire and taste and those of her mother, and taste is unveiled as a territory in dispute crossed by social and economic class mobility, gender identity, and intergenerational conflicts.

In this essay, I will analyze how "El budín esponjoso" cooks up a critique of the social grammar of consumption that governs individual and collective taste as a practical ideology of gendered and class power relations. Food as a language spoken by taste is the daily apprehension of reality. As the result of the daily cooking of power relations, taste organizes perceptions ideologically and politically through culinary grammars or gastronomies. In this sense, Uhart's philosophical and pedagogical perspectives, marked by her biography, converge in an authorial enunciation that distinguishes her treatment of the kitchen, food, and commensality from other writers' representations of food. In "El budín esponjoso," Uhart offers the reader a transformation at the level of the signified by turning an idealized middle-class culinary action that is very feminine, such as baking a delicious and delicate cake equivalent to a Torta Paradiso, into an intelligent concrete critique of consumption, gendered class relations, and class prerogatives. In the story, taste is a matter of market but also of experience. Cooking and eating are represented as acts of consumption; they materialize a feminine power lauded in an advertising and print culture that determines taste, social roles, and gender identities.[4]

My hypothesis is that through the microphysics of cooking, the author invites readers to question the referent of taste by showing the tensions within a social imaginary that materializes a series of actions and experiences such as cooking, guiding our perceptions and wiring us through our senses into a singular reality. The story illuminates a shifting moment in the status of cooking and culinary knowledge as a defining component of female domesticity and taste. The girl's strong desire for a tasteful experience associated with a traditional imaginary of romantic couples and weddings takes her on a culinary experience. Using a modern cake mix and lacking her mother's guidance, the girl fails in her purpose, but instead of internalizing the fiasco as her fault, she offers a critique of adults' relationship with consumption, failure, and daily life. In the end she learns that in the complex relation between production and women's representation, experience and exploration have been replaced by consumption, and what has been gained in time has been lost in sensory embodiment of the infinite meanings of daily spaces and experiences. The transformation of the signified cake through the sensorial descriptions exemplifies how taste is the result of a complex interaction between material reproduction and representations. Taste crystallizes patterns of consumption that become a tool for the daily ingestion of power relations and social hierarchies. Regardless of the result, Uhart still shows that cooking is an emancipatory experience, as it is the only manner in which the girl can contrast the entelechies sold by the publicity of new products (such as cake mix) and the full sensory experience of baking the cake she wants.

In the story, the kitchen as a locus of feminine identity and knowledge acquires a different significance. The girl wants to bake a cake but is expelled from the kitchen by her mother, who argues that children make disasters in the kitchen and sends her to cook in the shed. This initiates a transformation in the meaning of the cake and the kitchen—given the conditions imposed by the mother, the first turns into a piece of "crap," and the second becomes a space dominated by order and consumption. The kitchen is no longer the locus where feminine communities are congregated around pots, smells, concoctions, spices, exotic ingredients, cookbook recipes, and traditions dripping beyond generational, ethnic, and class differences. The transmission of culinary knowledge between generations is canceled by the role assumed by advertising, appliances, commercialization, and clear class divides. There is no inheritance of recipes and revelations of secrets, as could be observed in Ana Sampaolesi's "Pachacamac" (1997), Laura Esquivel's *Como agua para chocolate* (Like Water for Chocolate, 1989) and *Íntimas suculencias, tratado filosófico de la cocina* (2015), or Isabel Allende's stories in *Afrodita* (1997).[5]

For Uhart, the kitchen is not an allegory for a woman's own room for creativity and independence, as in Tununa Mercado's "Antieros" (1998). And cooking does not refer to writing, as in *Locas por la cocina* (1997) by Angélica Gorodischer et al. Ingredients, utensils, and recipes are not linked to the discovery of sensuality and the exploration of the body or to a feminist vision, such as in Rosario Castellanos's "Lección de cocina" (2012), Ángeles Mastretta's "Guiso feminista" (1992), or Ana Sampaolesi's "Sal en bife" (1997), or to an eroticism and the conflicts between the social imposition of the female figure and a blameless appetite, as in "Inmensamente Eunice" (1999) by Andrea Blanqué. There is no reminiscence of the intellectual shrewdness of Sor Juana Inés de la Cruz in Uhart's story; on the contrary, the philosophical questioning in Uhart's work results from her clever capturing of actions, movements, and words that exhibit the incarnated memories guiding our bodies in the perception of reality through cooking and consuming.

Bodies in "El budín esponjoso" reveal in their gestures and words a sensorial learning. In this way, the author connects the symbolic realm with that of a singular experience. The kitchen brings memories of mistreatment: a place where cabinets enclose and hide desires, secrets, and frustrations behind the fancy kitchenware. Chocolate, sugar, and flour come mixed with distrust and ingenuity. Pans and lids do not match and exhibit marks of past fires and overcooking; strainers get clogged; and mothers and daughters curdle gender and class identities through the discipline of soup and the promises of cakes. Each bite is digested with the taste imposed by a diet made of affect and normalizing power. "El budín esponjoso" offers a vigorous critique of the cultural and social prerogatives written symbolically in food and leaves readers wondering about its referent.

In the field of literary studies, particularly regarding Latin American literature and history, food has lent itself to the elaboration of a feminist gaze; it symbolically subverts knowledge framed under patriarchal domination. And the representation of food and food as a social situation has been approached from an interdisciplinary perspective,[6] and has received increasing interest in studies on material culture.[7] The configuration of consumption cultures intertwined with the shaping of gender and class identities across racial policies at the core of the grammar of taste are contributions from cultural studies and the sociology of labor and consumption, as well as from architecture, which has placed food and culinary practices in dialogue with other social practices and with economic structures.[8] A prolific and continuous corpus of critical perspectives sharpens the observation made by the French politician and lawyer Jean Anthelme Brillat-Savarin: we are not only what we eat, but how, when, and where we cook.

Worth noting are Paula Caldo's studies on gastronomy, culinary arts, education, gender identities, and the consumption of cookbooks in Argentina;[9] Rebekah Pite's work on iconic Argentine professional cook Petrona C. de Gandulfo;[10] Cuban Antonio José Ponte's essays, particularly his work on Nitza Villapol;[11] Alison Krögel's studies of the legacy of colonial extractive practices in the Andes; current culinary practices linked to the "foodie culture"; gendered economic strategies at community markets; and iconic and linguistic representation of food through film, literature, photography, and historical documents.[12] Compiled in a systematic way, *Comidas bastardas. Gastronomía, tradición e identidad en América Latina* (2013),[13] edited by Ángeles Mateo del Pino and Nieves

Pascual Soler, offers a rich series of essays that form an interdisciplinary perspective and present food as a system of signs that creates communities, patrimonies, power dynamics, and production relations.[14] As Sonia Montecino Aguirre has stated,[15] we do not eat anything before us—only what we symbolically understand as food, which refers us immediately to the body as a surface that turns into a tool for knowing and a sensorial record, and subjectivity as a domain in which thoughts and ideas have flavor. Taste both lives in the palate and is a grammar of the social order that creates a sense of belonging and memories.[16]

In her study on food, aesthetics, and philosophy, Carolyn Korsmeyer analyzes the visual representations of food and taste, emphasizing their haptic nature. The author "rescues" taste from its relegation as an "inferior" sense by looking back to the body and the personal quotidian experiences and connecting it to Pierre Bourdieu's notion of "habit."[17] Habit is that invisible confluence of economic, cultural, social, and educational factors that guides individuals' interpretation of the world and also orients perceptions, from the palate to the set of rules that we naturalize and apply when we read a recipe, set a table, and eat. Taste and commensality are social situations that are not accidental.[18] David Sutton observes that food is able to "both generate subjective commentary and encode powerful meanings [that] would seemingly make it ideal to wed to the topic of memory."[19] This statement makes sense as it brings to the conversation the field of the senses and perceptions, which can be assessed through the observations and experiences of micro-social situations—those actions and experiences that inhabit our domesticity.

The grammar of taste, as seen in "El budín esponjoso," is the set of rules shaping the intersection between the intimate/private and the public, and the way in which power dynamics are digested in between habits, rites, traditions, and also daily rebellions. Taste and commensality become key concepts in the analysis of this short story. Sutton suggests that we can comprehend the evocative power of food by understanding how the senses and perceptions work. Smell, touch, taste "have a much greater association with episodic than semantic memory, with the symbolic rather than the linguistic, and with recognition rather than recall . . . [which would] explain why taste and smell are so useful for encoding the random, yet no less powerful memories of context past."[20] Therefore, the world of perceptions that flow in and through the quotidian experience without us consciously noticing them are deeply connected to our sense of taste. In this sense, taste is an "internal" feeling or perception, a way of seeing things and comprehending reality. It is an embodied knowing that can either reaffirm or contest the very perceptions that lay out its conceptual foundation as part of our everyday "situated cognition" in which the body is constituted along with the world.[21]

In "El budín esponjoso" the transformations in the cake can be seen as a daring subversion of taste as a form of knowing that invests gender and class identities structured around consumption and tradition. In its opening lines, taste and sensory memory emerge as the key topics at hand. The narrator explains, "I wanted to bake a spongy pudding. I did not want to bake cookies because they do not have the third dimension. I eat cookies and it seems that they miss something; that is why people cannot stop eating them."[22] As Paula Caldo has noted, by the 1940s and 1950s the industrial or commercial stove in the food industry and the gas stove in the family home had replaced the economic stove (a kerosene-based stove), which broadened the public's access to certain foods, including pasta, crackers, and cookies.[23] And although certain refined products such as chocolates, French-like pastries, and some baked goods such as cakes, remained at the upper-class pastry shops, the industrialization of food allowed the middle classes and popular sectors access to some alternatives or equivalents.

Cake mixes, such as Exquisita, are emblematic of this. The cake mix became a clear example of the modernization of culinary practices associated with changes in the transmission of taste values and dissemination of culinary knowledge. In the previous decades, food and food supply companies sought endorsements from prominent figures such as Doña Petrona,[24] who advertised brand-name products in some of her recipes and television shows, and product brands and women's magazines that shared recipes guaranteeing their quality via an invocation of her name.[25]

As part of a diversification of its production, by 1959 Molinos Río de la Plata, one of the most important companies in the Argentine food industry, launched Exquisita, which promised to do something more than just simplify the baking process. Cake mixes condensed and simplified knowledge, as they required one to follow a few simple instructions; they saved time; they seemed more economical, as they required fewer ingredients; and they were perceived as more practical and clean.

Cake mixes opened up the possibility for popular sectors and working-class families to enjoy cake by preparing it at home, and, more importantly, made cakes available for a more varied array of social and domestic events. But, above all, cake mixes eliminated the shadow of baking failures. Before the creation of Exquisita the traditional Argentine *facturas* (Danish-like pastries) were the typical sweet treats for the working classes, while cakes and French-like pastries were designated for the middle classes, the commercial kitchen, and the food industry. But baking innovations made cookies and cakes accessible to all, drawing new lines for consumption, taste, and social differentiation in the crossover between gender and class. The story moves this passage from a formula based on culinary-art production and experience-based knowledge to one structured around consumption of cooking and kitchen aids more in line with personal comforts and home improvement models in certain domestic spaces such as the kitchen. The cake mix was better suited to the home's accelerating rhythms and to the gender expectations of the modern housewife. Initially, the girl's rejection of cookies would suggest a kind of longing for old times and a resistance to modernization (something apparently her mother does not resist), as she clearly announces that she is not interested in plain industrial or popular cookies (for the masses or the dogs), but in a cake that has an "aura" or "third dimension."

Consumerism and gender identity are clear in the narrator's appetite as she describes the cake's packaging: "[The cake] came beautifully packed within a small box: it was called the Paradise Cake. The box had printed a woman in a long dress: I cannot remember if it was a woman with a man or a woman alone; but if it was just a woman, she was waiting for a man."[26] Until the first decades of the twentieth century, the Torta Paradiso was manufactured and sold in Argentina by the industrial bakery brand Terrabusi. Its packaging had various designs, but the logo always showed a female silhouette holding an umbrella. Gender roles were prefigured by the press and advertising industries. They presented a sweet "feminine" palate for cakes and a taste for images that organizes the narrator's perceptions: "Just biting it softly, one could feel that all the mastication processes, swallowing, etc., were perfect. It was not like chewing cookies, which are for eating when we are bored; it was for thinking about the Paradise Cake in the afternoon and eating it, an afternoon of nice thoughts."[27] Publicity here functions at the level of social imaginary, recovering values fixed in memories and mixing them with intentionality, filling time and space with "floating signifiers" that inscribe taste as desire and connects material life with subjectivity: "When I saw the 'Spongy Pudding' recipe, I said: with this, I am going to bake something similar. I'll ask mom to let me use the economic oven for baking it. 'Not even in dreams,' she told me."[28] Perhaps what the girl is longing for in the evocation of the Torta Paradiso is the artisanal experience in the kitchen as a mechanism or medium to connect thoughts and perceptions.

The gas stove was widely promoted by Doña Petrona during the late 1920s, and by the 1930s and 1940s most middle-class homes were equipped with one. Although "El budín esponjoso" was published in the 1970s and there are no explicit historical references in the story itself, the mother's excuses for not letting the girl use the economic oven could be because children make messes in the kitchen, or because her mother was simply cooking less than in the past (the narrator says that the "black box" was almost always off). Despite the ambiguity of the era in regard to the kitchen appliances, this discrepancy between a daughter who wants a taste of Torta Paradiso, implying all those gender roles, and a mother who seems to adhere to more modern values (either she does not see her daughter in the kitchen or she does not cook anymore herself) reveals the complexity of the tensions between symbolic systems regarding cooking as a materialization of gender roles and the knowledge "assigned" to them.

Taste emerges in the confluence between consumption patterns, class and ethnic prerogatives, and gender identities. Kitchen appliances and food brands relying on famous professional cooks to endorse their products as well as chefs relying on brand sponsorship to reach their public was a dynamic that helped configure the culinary arts.[29] Taste was embedded in a menu of gender roles and taste would be felt as a feeling and desire. In the case of Torta Paradiso, the gender roles associated with it seem clear. Versions of the recipe locate its origin in the Lombardy region in Italy, where it is said that a bride baked this cake and offered it to a monk, who after tasting it named it "Torta Paradiso." By the late twentieth century the recipe was registered, becoming one of the best-known Italian cakes. It appears in the 1944 edition of *El libro de Doña Petrona* in the desserts section, along with the following cakes: Anniversary Cake, Birthday Cake, Almond Cake, Wedding Cake, Wedding with Tiers, Silver Anniversary Cake, Coconut Ta-Te-Ti, Delicious Cake, Fruitcake "Charo," Christmas Cake, Tennis, Esther, Argentinean Independence Cake, Angel Food Cake, Negrilla, 9 of July Cake, Boy's First Communion, Paradiso Cake or "Torta Paradiso," Soufflé, Supreme, and Pompadour Cake.[30]

A woman's life trajectory could be read in this list, which matches the imaginary of the young narrator. Recipes and cooking become a map of the senses and meanings through which women become desiring subjects. One of those afternoons of pretty thoughts while tasting Torta Paradiso prompts perfect body movements: a soft mastication, a perfect swallowing. The young cook wants to acquire and practice the knowledge that will take her to that moment. Once again, revising Doña Petrona's recipe for Torta Paradiso, we see that it was not a difficult task. The secret is simply a slow and controlled beating of the batter until it is smooth and consistent. The cake's preparation requires essential skills such as deep concentration and a connection with the batter through controlled movements of the arms and hands. The cake requires 10 egg yolks, 6 egg whites, 200 gm of powdered sugar, 150 gm of potato starch, 200 gm of flour, 1 lemon zest, 1 cc of vanilla essence, and 150 gm of melted butter. Doña Petrona's recipe emphasizes whisking to form a frothy batter and moving the mixture gently until folding in the flour and the potato starch, and incorporating the warm butter at the end. Clearly addressed to an already trained cook, the recipe does not offer details about how to avoid the collapse of the sponge during its time in the oven.

The appearance of the industrial oven allowed the mass production of certain foods (such as cookies) similar to the imported ones consumed by the upper classes.[31] Therefore, the narrator does not want the feel of "popular" cookies, but the fluffy, more prestigious touch of cake. However, either because children do not belong in kitchens or because her mother utilizes modern culinary products such as instant cake mix, the narrator embarks on the experience alone to prepare something similar to Torta Paradiso. The cake mix allows her to avoid the complex preparation; nevertheless, expelled from the kitchen and circumscribed to suboptimal conditions, the narrator is led to an experience that will impact her taste and her thinking: "In the shed, my mother was going to turn on a portable stove (it is dangerous, children should not use it) . . . maybe she did not care about death."[32] Nevertheless, the differences between the traditional Torta Paradiso and ones prepared with modern cake mixes is notorious. The first requires beating egg yolks and sugar at a constant pace for a sustained period until a fluffy consistency is achieved, and folding in flour, potato mix, and melted butter with extreme care to avoid a glutinous formation, while the second only requires beating flour, sugar, and the leaven mix with eggs. Both mixtures will rise, but the first is a genoise that melts in one's mouth while the second, although fluffy, remains a dense sponge cake. Clearly, preparing a sponge cake with the modern cake mix is less time consuming, yet the Torta Paradiso demands a presence in the kitchen that implies actions (a body) rooted in a different emotional and intellectual experience of daily life. And the cake mix box hides the complex process that the narrator wants to learn in order to avoid cookies, which lack that spongy texture.

The locus for culinary knowledge had changed and the kitchen had become more a place for the consumption (and exhibition) of objects rather than for complex meal preparation. The orality transposes in the narrator's voice the mother's justifications—children make a mess in the kitchen and should not handle dangerous things, therefore, let's take them both outside. Forced to bake the batter in a small pan, the young narrator follows every step in the recipe except one: avoid opening the oven while the cake rising. As she is cooking in an open space, in a pan with just a lid, she cannot observe the cake as it rises, something that could have been done through the modern gas oven's view-window: "But I wanted to check if it was already cooked; rather, I wanted to see how it was getting cooked. Same as a Japanese guy that had a nursery and used to get up every night to see how plants were growing."[33] Here we can find the tension between the symbolic systems that configure the mother's taste with that of the girl. It is her curiosity about the process that makes her craving for the traditional Torta Paradiso different from that of her mother, regardless of whether she is a modern or traditional housewife. The instant cake package may save the girl from some complications but it imposes a different taste on her own.

The girl's curiosity is not considered by the recipe. In fact, it is an internalized code (of patience or ignorance) that for baking success the oven should not be opened: "¡Qué manía!" (What a craze!) blurts out the mother when she sees the girl lifting the lid. Being curious about how things happen does not seem to be part of the culinary arts, which has rules to be accepted in sotto voce. Taste does not have to be questioned, but as a corpus of social and cultural knowledge it must be learned and accepted. A distanced observation as part of the experience seems to ruin the results: "The cake had turned dark brown and folded up in all directions: lengthwise and crosswise. It looked like a brown pastry, one of those called vigilantes."[34] Compactly folded in every direction, the Torta Paradiso resembles a "vigilante," a typical Argentinean stick-shaped pastry named by anarchist bakery workers, or *panaderos*, mostly Italians, who violently clashed with security guards and policemen during strikes and labor protests in the 1920s. To contest the brutal repression and incarceration of union leaders, as well as the complicit understanding between the church and the police, bakery workers created "vigilantes," a stick-shaped pastry resembling excrement, and "bolas de fraile," a ball-shaped pastry resembling friars' testicles. The culinary failure leads the young narrator to corroborate that her venturing into the baking experience herself elicited her mother's censorship. Although from the beginning of the story, taste as a social situation appears interrelated with consumption and power (the imaginary the girl adheres to in the description of the cake), taste as a feel depending always on the experiential sensation is subjected to the gesture of exploration, in this case, the girl's curiosity. Combined with the culinary restrictions imposed by her mother, caused too by a taste guided by the grammar of consumption (of food, ingredients, recipes, culinary appliances), curiosity pushes the girl to evaluate the process not as a culinary failure to feel ashamed of, but as a natural product of a bigger social recipe: "My mother said: 'It is to be expected, I already imagined that.' I thought that for adults making crap was something logical and inevitable."[35] Cooking is an experience that enables us to become conscious of our senses; it forces us to explore perception as part of our constant thought process. It is, ultimately, a form of rewiring through transformation. The cake mix eliminates the magic of that experience-changing taste. By avoiding any reference to a cake mix brand such as Exquisita, Uhart emancipates her narrator from consumption.

The refined Italian Torta Paradiso represents baking as the rarefied event, while its replacement, the modern cake mix in a box, confirms that mass-consumption baking is the event, rather than the experience of baking itself. The final product, a cake shaped like a vigilante, reveals that transformation of taste as a result of consumption and modernization in the kitchen occurs at the expense of the sensorial experience and imposes new perceptual codes. Only a narrator with a spirit of innocence and exploration—as that of a child in the kitchen—can visualize how reality is apprehended in small gestures, through every bite and every perception. Between the enchantment of baking a cake and the strangeness of the product there is a string of small events, movements—those of cooking—through which bodies are alert despite trivial repetitions that allow us to approach the unknowable of the real or the singularity that composes reality. And what was the referent of taste in this story other than the unattainable or the unstable meaning feasible only through the quotidian experience?

"El budín esponjoso" is a metaphysical exploration of the small, sensorial aspects of daily life, and as such, it takes the reader into an inquiry of the senses: touch, taste, smell, sight, and hearing are all present through the orality transposed in the text, driving us to the uncontrolled flow of certain actions, making us face the importance of failure as a learning tool and as part of this embodiment. If Torta Paradiso requires an embodiment of the kitchen by sensing the air forming into the batter, the modern cake mix requires only following instructions. The story articulates the expectations of consumption inherent in both mother and daughter. But at the same time, through the narration, it brings to the surface the tension between two symbolic systems that, despite not being explicitly and clearly defined as opposites regarding gender values, are distinct in the materiality that they refer to: the girl still wants to experiment as a constitutive part of her identity and her learning, and her mother wants to avoid the experience and the failures by consuming. She sees consumption itself as the experience. As a pan out of the oven, Uhart leaves us at the door of the referent. What is taste if not the result of a constant experience of contradictions, negotiations, resignations, failures, and rebellions? What makes Torta Paradiso delightful is the girl's desire to experiment with cooking, regardless of the values associated with that particular cake. She wants to embody the kitchen as a sensorial adventure. Uhart dissipates any doubt about it through the detailed description of the action of baking. It was not the girl's baking failure that made the cake inedible, but her mother's inability to guide her in her exploration. With this story, Uhart opens the door for emancipation through experience. In the end, the girl realizes a terrible truth: for adults, baking a cake has become a matter of mechanical appetite rather than one of desire.

Notes

1. Hebe Uhart, *Relatos reunidos* (Buenos Aires: Alfaguara, 2010), 10. Translations are my own throughout the chapter.
2. Graciela Speranza, prologue to *Relatos reunidos*, by Herbe Uhart (Buenos Aires: Alfaguara, 2010), 11.
3. Adrián Ferrero, "Entrevista a Hebe Uhart," *Confluencia* 30, no. 2 (Spring 2015): 83.
4. Oscar Traversa, ed., *Cuerpos de papel II. Figuraciones del cuerpo en la prensa 1940–1970* (Buenos Aires: Santiago Arcos Editor, 2007), 18.
5. See Maite Zubiaurre, "Culinary Eros in Contemporary Hispanic Female Fiction: From Kitchen Tales to Table Narratives," *College Literature* 33, no. 3 (Summer 2006): 29–51.

6. Jean-Pierre Poulain, *The Sociology of Food: Eating and the Place of Food in Society* (New York: Bloomsbury Academic, 2017).
7. Emblematic are Rebecca Earle's studies on food, bodies, Spanish conquest, and colonial power dynamics. Rebecca Earle, "European Cuisine and the Columbian Exchange," *Food and History* 7, no. 1 (2010): 3–10; Rebecca Earle, *The Body of Conquistador: Food, Race and the Colonial Experience in Spanish America, 1492–1700* (Cambridge: Cambridge University, 2012); Rebecca Earle, "Food, Colonialism and the Quantum of Happiness," *History Workshop Journal* 84 (October 2017): 170–93. These add to the contributions made in the field of cultural anthropology by classic studies that establish the relationship between food and language such as Claude Lévi-Strauss, "The Culinary Triangle," in *Food and Culture: A Reader*, ed. Carole Counihan and Penny Van Esterik (New York: Routledge, 2008), 40–47. Others reveal conceptions of witchcraft and practices of eroticism in the connection between class, gender, and racial demarcations in the preparation and consumption of chocolate during pre-Hispanic and colonial times, such as Martha Few, "Chocolate, Sex, and Disorderly Women in Late-Seventeenth and Early-Eighteenth Century Guatemala," *Ethnohistory* 52, no. 4 (2005): 673–87. Roland Barthes in "Toward a Psychosociology of Contemporary Food Consumption," in *Food and Culture: A Reader*, 28–35, proposes food as a system of communication that possesses a nostalgic value that wires past, present, and future together regardless of the latitudes.
8. Inés Pérez, *El hogar tecnificado. Familias, género y vida cotidiana 1940–1970* (Buenos Aires: Biblos, 2012), 107–8.
9. Paula Caldo, "En la radio, en el libro y en la televisión, Petrona enseña a cocinar. La transmisión del saber culinario, Argentina (1928–1960)," *Edução Unisinos* 20, no. 3 (September–December 2016): 319–27; Paula Caldo, "Leer, comprar y cocinar. Una aproximación a los aportes de los recetarios de cocina en el proceso de construcción de las mujeres amas de casa y consumidoras, Argentina 1880–1940," *Revista Sociedad y Economía* no. 24 (January–June 2013): 47–70; Paula Caldo, "Pequeñas cocineras para grandes amas de casa . . . La propuesta pedagógica de Ángel Bassi para las escuelas argentinas, 1914–1920," *Temas de Mujeres* 5, no 5 (2009): 33–50; Paula Caldo, "Recetas, ecónomas, marcas y publicidades: la educación de las mujeres cocineras de la sociedad de consumo (Argentina, 1920–1945)," *Arenal* 20, no. 1 (January–June 2013): 159–90.
10. Petrona C. de Gandulfo, *El libro de Doña Petrona. 1000 Recetas Culinarias por Petrona C. de Gandulfo* (Buenos Aires: Editorial Atlántida, 1944); Angélica Gorodischer and Ana Sampaolesi, eds., *Locas por la cocina* (Buenos Aires: Biblos, 1997).
11. Antonio José Ponte, *Las comidas profundas* (Rosario, Argentina: Beatriz Viterbo, 2010); Antonio José Ponte, "¿Quién va a comerse lo que esa mujer cocina?," *Ddc*, March 2, 2012, https://cubamaterial.com/blog/quien-va-a-comerse-lo-que-esa-mujer-cocina-por-antonio-jose-ponte/.
12. Krögel's work on food and resistance in the Andes by means of the concept of "food-landscapes" is particularly vital for integrating the world of symbolic figurations of food into the material production of daily life where those representations conform to the "apprehension" of social and racial hierarchies within the

economy and food production. See Alison Krögel, *Food, Power, and Resistance in the Andes: Exploring Quechua Verbal and Visual Narratives* (Plymouth, UK: Lexington Books, 2012).

13. Ángeles Mateo del Pino and Nieves Pascual Soler, eds., *Comidas Bastardas. Gastronomía, tradición e identidad en América Latina* (Santiago: Editorial Cuarto Propio, 2013).
14. Focusing on gastronomy as the culinary art that speaks to food preparation and consumption, and the link between food manipulation and commensality, the volume includes studies such as those on tamales by Meredith Abarca, "Receta de una memoria sensorial para tamales: Eduardo Machado," 387–407; as well as those on corn, chicha, and music such as Adriana I. Churampi Ramírez, "Who Is Afraid of . . . Chicha?," 269–85. Churampi Ramirez analyzes key notions related to the cultural heterogeneity of Latin America such as *mestizaje*, syncretism, and transculturation.
15. Sonia Montecino Aguirre, *La olla deleitosa* (Santiago: Catalonia, 2005), 11.
16. Victoria Pitts-Taylor, *The Brain's Body: Neuroscience and Corporeal Politics* (Durham, NC: Duke University Press, 2016), 44–45.
17. In *El sentido del gusto. Comida, estética y filosofía* (Barcelona: Paidós, 2002), 22, Carolyn Korsmeyer analyzes how the values embedded in the hierarchy of senses penetrate representational systems that are exhibited and explored in food representations. Pablo Maurette's observations in *El sentido olvidado. Ensayos sobre el tacto* (Buenos Aires: Mardulce, 2015), 56–67, about touch as a sense associated with vision are interesting regarding taste. An image, a sound, or a smell moves us and that perception is haptic in the sense that we can feel it, which is why looking at something "is" a haptic experience. However, as Korsmeyer has pointed out, vision and hearing are considered "objective" senses as they operate at some distance from the object, which means a kind of separation between perception and feeling or sensation, whereas with taste, smell, and touch, Korsmeyer observes that sensation or feeling is experienced as if they were "internal" (45–46). Such distinctions have run across classical philosophy as a form of hierarchizing knowledge, and, as a revision of phenomenology indicates, the information that we obtain from the senses is concrete, specific, and circumscribed to the here and now.
18. Pierre Bourdieu, *Distinction: A Social Critique of Judgement of Taste* (London: Routledge, 1986), 136.
19. David Sutton, *Remembrance of Repasts: An Anthropology of Food and Memory* (Oxford: Berg, 2001), 6.
20. Sutton, *Remembrance of Repasts*, 102.
21. Pitts-Taylor, *The Brain's Body*, 35, 46.
22. Uhart, *Relatos reunidos*, 175.
23. Caldo, "En la radio," 324.
24. Rebekah E. Pite, *La mesa está servida. Doña Petrona C. De Gandulfo y la domesticidad en la Argentina del siglo XX* (Buenos Aires: Edhasa, 2016), 48.
25. Pite, *La mesa está servida*, 48–51; Caldo, "En la radio," 326.
26. Uhart, *Relatos reunidos*, 175.
27. Uhart, *Relatos reunidos*, 175.
28. Uhart, *Relatos reunidos*, 175.

29. Pite, *La mesa está servida*, 46–49.
30. Gandulfo, *El libro de Doña Petrona*, 329.
31. Caldo, "En la radio," 324–25.
32. Uhart, *Relatos reunidos*, 176.
33. Uhart, *Relatos reunidos*, 177.
34. Uhart, *Relatos reunidos*, 178.
35. Uhart, *Relatos reunidos*, 178.

PART IV

Latin American Food Writing

Between History and Aesthetics

CHAPTER 11

The Poetics of Gastronomic History

Salvador Novo's Cocina mexicana

IGNACIO M. SÁNCHEZ PRADO

The study of gastronomical texts and literature from the perspective of academic literary studies has been growing in recent years but remains a critical practice with limited cartographies and significant blind spots. In a 2014 overview focused on works in English, Joan Fitzpatrick catalogs a series of approaches to the connection between food and literature, including the use of food to understand the relationship between body and subjectivity, the historical specificity of food and its objects, the nature of the representation of food, the use of food studies to open up the canon to alternative forms of writing (including cookbooks), and the intersection of food studies and gender studies to unearth and value literature written by women.[1] Although scholarship shaped around these themes and paradigms has shown the value of food studies for literary studies, the development of approaches in understanding the dimension of literature remains a pending agenda. In Mexico, home of the one of the most complex traditions of gastronomy in the world, including the cuisine first included in UNESCO's Intangible Cultural Patrimony program, food studies remain firmly grounded in disciplines like history and anthropology.[2]

In literary studies, most efforts focused on Mexico have been sporadic, usually spread out in individual essays and the occasional conference.[3] This is nonetheless surprising, because some of Mexico's major figures have made significant contributions to the subject, even books about food, from Alfonso Reyes to Fernando del Paso and Adolfo Castañón. As a first approximation to this corpus, in what follows I will propose the idea of a poetics of gastronomic history to account for the ways that writings about food may be read within literary criticism. However, I am not proposing a close reading of literary texts to describe their formal traits or their historicity. Instead, I follow Caroline Levine's idea of the "affordance of form" to understand literary forms as structuring principles with a dynamic relationship to the social, and with the understanding that forms are capable of performing work in the realms of the political, the social, and the cultural.[4] Methodologically speaking, Levine's approach proposes the study of literary form in relationship to other forms to understand questions such as the "specific order" imposed by every form or the ways in which "literary and social forms come into contact and affect one another, without presuming that one is the ground or cause of the other."[5]

Given that this is a short text, my discussion will be centered on one of the most important works in Mexican culinary literature, Salvador Novo's *Cocina mexicana. Historia gastronómica de la ciudad de México* (1967).[6] The book is a key document of Mexico's gastronomical history and it is often cited as an authoritative source on the matter by scholars in different disciplines. In his discussion of the history of histories of Mexican food, José Luis Juárez López argues that Novo is part of a group of people he calls "apologists." Juárez López argues that *Cocina mexicana*, along with shorter pieces on food by the author from preceding years, is the key text that followed a period dominated by "codifiers" who tied culinary discussions to the definition of Mexico's national essence, under the umbrella of efforts by the Mexican government to showcase their cuisine at national and international levels.[7] Over time, Juárez López concludes, the book would become paradigmatic as a model for writing about food in subsequent decades for various reasons: Novo's standing as the official chronicler of Mexico City and his reputation as an erudite and a gourmand, the consistent reprinting and republication of the book, the quality of the book's structure and historical depth, the appeal of its argument in defense of Mexican food against foreign influences and other factors.[8] While this description aptly describes the nature of the narrative and the content of the book as a historical source, it does not quite account for the literary reasons behind the book's importance and influence. These are related to the way that the historical form in which Novo thrived, the literary chronicle, provided unique ways to engage the social and to use prose and narrative to account for the cultural phenomenon of culinary history, an engagement that the technical writings of anthropologists and the straightforward culinary works of chefs and cooks could not achieve.

Cocina mexicana is structured as a meal divided into three courses, corresponding to pre-Columbian Mexico, the colonial period or "Virreinato," and the "Siglo de las Luces" (i.e., the nineteenth century or the Century of Lights, an Enlightenment reference influenced by French cuisine). It is followed by dessert, which corresponds to the twentieth century up to his own time. Subsequently there is a menu of texts cited in the history, from excerpts about the Aztecs from Bernardino de Sahagún's sixteenth-century *Historia general de las cosas de la Nueva España* to Novo's own famous 1946 chapter on Mexican food from his chronicle *Nueva grandeza mexicana*. The book finishes with a *sobremesa* (a term that refers to the post-meal conversation) of five menus from presidential meals of different periods and a *despensa* (pantry) of books on Mexican culinary history. The book has been reedited ten times from its original publication to 2010, and each edition keeps the same text but gradually adds more illustrations, going from a simple set of icons between sections in early editions to being accompanied by various glossy photos and color prints in the latest release. To stay within the question of literary form I will limit myself to the Novo's writing, but the materiality of the book over time would certainly be an interesting object to study alongside a history of cookbooks and their editorial traits in Mexico, a work that to my knowledge has not been pursued in either literary or cultural terms.

Given the centrality of the text in Mexican culinary historiography and the copious academic and critical bibliography around Novo—primarily focusing on his poetry, his role as a prominent intellectual and chronicler in midcentury Mexico, and his identity as one of the first Mexican figures to perform his homosexuality in the open—it is significant that *Cocina mexicana* is rarely the focus of scholars. Yet the book is thoroughly readable within Novo's work and provides new dimensions to the evolution of his literary style. In the period that concerns me, his most important work relates to the chronicle, a genre of great historical importance to Mexican literature. As various scholars have discussed, the chronicle (or *crónica*) traces back to various nonfiction genres, from the writings of the Spanish conquest to journalistic pieces, and has a particularly important role in understanding both the effects of urban development and the contact between lettered and popular culture.[9] Novo is perhaps the single most important writer in the chronicle genre in midcentury Mexico and it is possible to claim that his writings established a before and after in the genre. Mary K. Long characterizes Novo's work in this way: "Novo took advantage of the chronicle's established function of defining national identity in order to create a space for articulating a new modern identity for himself and his readers while also renovating the form."[10]

Cocina mexicana is a pinnacle in this project, by virtue of which the chronicle form shapes and is shaped by the social forms of both Mexican post-revolutionary nationalism and capitalist modernity. Indeed, as Viviane Mahieux notes regarding Novo's work in the 1920s and 1930s, "Novo's conceptualization of the role of literature, and more specifically of the chronicle, works from an intimate complicity between the intellectual and the public sphere."[11] This role of literature was, according to Mahieux, Novo's response to the idea of the post-revolutionary intellectual by deploying frivolity and provocation to question the idea of the intellectual as a "solemn guide for a nation," harnessing "the newfound cultural significance of commercial media."[12] As the decades progressed, Novo evolved toward a perspective organically imbued with the dynamics of Mexico City culture at a time in which the country enjoyed unprecedented economic growth (the period from roughly 1940–60 is referred to as the "Mexican miracle"), manifested in particular by the acceleration of urbanization and the gradual consolidation of Mexico City as a megalopolis.[13] The organic relationship between this morphing city and Novo's work in the chronicle form was crucial for the development of a new relationship between literary form and social form in this period. As Juan G. Gelpí argues, "modernization also brought along a rearticulation of the ways in which the capital's inhabitants conceive culture and the ways in which their subjectivity exercises of the right to the city."[14] As a variant of this kind of writing, *Cocina mexicana* creates a hybrid form by structuring culinary history, the chronicle, and other practices like the anthology into a menu shaped by various forms of cultural and social praxis, from nationalist historiography, to urban flânerie and other forms of observation in the modern city, to the experience of dining.

In *Cocina mexicana*, the basic premise of a writing form that seeks to engage the forms of the social is visible on the very first paragraph of the preface, titled "Hors d'oeuvre":

> The Nahuas had various words to qualify beauty, to signal the value of things. The beauty implied in a flower allowed for the noun XÓCHITL to be used as an adjective, and the same could be done

with QUETZAL, or with CHALCHIUH, or with YECTLI—a good, upright thing. These words, used as adjectives, confer the idea of preciousness.

But a verb—CUA—is the one that most genially created adverbs and adjectives that would express beauty and goodness as that which is assimilable; that which delights and seizes not only the sight, but the heard: the spirit and the flesh.

This verb, CUA, means to eat. The adjective CUALLI means at the same time the beautiful and the good: that is: the edible, the assimilable: that which is good for you and therefore good.[15]

After developing the etymology of the word further, Novo states:

> Under the advocation of the nahuas, let's then speak of what is CUALLI, in its sense of edible. Let's hope that I achieve for these pages to also become CUALLI in the other sense; that I am to the CUALTIN—good and saintly—eyes of you, a CUALNEZCATLATOANI.[16]

In this passage, we can see Novo's performative prose at work. Although its philological and erudite nature is unquestionable, this knowledge is deployed in a thoroughly modern form of writing in which the playful cadence of his prose is in itself a way to capture the rhythm and pace of urban life. For Novo, the chronicle is an instrument of great historical depth and genealogy that has the ability to render its subject matter as contemporary and immediate to its readers, appealing to them through intellectual and affective means. The concept of "Cualneztlatoani" agglutinates the term "tlatoani," which refers to the ruler of the Nahuas but also means "he who speaks," with the qualifier "cualnez," a specific variation of "cualli" that implies not only goodness but also grace. Although he uses the complex variations of Náhuatl to convey this point Novo is in fact constructing his speech on the basis of his modern persona as a dandy, whose grace and elegance are essential elements of his literary authority.

Long highlights Novo's "growing awareness of the importance of performance in individual self-presentation accompanied by a willingness to change both Arielist ideals about the role of knowledge in the formation of national identity as well as canonical post-revolutionary nationalism. The rhythms of advertising inform these views of identity and at the same time are central to the renovation of the form."[17] Novo lived during a time when the avant-garde visual and literary arts often coincided with the change in visual and discursive regimes of the public sphere via advertising and other media, and, as Sergio Delgado Moya defines it, the "aesthetics of consumer culture" was a central experiential and social aspect of growing cities in Mexico and elsewhere in the Americas.[18] In this context, Novo threads the aforementioned passage with various social, linguistic, and historical forms in *Cocina mexicana*. Prosody itself connects resources used by publicity discourse (like alliteration, which Novo utilized in writing slogans for consumer products) with a historical knowledge of pre-Columbian Náhuatl culture that was becoming well-known due to the translation and publication of Aztec poets around that time and to the growing popularity of the Museo Nacional de Antropología, which houses archeological discoveries from pre-Columbian civilizations. This is a work of mediation typical between historical moments and cultural forms central to Novo's writing. Salvador Oropesa describes the writing of Novo's chronicles as connecting "the 'traditional' Mexico of the Porfiriato and the new Mexico City of immigrants."[19] Novo's historical and cultural mediations are not connections between a lost past and the present, but rather articulations of disparate elements of the contemporary that remain aporetic or at least frictional within the rhythms and dynamics of social and cultural forms. Indeed, the use of Náhuatl in Novo's "Hors d'oeuvre" is not rare for a Mexican of the era, not only because the language was present in everyday life through toponyms and residual words in speech, but also because cultural efforts to foster pre-Columbian culture as a source of nationhood were thriving at the time.[20] It is the role of the chronicler to use literary form as a way to render thinkable the articulation within social form of elements that coexist regardless of their apparent disparity.

References to Nahua culture are as much a claim to historical roots as they are an experience of the modern nation. Levine argues that prosody in particular and the rhythms of literary and poetic form in general "match or mirror lived temporalities" and they engage social forms given that "both seek to control time but they do so in different and sometimes contending ways."[21] Novo uses language and prosody to formulate a history of food that structures a sense of time—a national time with deep layers and complex affects and experiences—that is threatened by a competing social form: that of Americanized capitalist modernity, which, as a consequence of the "Mexican miracle," was a significant part of everyday urban life. This is a concern of Novo's work with the chronicle: as much as he embraces the cosmopolitan and cultural aspects brought about by urbanization, he often highlights the need to understand the multiple sedimentations required for the formation of cultural and social experience. In his 1946 chronicle *Nueva grandeza mexicana* he used the language of rhythm and time to describe the transition between the Porfirian city of the early twentieth century and the post-revolutionary *metropoli* of his time:

> Every commotion, by shaking things up, accelerates the rhythm of life. Man aspires to win time, to abolish space. . . . Retrospectively, it is nothing but natural that the revolution, that shaking up of our Porfirian inertia, prior to the world wars and the Russian revolution, coincided in Mexico City with an acceleration of transports.[22]

What Novo describes in this passage is precisely the mutual engagement of dynamic forms between the social, the cultural, and the textual: the acceleration of politics (the Revolution) and of space (urbanization) is woven together with that of transportation, which in turn is an acceleration of experience. The chronicle is the genre that captures this, because its varied genealogies have always already shaped its form at the linguistic and structural level to radical transformations of the forms of the social. The chronicles of the conquest and afterward created new regimes of language through the use of catachresis and allegory, responding to a form of the world that had dramatically changed with the discovery of the Americas. Oropesa notes that "Novo uses the neo-baroque as the system to describe the city because it enables him to unmask the reality of the metropolis without removing that mask."[23] Oropesa also notes that the neobaroque allows Novo to say more than what is visible and exemplifies with the use of an anachronistic preposition the staleness of a social institution.

One could take the point about Novo's neobaroque even further. Mabel Moraña notes that the baroque has an "epistemological operational capacity with respect of discourses that accompanied the entrance of Latin America to the successive instances of globalized modernity." As such, the baroque became "one of the principal mechanisms in the process of transculturation" as well as a "fundamental piece in the process of construction of differentiated cultural identities."[24] Novo's neobaroque functions in *Cocina mexicana* by narrating food history through texts that used baroque procedure to mediate difference and transculturation across historical modernizations. The chronicles of Bernardino de Sahagún, which Novo uses as source and model for his pre-Columbian and colonial "courses," are case in point. As Walden Browne argues, Sahagún's writing, heterogenous in its topic and particular in its language, enacted "the movement from the particularity of the semantic inconsistencies between languages (problems of translation) to a more generalized revision of a historical worldview," a description that fits the Oropesa's characterization of mediation in Novo.[25] Novo wrote from this tradition of shaping literary form in order to shape history, adding the rhythms of the contemporary to the rhythms of history that he extracted from the archive.

His discussion of avocados, for example, departs from three chronicles facing the fruit *ahuacatl*, unknown to the Spanish at the time of the conquest. Sahagún is cited in a passage that, following Browne's characterization, seeks to translate the word by enacting a careful description of the physical features of the fruit, along with warnings related to its social use (such as the avoidance of the avocado by lactating women) to a final judgment that locates the fruit in the material and sensorial world of his implied reader: "very good to eat and precious."[26] Novo follows by citing the writings of Gonzalo Fernández de Oviedo, whose writings instructed Europeans about the plants of the Indies and whose characterization of the avocado is based on that of the pear. According to Novo, Oviedo "disconcerts us," assuming that the linguistic short circuit that describes an avocado through the shape of a fruit that otherwise is quite different affects the very world that is being constructed.[27] Finally, he cites the thorough descriptions of the naturalist Francisco Hernández, which finally introduces the fruit into a scientific catalog of the time. Up to this point, Novo's tracing of the history of the avocado is based upon a tracing of the ways in which different forms of chronicle gradually integrated the rare fruit to the world of Europeans, from its translation (Sahagún), to its misrecognition (Oviedo), to its institutionalization in science (Hernández). Yet, the point of the historical archive is not a matter of mere erudition, but rather an enactment of the affective and physical pleasures of a fruit that required major textual intervention to even become a form in historical memory. It is also to understand how the fruit shapes and is shaped by everyday life and historical merging. By 1967, the social form of avocado consumption is narrated through the different layers of history in counterpoint and tension with the new markers of difference, including the flow of modern consumption. After extolling the virtues of avocados' "excelsitud autónoma" (autonomous excellence), that is, its beauty in itself, he begins to ponder mixture:

> It withstands even being shredded and showered in that adulteration of its old acquaintance the tomato that is *ketchup*, in an avocado

> cocktail. . . . Even dessert, of course, part of an American treat, in the form of ice cream, or avocado *mousse* (purée, lime juice, sugar, cream, gelatin—and to the fridge). It is clear that guacamole is the perfect work of art, the legitimate use of the three Nahua ingredients that integrate it: avocado, tomato and chile.[28]

This description uses a mixture of verbal and stylistic marks to create a certain tempo through the form. In the passage describing foreign uses of the avocado, the italics embody an estrangement from the text that develops into a faster, more economic prose: the ice cream or mousse is an image that does not even reach a conclusion and ends up delivering a mere list in parenthesis, with the fridge enunciated almost as a condemnation. Conversely, the description of guacamole begins with a more traditional construction ("Claro es," from a more intellectual form of Spanish) preceding the description of a "perfect work of art" and ending with a list in which the three ingredients, not rushed into a parenthesis, are listed in their strength and autonomy with a conjunction that conveys closeness and is denied to the list in parenthesis. Novo's writing enacts form from the details of his word choices up to the symbolic construction of the transculturation process it describes.

As Novo moves from the historical to the contemporary, and as the focus on Mexico City's modernization becomes the central theme of the book, the procedures described up to this point render visible the interaction of the chronicle form with the intense formation of the city as the space and cipher of the social forms of modernization. The city forces writers, even those like Novo who hold on to conservative ideas of culture and society even when they themselves embody cultural and sexual difference, to grapple with a knowledge of the everyday that requires unprecedented dedication and depth. Novo was no progressive: even if his very public homosexuality placed him ahead of his time in terms of sexual identity, he was a champion of elitist societal and cultural norms. At the same time, the "exhibitionism" that Novo frequently performed, as well as his penchant for the vulgar, were essential for his interventions. As Javier Guerrero notes, Novo's writings "open space to the uncomfortable inscription of the popular and the vulgar in the vast Latin American scene."[29] This "uncomfortable inscription," manifested by Novo in the tension between the lettered and the popular, the national and the cosmopolitan, confronts emerging regimes of knowledge and form that explode with the advent of the city as the center of national life.

This was something embedded in his choice of Mexico City as the ideological center of Mexican gastronomy and not a place with a large indigenous population like Oaxaca, as many Mexican gastronomes do today.[30] Novo's multilayered recourse to the chronicle as both a technology for the transformation of the historical into a discourse of everyday life, and a textuality that captures the present in its rhythms and acceleration, is thoroughly embedded in the epistemological revolutions that were forced by the radical transformations and visualizations of the quotidian as an object of knowledge. Henri Lefebvre's famous and monumental work on the matter explained this very point: "Daily life, like language, contains manifest forms and deep structures that are implicit in its operations, yet concealed through them."[31] This argument coincides in approach and terminology with Levine's idea of form, and notes the formal parallels between writing and everyday life as forms connected through epistemological and aesthetic procedures, which mutually shape their deep structures. Novo's writing, in its appeal to the modern and the vulgar, is a clear example of the chronicle as a modern literary genre that, at least in Mexico, renders visible and structures itself around the poetics of the exchange between daily life and language.

This final point can be illustrated when one sees how Novo deploys the poetics of gastronomy and the chronicle form. In the chapter titled "Dessert" (Novo uses the English word), he debates the survival of the taco and the gradual growth of the sandwich. This concern was particular to the time because of the increase in popularity of processed white bread due to the emergence of Bimbo, still today Mexico's dominant bread corporation, in 1945. As Robert Weis has studied, Novo attributed the introduction of white bread in his country to Ulysses S. Grant's troops during the US invasion of Mexico in 1846, and he saw it not only as an object of cultural imperialism, but also as a degradation of the gastronomical experience due to corporate homogenization.[32] Commercial white bread can be seen in the context of the discussions I have set throughout this article as an object that leads to new social forms in the practice of gastronomy (the popularization of the US-style ham and cheese sandwich at the expense of both the taco and the torta), and that the chronicler must engage. Novo accounts for this change:

> The intelligent Nahuatl custom of hoisting from the pot to the mouth the portion that will be eaten in one bite, after wrapping it in the also edible tortilla spoon that would be the farinaceous

> accompaniment that Westerners find in the bread that is gobbled up separately: that intelligent custom, it is the glorious precedent of the combinations of simultaneously enjoyed music and accompaniment, that would discover each other in the taco: they would mix themselves in the seraphic compound torta, and would degenerate themselves to the point of the geometrical, insipid and pale perfection of the sandwich.[33]

It is in this passage that the chronicle of Mexican food finds the poetics of gastronomic history: a textual representation of the transforming form of the taco into sandwich, linguistically and formally restored to its origin through its literary resources. In the combination of the elegantly neobaroque prose, the dialectical contrast between Mexico and foreign influence, and the celebration of the torta's *mestizaje*, Novo's literary form constructs its rhythms in engagement with the social.

In her argument for the idea of form, Levine advocates for "a new formalism" that "will have to take account of the temporal patterns of art and life as organizing and shaping, yes, but also as plural and colliding, jumbled and constantly altered, each, thanks to the others, incapable of imposing its own dominant order."[34] It is my claim here that what I call the "poetics of gastronomic history" in Novo's work, along with his work in the chronicle genre, provides a window to perform this critical task. This entails the idea that the role of literary studies in the larger context of food studies is not merely the representation of food, or of social identities through food. It is also not a call to perform close critical readings of gastronomic literature that focus on their philological or aesthetic value. Rather, it means unfolding those strategies to understand gastronomic history and writing as cultural forms very closely intertwined with the forms, scaffolds, rhythms, and affects of the social. The intensity of gastronomy as an everyday practice and the impossibility of fully fixing it into established forms of representation allow texts like *Cocina mexicana* to be the points of inflexion of a diversity of social and cultural flows at any given point in time: in Novo's case, diachronically in terms of his deployment of a history that traces back to pre-Columbian times and synchronically in terms of accounting for the sweeping forces of modernization. The intersection between these flows is both dialectic and rhythmic. As Lefebvre puts it, "Dialectical analysis observes or constitutes the relations between three terms which change according to circumstance, going from conflict to alliance and back again. This in presence of the *world*, to the extent that it features relations of past-present-future."[35]

Thus, the analysis "does not isolate an object, a subject, or relation" but rather "seeks to grasp a moving but determinate complexity."[36] Novo was the master of capturing, in his chronicles, the "determinate complexity" of Mexico's midcentury modernization, as well as the word in its temporal relations. In *Cocina mexicana*, gastronomical history opens the space for food studies in literature to be, first and foremost, a critique of the determinate complexity of the relations between social and cultural form.

Notes

1. Joan Fitzpatrick, "Food and Literature. An Overview," in *Routledge International Handbook of Food Studies*, ed. Ken Albala (London: Routledge, 2013), 122–23.
2. For Mexico's inclusion in UNESCO's program, see Ronda L. Brulotte and Alvin Starkman, "Caldo de Piedra and Claiming Pre-Hispanic Cuisine as Cultural Heritage," in *Edible Identities: Food as Cultural Heritage*, ed. Ronda Brulotte and Michael A. Di Giovine (London: Routledge, 2016), 109–23.
3. The most significant effort of which I am aware is Sara Poot Herrera, ed., *En gusto se comen géneros. Congreso Internacional Comida y Literatura*, 3 vols. (Mérida, Mexico: Instituto de Cultura de Yucatán, 2003), which gathers papers from a conference held in Mexico. Yet, the lack of monographs on the matter is significant.
4. Caroline Levine, *Forms: Whole, Rhythm, Hierarchy, Network* (Princeton, NJ: Princeton University Press, 2015), 6.
5. Levine, *Forms*, 22
6. In this essay, I will cite from the latest edition: Salvador Novo, *Cocina mexicana. Historia gastronómica de la ciudad de México* (Mexico City: Porrúa, 2010). Translations are my own throughout the chapter.
7. José Luis Juárez López, *Nacionalismo culinario. La cocina mexicana en el siglo XX* (Mexico City: Consejo Nacional para la Cultura y las Artes, 2008), 172–73.
8. Juárez López, *Nacionalismo culinario*, 182–83.
9. See Ignacio Corona and Beth E. Jorgensen, ed., *The Contemporary Mexican Chronicle: Theoretical Perspectives on the Liminal Genre* (Albany: State University of New York Press, 2002); Carlos Monsiváis, ed., *A ustedes les consta. Antología de la crónica en México* (Mexico City: Era, 2003); Esperança Bielsa, *The Latin American Urban Crónica: Between Literature and Mass Culture* (Lanham, MD: Lexington Books, 2006); Juan Gelpí, *Ejercer la ciudad en el México moderno* (Buenos Aires: Corregidor, 2017).
10. Mary K. Long, "Writing the City: The Chronicles of Salvador Novo," in Corona and Jorgensen, *The Contemporary Mexican Chronicle*, 181.
11. Viviane Mahieux, *Urban Chronicles in Latin America: The Shared Intimacy of Everyday Life* (Austin: University of Texas Press, 2011), 124.
12. Mahieux, *Urban Chronicles in Latin America*, 97.
13. For the socioeconomic conditions of this period see John W. Sherman, "The Mexican 'Miracle' and Its Collapse," in *The Oxford History of Mexico*, ed.

William H. Beezley and Michael C. Meyer (Oxford: Oxford University Press, 2000), 537–68.

14. "Supuso también una rearticulación de los modos en que los habitantes de la capital conciben la cultura y las maneras en que su subjetividad ejerce la ciudad." Juan G. Gelpí, *Ejercer la ciudad en el México moderno*, 9. I translate the verb "ejercer" as "exercise the right" to better convey the meaning of Gelpí's text, to avoid the sense of physical exercise, which in Spanish corresponds to a different word ("ejercitarse").

15. "Los nahuas disponían de varias palabras para calificar la hermosura, para señalar el valor de las cosas. La belleza implícita en una flor permitía adjetivar el sustantivo XÓCHITL, y hacer lo mismo con QUETZAL, o con CHALCHIUH, o con YECTLI—cosa buena, recta. Estas palabras, usadas como adjetivo, confieren idea de preciosidad.

    Pero un verbo—CUA—es el que más genialmente creó adverbios y adjetivos que expresen belleza y bondad como lo que es asimilable, lo que deleita, y aprovecha no sólo a la vista y al corazón: al espíritu y a la carne.

    Este verbo, CUA, significa comer. El adjetivo CUALLI significa a la vez lo bello y lo bueno: esto es: lo comestible, lo asimilable: lo que hace bien, y es por ello bueno." Novo, *Cocina mexicana*, ix. Words in capital letters refer to terms in Náhuatl.

16. "Bajo la advocación de los nahuas, vamos pues a hablar de lo que es CUALLI en su sentido de comestible. Ojalá logre yo que estas páginas también resulten CUALLI en el otro sentido; que sea a los CUALTIN—buenos y santos—ojos de ustedes, un CUALNEZTLATOANI." Novo, *Cocina mexicana*, x.

17. Long, "Writing the City," 181–82.

18. Sergio Delgado Moya, *Delirious Consumption: Aesthetics of Consumer Capitalism in Mexico and Brazil* (Austin: University of Texas Press, 2017), 4–10.

19. Salvador Oropesa, *The Contemporáneos Group: Rewriting Mexico in the Thirties and Forties* (Austin: University of Texas Press, 2003), 138.

20. On the recovery of pre-Columbian texts, see Ignacio M. Sánchez Prado, "The Pre-Columbian Past as a Project: Miguel León Portilla and Hispanism," in *Ideologies of Hispanism*, ed. Mabel Moraña (Nashville: Vanderbilt University Press, 2005), 40–61. On the role of the anthropology museum in Mexican national culture, see Mary K. Coffey, *How Revolutionary Art Became Official Culture: Murals, Museums and the Mexican State* (Durham, NC: Duke University Press, 2012), 124–77.

21. Levine, *Forms*, 74.

22. "Toda conmoción, al sacudir, acelera el ritmo de la vida. El hombre aspira a ganar tiempo, a abolir el espacio. . . . Retrospectivamente, pues, sino natural que la Revolución, ese sacudimiento de nuestra inercia porfiriana, anterior a las guerras mundiales y a la revolución rusa, coincidiera en la ciudad de México con una aceleración de los transportes." Salvador Novo, *Nueva grandeza mexicana. Ensayo sobre la ciudad de México y sus alrededores en 1946* (Mexico City: Consejo Nacional para la Cultura y las Artes, 1992), 23.

23. Oropesa, *The Contemporáneos Group*, 23.

24. Mabel Moraña, "Baroque/Neobaroque/Ultrabarroque: Disruptives Readings of Modernity," in *Hispanic Baroques: Reading Cultures in Contexts*, ed. Nicholas

Spadaccini and Luis Martín-Estudillo (Nashville: Vanderbilt University Press, 2005), 242.

25. Walden Browne, *Sahagún and the Transition to Modernity* (Norman: University of Oklahoma Press, 2000), 122–23.
26. "Son muy buenas de comer y preciosas" in Novo, *Cocina mexicana*, 34–35.
27. "Nos desconcierta" in Novo, *Cocina mexicana*, 35.
28. "Aguanta hasta que lo desmenucen y bañen en esa adulteración de su viejo conocido el tomate que es el *catsup*, en un coctel de aguacate. . . . Hasta el postre, claro, de una minuta norteamericana, en forma de helado o *mousse* de aguacate (puré, jugo de limón, azúcar, crema, gelatina—y al refrigerador). Claro es que el guacamole es la obra de arte perfecta, el empleo legítimo de los tres elementos nahuas que lo integran: aguacate, tomate y chile." Novo, *Cocina mexicana*, 37.
29. "Espacio a la incómoda inscripción de lo popular y lo vulgar en la vasta escena literaria latinoamericana." Javier Guerrero, "Continente vulgar. Salvador Novo en Hollywood," *Revista de Estudios Hispánicos* 51 (2017): 37. For a good discussion of Novo's travel writing in terms of his performance, see Javier Guerrero, *Tecnologías del cuerpo. Exhibicionismo y visualidad en América Latina* (Madrid: Iberoamericana Vervuert, 2014), 109–59.
30. The discussion of which region represents Mexican food exceeds my current purposes, but I have discussed it elsewhere. See Ignacio M. Sánchez Prado, "Diana Kennedy, Rick Bayless and the Imagination of 'Authentic' Mexican Food," *Bulletin of Spanish Studies* 97, no 4 (2019): 567–92.
31. Henri Lefebvre, *Critique of Everyday Life: The One-Volume Edition* (London: Verso, 2014), 678.
32. Robert Weis, "Por la verdad del Osito Bimbo. Intelectuales de élite, la cultura nacional y la industrialización de la comida en México," *Brújula* 1, no. 1 (2002): 96–98.
33. "La inteligente costumbre náhuatl de izar de la cazuela a la boca la porción que se va a comer de una vez, después de envolverla en la también comestible cuchara de tortilla que será el acompañamiento farináceo que los occidentales encuentran en el pan engullido aparte: aquella inteligente costumbre, es el glorioso antecedente de las combinaciones de música y acompañamiento simultáneamente disfrutados, que se descubrirían en el taco: se mestizarían en la torta compuesta, y degenerarían hasta la perfección geométrica, insípida y pálida del sándwich." Novo, *Cocina mexicana*. 154. I translate the verb "mestizar" as "mixing," but one should remember that this also alludes to *mestizaje*, the idea of the mixture of the Spanish and the indigenous as the core identity of Mexico.
34. Levine, *Forms*, 81.
35. Henri Lefebvre, *Rhythmanalysis: Space, Time and Everyday Life*, trans. Stuart Elden and Gerald Moore (London: Bloomsbury, 2013), 21
36. Lefebvre, *Rhythmanalysis*, 21.

CHAPTER 12

Food, Hunger, and Identity in Martín Caparrós's Travel Writing

ÁNGEL T. TUNINETTI

One of the main characteristics of travel literature is its diversity and the variety of topics that it can cover. Travel always involves an encounter with the different, the unknown, the unexpected, and in this encounter with the "other," food plays a central role. While a traveler may have little interaction with the other aspects of trekked lands, food is an unavoidable necessity. However, it has not always been central to their writing, as Renée Valeri has pointed out:

> Historically, little is known about travelers' food. It may be said that in general those who could took their food (and even people in charge of preparing it) with them, which meant that they tried to emulate their usual food habits. Others would make do with the local fare at wayside inns or the tables of hospitable notables. After the emergence of restaurants at the beginning of the nineteenth century in Europe, an internationalized bourgeois cuisine became available to travelers.[1]

However, in contemporary travel writing the presence of food is more prevalent and its roles can be multiple: from a motivation to travel, as for many gastronomic travelers of today, to a way to mark differences, to affirm national characteristics, or to express their moral convictions or doubts. To exemplify some of these roles, I will use the work of Martín Caparrós, a prolific writer both in fiction and nonfiction. It is in the later genre in which he has become a referent of the literary movement usually referred as "Nueva crónica Latinoamericana" or the "Nuevos cronistas de Indias."

This contemporary movement of *cronistas* (chroniclers or nonfiction writers) has a long tradition in Latin America, and the *crónica* as a genre holds a place of prominence in Latin American literature. Since the late fifteenth century, travel literature has played a very important role in Latin America. In fact, it can be said that Latin American literature began with the detailed travel narratives written by Spanish colonizers, the "cronistas de Indias." There is a very significant body of literary criticism that deals with the impact and influence of travel literature in the development of Latin American literature. In his Nobel Prize speech in 1982, Gabriel García Márquez acknowledged the debt of contemporary literature to the "cronistas de Indias."

Since colonial times, the *crónica* has become a well-represented genre in Latin America, and it had a significant impact during the Modernismo, a literary movement that arose in the region during the last two decades of the nineteenth century and the beginnings of the twentieth century. As Susana Rotker has argued in her book *La invención de la crónica* (1992), the modernist *crónica* as cultivated by well-known writers like Ruben Darío, José Martí, Manuel Gutiérrez Nájera, and Leopoldo Lugones shows all the characteristics that will define New Journalism internationally decades later.

Since the last decades of the twentieth century, the *crónica* is experiencing a boom, fueled by magazines such as *Gatopardo*, *El malpensante*, *Letras libres*, *Orsái*, and *Marcapasos*, and by an outstanding group of writers who have taken the genre to new heights. While these *nuevos cronistas* deal with a wide range of topics, travel plays a crucial role, and some of the best pages, or book compilations, are on travel.

One of these writers is Martín Caparrós. Born in Buenos Aires in 1957, he has been widely published in both fiction and nonfiction, and his journalistic career expands to radio and television. He has released the titles *¡Dios mío! Un viaje por la India en busca de Sai Baba* (My God! A Trip through India Looking for Sai Baba, 1994) and *El interior* (The Hinterlands, 2006), and his shorter travel reports have been compiled into collections including *Larga distancia* (Long Distance, 1992), *La guerra moderna. Nuevas crónicas de larga distancia* (The Modern War: New Long-Distance Chronicles, 1999). Other essay collections of Caparrós's are not comprised strictly of travel narratives, but they include many references to his travels; among these are *Una luna* (One Moon, 2009) and *El hambre* (The Hunger, 2014).

Using the author's books to reflect on food is especially pertinent as it is a topic central to his reflections on culture; he began his journalistic career as a restaurant critic. In *El hambre*, he writes:

> To eat is to act on our belonging to a culture: each community has its rules on what to eat and how to eat it. The cricket that is a delicacy in China would be anathema in my neighborhood and a relief from necessity in this neighborhood [in Africa]. A Big Mac would be food for poor and marginal people in New York and a privilege of rich kids in Managua or Kishinev [Chişnău]. Pork will come back as precious ham in Jabugo [Spain] and will unite Muslims and Jews in their absolute repulsion, and so on. But it is not only what we eat, but, of course, how we eat it: each culture sees as natural the way in which we eat.[2]

And a few paragraphs later:

> To eat is to write, to structure oneself up: each culture writes their self-narratives each day with the foods they eat, the way they eat them, the way they think about, remember them, yearn for them. One of the characteristics less considered about hunger is that it makes you eat always the same. Food variety is a modern myth, a myth of rich countries. Through history, the majority of people ate more or less the same things every day of their lives. Gastronomy—the art of variety in what we eat—is a specialty that, for thousands of years, was as spread as mother-of-pearl jewelry or fly-fishing.[3]

Food, therefore, is an excellent way to define us and confront us with otherness.

Travel, Food, and the "Other"

As mentioned above, food is unavoidable for the traveler, and therefore, it could be a source of anxiety, and a way of experiencing and communing with otherness. The more exotic the location, the more difficult it could become to find suitable food, but on the other hand, the more authentic the experience of finding what is different, which is the essence of travel.

Caparrós's *Larga distancia* is particularly important for the purpose of this analysis. Originally published in 1992 and republished in 2004, it includes travelogues to Hong Kong, Bolivia, Moscow, Haiti, Mato Grosso, and China, along with fictional texts and historical recreations. But almost more important than the chronicles themselves are the short texts in italics inserted between chapters, texts that reflect and theorize on travel literature and the representation of the "other," providing a theoretical framework to read travel literature in a world where distances have disappeared:

> To travel to tell about it has, also, in these times of airplanes and televisions, an archaic note. As they are so many other archaic pleasures. The pleasure, in this case, of letting itself be narrated, with a clearly arbitrary gaze: the narrative of a trip, the minuscule fragment of a life. And for me, the pleasure of changing the supposedly neutral gaze of the reporter into a capricious eye.[4]

This capricious eye is the perfect instrument to explore this fluid space of the travel chronicle, always in transit. This can be observed when he describes the uncertainties the traveler faces when arriving at a new destination, and at the departure the tension comes from not having been able of fulfill one's expectations. The traveler has to find a way to dispose of the food he brought with him to Moscow, bought in the initial fear of not being able to find food: "The tuna cans and crackers and nuts that I brought to Moscow, ready for the famine, and the embarrassment of not knowing what to do with them when it was time to leave."[5] To his relief, he cannot fulfill the ritual of eating dog in China:

> Some other times, the results of a trip are such as that night in Yang Shuo, when I ordered dog. I was about to leave, I had no more than two or three days left in China, and until then I had resisted the obligation. . . . That night, in the restaurant at the hotel in Yang Shuo, nobody else was there; they have a menu in English, and when I saw that they had dog, I couldn't find an acceptable reason to not order it. The waitress looked at me curiously. It was almost impossible to explain it to her. I still considered it hard to eat dog, but it was also hard to feel that way: I had to order it. Traveling needs those bad versions of an adventure: traveling sometimes imposes the obligation of the different. . . . If you are in China, you are supposed to do those things that only China offers. . . . It is necessary to fulfill the myths. And, in the best cases, the trip will be a confrontation between your previous myths, and the ones you are building at that time. A few minutes later the waitress came back . . . and told me that they didn't have any dog left. Now, when I remember my relief, I suspect that in fact they never had dog, because the travelers are not the only victims of traveling.[6]

Many of the book's memorable moments are related to culinary experiences, good and bad. Toward the end there is a long list of things and experiences that represent travel for the author, and food plays a significant role:

> And the smell of cilantro in Bolivia, of ginger in Suzhou, the smell of the garbage in Port-au-Prince, a perfume that I never used in Moscow but always makes me think of Moscow, and the inedible ham in a hotel in São Paolo, the mole sauce in that market in Tepoztlán, the reddish water coming from the faucets in the Chapare.[7]

Culinary experiences are an essential part of the travel experience, and a way of knowing where we are: "Last night I had foie gras for dinner and it was in Paris; tonight, corn grits with cheese in Kishinev, capital of Moldova. There is something in these jumps that attracts me more than anything."[8]

And the differences between cultures:

> In Spain places to eat are decent. I said: in each country the gastronomic business works in very different ways. French restaurants want to be sophisticated—and don't always succeed; Italian restaurants are stingy and cheat you; Dutch restaurants are incredibly expensive. In Spain, instead, restaurants serve a lot of food cheaply, even when sometimes it is not very tasty. But I respect a country that doesn't cheat you when it feeds you.[9]

Travel, Food, and National Identity

Travel literature played a seminal role in the definition and consolidation of national identity in Argentina, especially during the nineteenth century. From Darwin to Chatwin, scores of European travelers narrated their trips through South America, and their narrations are a crucial component in the development of its literature, as Adolfo Prieto demonstrated in his book *English Travelers and the Emergence of Argentine Literature* (1996). Besides the European chronicles, a significant number of travelogues written by Argentine authors came to play an essential role in the process of defining the nation. At the end of the nineteenth century and the beginning of the twentieth century, a cadre of travelers (scientists, military officers, diplomats, journalists) wrote numerous narratives of their trips to the most remote hinterlands, adding these regions to the new nation symbolically (and in some cases practically, since some of the travelers were members of surveying expeditions in charge of marking the country's borders). At the same time, following the model of the European Grand Tour, members of the ruling class would narrate their trips to Europe, and in some cases to the United States, therefore providing an aspirational model of development for the new republic.

From the European travelers who described the land and served as inspiration for the emerging Argentine novel to the native travelers who went to the borderlands to integrate those forgotten territories into the new nation, travel narratives helped consolidate and integrate the country. Once those issues were settled, however, travel literature lost relevance for most of the twentieth century.

The issue of nationhood had not disappeared, but during the mid-twentieth century the matter of identity became more prominent, and while there were no significant travelogues released there were many essay compilations dealing with the meaning and essence of Argentine identity. The end of the twentieth century brought significant changes: the failure of the neoliberal financial and political model imposed during the 1990s culminated with the catastrophic collapse of the Argentine economy in 2001. In less than a century, Argentina had gone from being one of the richest and most promising countries of the world ("the breadbasket of the world" as we used to say) to one of the poorest, with children dying of starvation and retired people committing suicide after losing their life savings.

These events fueled a cultural crisis in which the debate about what defines one as a member of a nation came back to center stage. *Crónicas* would appear as the ideal genre to reflect on the changing character of national identity in the contemporary world. Nationalism then acts as a filter, a gaze that provides us with a way of looking at the world, as Caparrós explains in *Larga distancia*:

> Problems of the gaze: If I were American, for example, it would be easier to travel. I would have, to start, a way to look at the world. There are American movies and guidebooks and novels that take place in every possible place; there is an American narration about everything. And, at the same time, being American is a strong concept everywhere, it means something, it conditions what is seen. Even if I were English: there is no place in the world that has not been read by the English, and I could gaze confidently upon my surroundings as if my presence in that beach were a remake of a trip made by a probable great-grandfather, founder of an empire. Or French: there is no place in the world that has not been thought and

> interpreted by the French, and I could take cover in the verbosity of the eighteenth century digested by Sartre or Barthes, and find ready-to-wear myths and reasons in every corner.
>
> But I am—almost—Argentine, and that means that there is no given way: I have to invent the ways of the gaze, I have to look upon the world alone, without real or imaginary company. Or with any company: to create my own tradition all the time, as an even more imperfect Frankenstein, as somebody who always starts again: The Eye of the Motherland.[10]

It is in this context that Caparrós wrote his most ambitious travel book, dealing with the country's "interior" (hinterland or backlands), historically considered to be the underdeveloped counterpart to the cosmopolitan Buenos Aires.

El interior is a more traditional travel narrative than *Larga distancia*.[11] In 2005 the author traveled thirty thousand kilometers during five months in his car, covering the northern half of Argentina. The result is a narrative of more than six hundred pages, divided around itineraries (from here to there), in which the narrator pays more attention to human stories than to the landscape. More importantly, it includes frequent reflections by the narrator on the goal of the trip: to look for a country, his own: "If you have to look for something, it is better to look for what you never lost. Argentina is an invention, an abstraction, a way of supposing that all I am going to cross from now on is a unit. Argentina is the only country to which I never arrived."[12]

The search starts from a skeptical perspective:

> It would be reassuring to be able to say that I am looking for the essence of the motherland, or, at least, to have reasons to think that we are something all together. It would be a relief to have a mission. But I don't aspire to that. I would be happy knowing what I am looking for. Maybe, on the road, I'll find it.[13]

He makes clear that national identity is a creation: "I wondered, to start, what would I have to look at: how do you put together a country."[14]

Food would play a significant role in this search for the national identity, and the conflicts between regional cultures and their plight against the pressures of national homogenization and globalization. Caparrós's trip covers two very different regions of Argentina. In the first half of the book he travels through the Northeast, a lush subtropical area dominated by big rivers, with culinary influences from the Guaraní indigenous people and the neighboring countries of Brazil and Paraguay. In the second part of the book he covers the Northwest, a very traditional region of highlands with a significant indigenous presence that was once part of the Inca empire.

Such diversity makes it difficult to find a national essence. There are identity marks in the simplest foodways, linguistic codes that can be recognized anywhere in a country: "I go into a grocery store and I recognize it. Argentina is that: a place in which I can go into a grocery store, even here, in San Antonio de los Cobres, and ask for 100 [grams] of salami and 100 [grams] of cheese and know that they know, that they understood: this must be the Motherland."[15]

There are certain customs that make him believe it is possible to find some things that are originally Argentine, but his comparisons with other countries in the region further complicates the issue. He describes the local mate when visiting Misiones, the province where most of the yerba mate, the leaves used for the infusion,[16] are cultivated:

> Land of mate: this is the land of mate. I like to drink mate, but also it touches me: I want to cherish this tradition as a soft weak undernourished baby glyptodon. Globalization is, above all, the most extraordinary process of cultural unification in history. Lately we all listen to the same music, we all drink the same waters with bubbles, we all eat the same ground beef patties in soft bread, we all wear the same weird German invention, pants. That's the reason why it is so extraordinary that a small tribe persists in a ritual that nobody else practices. The inhabitants of the Paraná and Uruguay river basins like to suck from a hot metal straw that we put inside an emptied gourd so the water we pour in comes out with the flavor of an herb: a bitter liquid that nobody else understands, a sharing ritual than nobody else shares. There are in the world few drinks so local. Sucking and sucking a hot metal straw.
>
> For me—for me, at least—to be Argentine is also to drink mate.
>
> And, besides, it has been rekindled. When I was a child we didn't drink mate. I say: Argentina was full of people that didn't drink mate. Mate was, back then, a thing of old and poor people. In the last years—ten, fifteen years—it spread everywhere. I remember, for example, the newsrooms during my first years: a lot of journalists had a bottle of gin in their drawers, and you never saw mate. Now, gourds are everywhere. And there are mate bars, and hot water vending machines, and readymade mates in the supermarkets and fashion straws. . . . Mate is everywhere but it is—so precise, so

clearly—from these lands: here it is produced, here it is drunk all the time. Misiones: the red and the green, land and yerba.

> You can argue then: to be Argentine is like being a gaucho or Paraguayan or Uruguayan. It is curious to see how an identity—an old rite—destroys the new borders.[17]

As we can see, even if mate seems to hold a cue to Argentine national identity, what to do with the fact that Uruguayans and Paraguayans also drink mate with a passion, and consider it part of their identity?

In the case of mate, we have a tradition from the periphery of the country that has become central to the national identity, but that is not always the case. Many of the so-called national traditions have been imposed, almost in a colonial way, by Buenos Aires:

> I confess to him that I had never thought that, among the forms of inequality between the Capital and the Interior, there was also gastronomic inequality. The porteño looks at me with surprise, and then we laugh. I had never thought about gastronomic inequality but I think the porteño from Itá Ibaté is right. The port of Buenos Aires imposed on Argentina its foods and made it one of the poorest countries in the western hemisphere regarding gastronomy. The national table is an unstoppable repetition of the same sausages and blood sausages, chunks of grilled meat, milanesas, pizzas, empanadas, and pasta. There are almost no regional differences: it is as difficult to eat surubí in Corrientes as locro in Catamarca. Lately some pressure from foreign tourism and the influence of globalization—that enjoy certain peculiarities, to have world food there must be a world of diverse foods—caused the reappearance of some local dishes. But they are few, and not always easy to find in the Interior, their place of origin. In Buenos Aires, instead, it is possible to eat with more diversity.[18]

The realization of this inequality is reinforced many times at different locations, when the narrator tries to find traditional local foods in their places of origin. For example, when he tries to eat *locro* in the northwest region, and find out how health concerns imposed by the upper classes limit the availability of certain dishes:

> I want to eat locro; I can't find it. I ask in two or three restaurants and they don't have it. Then I ask a taxi driver, and he tells me no, in that area no, but maybe near the bus station you can find it, and before I say anything he calms me down:

> —But it's clean. What happens is that here downtown is the rich people's area, and the doctors are always around and they say things, so, what restaurant will dare to cook locro?[19]

Even when he eventually finds local delicacies, it is evident that those dishes or ingredients are not easily available and/or accepted:

> I eat yacaré. I say: I ingest this vernacular reptile. . . . The critter is small: Normally—normally?—only the tail is eaten, but these are coming from a farm and they can be eaten whole, he explains to me, and he tells me that in his kitchen they also cook sopa paraguaya and chipa guazu . . . and that they are the kind of things that any local resident in Formosa eats at home or in a neighborhood dinner, but when they go to a restaurant it doesn't sound sophisticated, so they order the same milanesas pasta meat as always.
>
> —Here most people still say that this is food for poor people and reject it.
>
> In marginal places, local food still has that karma. The yacaré arrives fried in small pieces: it has the light texture and consistency of chicken and a slight taste of river fish. The fried manioc works perfectly as a side dish, and I eat them as if I am fighting against the gastronomic uniformity of the motherland.[20]

The traveler has a clear agenda: to rescue local foods and to find in them elements that would make them representatives of the national identity. On several occasions, he insists on the prevalence of beef in the Argentine diet as part of the aspiration of every inhabitant of the country: "An Argentine doesn't need much, his asadito [grilled beef], his glass of wine, his soccer match, his family."[21]

But even a simple ingredient like beef can mark the differences between the capital and the interior, as we can see when the writer is more surprised by a different way of eating beef than by more exotic ingredients:

> Don Felix is enthusiastic and tells me that until he was thirty he worked around: in a mechanic garage in Parque Patricios, in the coal mines of Rio Turbio, and I don't know in how many other places but, around twenty years ago, he decided to come back to his region because he missed it so much. . . . He tells me that the best foods are the ones he prepares with his friends, and starts giving me recipes for hare, armadillo, ñandú, kid goat, hen, guanaco, and even skunk. The one that impresses me the most is the one for cow head:
>
> —For the head, you have to give it time. Early in the morning,

when you get up, you make a big hole in the ground and start a fire. You leave the fire for two or three hours. Then you take everything out and put the cow head inside. But before you have to wrap it in burlap and then cover it in mud so it doesn't overcook. First you have to clean it, of course, and season it with some adobo and chimichurri. You put it inside and you cover it with soil and let it cook there, with that heat, eight nine ten hours. . . . You can't imagine how good it is. You eat everything, the tongue, the cheeks, everything.[22]

The tensions between center and periphery, capital and interior, are not the only ones that define Argentine foodways. Equally important are the pressures from outside the country, both at the regional and global level. For example, in Misiones, a province wedged between Paraguay and Brazil, it is the Brazilian influence that changes the traditions:

> I guzzle fat. More fat. For days now I eat these endless hecatombs that Brazilians call espeto corrido: sausages blood sausages kidneys chinchulines beef ribs pork ribs flank steak. . . . Infinite parade of meats with many salads and fry manioc. Here in Misiones it is very difficult to find meat prepared in a different way. The word "espeto" is now Spanish. Espeto has become the traditional food of this province. I look for dorados or surubies or pacues and, disappointed, cannot find them.[23]

However, the main threat to identity is not coming from neighboring countries, but from globalization, and the effect of national homogenization coming from the capital is reproduced at the world level:

> The Motherland effect hides in the supermarket: I went into a supermarket and I found the same groceries, with the same brands that you already know. The Motherland is bagley, cruz del sur, cepita, cocacola, hellmanns, la campagnola, colgate. If this tendency continues we'll achieve it: there will be less and less national brands, there will be less national references: there will be no more borders in the world.[24]

In this list, we can appreciate the mix of national brands (Bagley, Cruz del Sur, Cepita, La Campagnola) with global brands (Coca-Cola, Hellmanns, Colgate). The politics of food in *El interior* are structured around two axes: the internal conflict between regional foodways and the homogenizing influence of Buenos Aires, and the external conflict—how to retain national culinary traditions against the forces of globalization—and the author concludes, after his search for national identity, that the whole country is a contact zone: "Somos, en cualquier sitio, una frontera" (We are, everywhere, a border).[25]

Hunger, Satiety, and the Moral Conflicts of the Traveler

Not all the *cronistas* agree on the role of social and political engagement of their writing. In the case of Caparrós, his engagement is evident, and it has become more prominent recently.[26] However, his style is never preachy, and the narrator is always questioning his position in the world in relation to his topics. In that sense, Caparrós's writing is so self-reflective that the narrator can be considered the main character of the *crónicas*.[27] Two recent books, *Una luna* and *El hambre*, deal with difficult topics. *Una luna* is a compilation of articles written in twenty-eight days while under contract by the United Nations to interview migrants in different countries; *El hambre* is a six-hundred-page reflection on the causes and consequences of hunger in the world. Obviously, the topic of food is omnipresent in the latter book, but it also plays an important role in *Una luna*, as it is subtitled *Diario de hiperviaje* (Journal of Hypertravel) and food serves to mark the distance not only between the places but between the possibilities to access food. While the narrator prepares for the interviews, he is always reflecting on his own privileges: "But before going to meet my two black guys, I'm going to the Ritz for lunch: marble, linen tablecloth, tuna marmitako, and duck magret in pink grapefruit sauce";[28] or:

> I eat shrimp on coconut milk paired with a South African Chardonnay—the richest eat rich on the planes. I watch a channel on the little screen—the richest have more channels in our little screen—that shows the culinary richness of Iceland. Suddenly I think of the poverty in Zambia waiting for me tomorrow and I change to the news.[29]

The narrator's moral conflict between the life he leads and the realities he reports becomes acute when confronted with the stark realities of life in the poorest regions of the world:

> When she was telling me about the ball of millet flour she would eat every day of her life and I asked her if she really ate that ball of millet every day of her life and we had a culture shock:
>
> —Well, every day I can.

> She lowered her eyes, embarrassed, and I felt like a doormat, and we kept talking about her foodstuffs and lack of them . . . [30]

This contrast is not limited to the experiences of the traveler, but to the availability of food to different people in the same country. When researching the issue of hunger in India, Caparrós details in three long paragraphs the list of food items available in a breakfast buffet, to conclude: "Fortunately, each dish has a label. The buffet at the Taj Hotel, the best in Mumbai, includes two glasses of Moët & Chandon and costs 3,500 rupees plus taxes. Taxes are not that high."[31]

The problem that Caparrós tackles directly is how to talk about these issues without becoming part of the system of exploitation that creates them: "How to tell so much about misery without falling into a miserabilismo [miserabilism] in the fashion of a small tear for the pain of the other? And, even before: Why to write about so much misery? Very often to write about misery is a way of using it."[32]

Reading these books and their extreme situations of human pain and poverty, one feels on the one hand the fascination of reading a very engaging and well-written text, but on the other a certain embarrassment in being part of the exploitation of that misery, the feeling of observing something obscene, related to what has been called the "pornification" of culture. One of the central arguments of pornography's opponents is that it trivializes sex and desensitizes its consumers to real intimate experiences. Drawing an analogy, these *crónicas* or *pornocrónicas* on world miseries, even when written with the explicit or implicit goal of denouncing such problems, lose some of their impact due to its high level of stylization and metareflection.

The first use of the concept of porn outside the sexual realm was precisely on food, when Rosalind Coward developed the expression "food porn" in her 1985 book *Female Desires: How They Are Sought, Bought and Packaged*. In the chapter "Naughty but Nice: Food Pornography," she describes the picture of a glamorous breakfast in the magazine *Slimmer*: "This pleasure in looking at the supposedly forbidden is reminiscent of another form of guilty-but-indulgent looking, that of sexual pornography."[33] We can relate this concept of guilt with the feeling we have when reading these chronicles of disasters and extremely daunting situations in a book like *El hambre*. We are reading a book about people literally dying of hunger and thinking about what we'll eat for dinner.

These voyeuristic and contradictory aspects of the *crónicas* does not go unnoticed by Caparrós, who also brings up the pornographic perspective:

> This is the true division of classes, the most terrible division of classes: the ones that worry about what we are going to do tomorrow, and the ones that worry about what are they going to eat tomorrow. And this is the cruelty of Africa, that shows that too much. Africa is obscene, in the truest meaning of the word. Or pornographic, if we accept that some people get aroused by this. If stupid political correctness hadn't prevailed, Americans and Europeans and some other people could organize tours to Liberia, Ethiopia, Zambia, Mozambique, to enjoy that difference, with the palpable and brutal confirmation of that difference: crown of their success. But some people already do that, often, shamefully, when they contribute one hundred dollars or some euros for the African kids, the hunger in the world, AIDS in black and white. The cruel, horribly cruel reality of Africa is that it tells you loudly what you already know, softly: that the world is shit. And that it is so easy to accept.[34]

It is in this acceptance of the world's ills where we need caution not to fall into the trap of believing that, just because we are reading a *crónica* denouncing this hunger, that we are doing something to solve the problem. Jesse Kavadlo, in studying the concept of pornography in relation to TV reality shows, writes:

> Indeed, panting over housing classifieds or salivating in front of Rachael Ray shares elements with pornography; each in its liminal space between real and fantasy seems attainable and seems to take place in real time with real people. Yet the average person viewing a cooking show, or reading the real estate advertisements in the *New York Times*, like the average person watching pornography, possesses the illusion of possible participation more than the actual prospect of making it real. . . . Purveyors of all categories of porn perform so the viewer doesn't have to.[35]

Of course, Caparrós is fully aware of this, and of what ultimately can be the value of his book, a way of purging the guilt of being part of the system that allows so many people to suffer and die from hunger: "The current, modern, progressive way of the classic religious redemption: they pass the basket, you drop a coin. (Or, if not, you write this book)."[36]

Conclusions

The topic of food is intrinsically relevant to travel literature, as it allows the traveler (and therefore the reader) to explore issues of identity, nationalism, and privilege. In the case of Caparrós, if in the first two parts of this essay we explored how food allows the writer-traveler to define their own identity in contrast with the "other," in *El hambre* we reach the most extreme situation: the ethical aspects of gastronomy and the chasm between those who have food and those who do not, a chasm that defies the limits of empathy and understanding.

Notes

1. Renée Valeri, "Travel," in *Encyclopedia of Food and Culture* (New York: Scribner, 2003), 416.
2. Martín Caparrós, *El hambre* (Buenos Aires: Planeta, 2014), 243. Caparrós's books have not been translated into English. All the translations in this chapter are mine; I have tried as much as possible to reproduce the author's peculiar colloquial style and use of punctuation.
3. Caparrós, *El hambre*, 244.
4. Martín Caparrós, *Larga distancia* (Buenos Aires: Seix Barral, 2004), 15.
5. Caparrós, *Larga distancia*, 248.
6. Caparrós, *Larga distancia*, 191–92.
7. Caparrós, *Larga distancia*, 250.
8. Martín Caparrós, *Una luna. Diario de hiperviaje* (Barcelona: Anagrama, 2009), 17.
9. Caparrós, *Una luna*, 121.
10. Caparrós, *Larga distancia*, 35–36.
11. I use "hinterlands" as a possible translation, but it is a poor substitute for the implications of the phrase *el interior* in Argentina. "Hinterlands" evokes remote, faraway lands, while *el interior* is, essentially, every part of Argentina outside of Buenos Aires.
12. Martín Caparrós, *El interior* (Buenos Aires: Seix Barral, 2009), 5.
13. Caparrós, *El interior*, 6.
14. Caparrós, *El interior*, 17.
15. San Antonio de los Cobres is a remote town at the foothills of the Andes in Salta, located in northern Argentina; Caparrós, *El interior*, 421.
16. Plant used to prepare the mate infusion (*Ilex paraguariensis*).
17. Caparrós, *El interior*, 106.
18. A *porteño* is an inhabitant of the capital, Buenos Aires (the port city). *Milanesa* is breaded meat, similar to schnitzel, that arrived in Argentina with the Italian immigrants; empanadas are meat pies; *surubí* is a river fish from the Amazon

and Paraná river basins; *locro* is a traditional stew with corn, beans, other vegetables, and meats. Caparrós, *El interior*, 166.

19. Caparrós, *El interior*, 467.
20. *Yacaré* is a species of alligator from South America; *sopa paraguaya* and *chipa guazú* are different styles of corn bread common in Paraguay and northeastern Argentina; Formosa is the northern province in Argentina on the border with Paraguay. Caparrós, *El interior*, 208–9.
21. Caparrós, *El interior*, 17.
22. A ñandú is a South American bird similar to an ostrich; a guanaco is a South American wild camelid similar to a llama. Caparrós, *El interior*, 500–501.
23. *Espeto corrido* is a modality of restaurants that originated in Brazil in which you are served all-you-can-eat grilled meats skewered onto a sword; *chinchulines* is a cow's small intestine, one of the common components of a grilled barbecue; *pacues* are different species of freshwater fish native of the region. Caparrós, *El interior*, 155.
24. Caparrós, *El interior*, 261.
25. Caparrós, *El interior*, 464.
26. See María Angulo Egea, "El realismo intransigente del periodismo literario de Martín Caparrós. Compromiso político, sentido histórico y voluntad de estilo," in *Estudios sobre el Mensaje Periodístico*, 22, no 2 (2016): 627–45.
27. María Moreno, "El pintor de la vida moderna," *Página 12*, September 12, 2003, https://www.pagina12.com.ar/diario/suplementos/libros/10-737-2003-09-14.html.
28. Fish stew from the Basque country of Spain. Caparrós, *Una luna*, 105.
29. Caparrós, *Una luna*, 138.
30. Caparrós, *El hambre*, 9.
31. Caparrós, *El hambre*, 193.
32. Caparrós, *El hambre*, 12.
33. Rosalind Coward, *Female Desires: How They Are Sought, Bought and Packaged* (New York: Grove Weidenfeld, 1985), 101.
34. Caparrós, *Una luna*, 55.
35. Jesse Kavadlo, "*Fear Factor*: Pornography, Reality Television, and Red State America," in *Pop-porn: Pornography in American Culture*, ed. Ann C. Hall and Mardia J. Bishop (Westport, CT: Praeger, 2007), 100.
36. Caparrós, *El hambre*, 449–50.

CHAPTER 13

American Counterpoints

Barbacoa and Barbecue beyond Nation

RUSSELL COBB

In a low-slung two-tone green building on San Antonio's working-class west side, García's Mexican Food To-Go serves a dish that crosses an unwritten racial and national divide in Southwestern cuisine. The dish—barbecue brisket tacos—has made this unpretentious eatery rightly famous, by combining two staples of the Southwestern diet: tacos and barbecued beef. The brisket tacos make a simple dish, with a couple of strips of smoked brisket laid inside a white flour tortilla, accompanied by a dollop of guacamole. The result is a Tex-Mex alternative to the much more standard meal: the combination plates of cheese enchiladas and ground beef burritos served at mainstream restaurants throughout the region.

Scholars of contemporary Mexican foodways have pointed to a reassertion of "authenticity" in recent years among restaurateurs on both sides of the border. Even in places on the borderlands such as Tijuana, high-profile restaurants have cultivated "alta cocina mexicana" (high Mexican cuisine) originating in central and southern regions of Mexico, such as Puebla and Oaxaca, at the expense of the more transnational varieties of Cali-Mex or Tex-Mex.[1] Mexican chefs have cultivated the idea of "authentic Mexican cuisine" as a bulwark against creeping Americanization of the borderlands, and perhaps as a subtle political message in an age of anti-immigrant paranoia. As Jeffrey Pilcher has noted, "the global presence of Americanized tacos has provoked outrage from many Mexicans, who take patriotic pride in their national cuisine."[2]

On the US side of the border, there is also little room for a literary appreciation of Tex-Mex specialties like the brisket taco. The violent encounter between Anglos and Mexicans in the nineteenth century in the southwestern United States left the victorious white settlers with a feeling of cultural—and culinary—superiority to their Mexican counterparts. Mario Montaño notes that many of the slurs ("beaners," "greasers," etc.) invented by Anglos for Mexicans revolved around the latter's foodways. It was only later, as Anglo-American cultural hegemony was firmly established, that certain foods (fajitas, menudo, etc.) achieved a degree of respectability in the white mainstream.[3] Anglo food companies such as Gebhardt Mexican Foods made Mexican food "safe" for white consumption, even though a certain kind of consumer knew that they were getting a bland offshoot of the original. This has led, in more contemporary times, to a frenzied pursuit of "authentic" Mexican food. The supposed authenticity of interior Mexican cuisine has acquired a degree of prestige the hybrid form of Tex-Mex never achieved, even after some forms of Mexican cooking made their way into the US American mainstream. From Diana Kennedy's cookbooks to Rick Bayless's widely popular books and television shows, "alta cocina mexicana," with its emphasis on cooking delicacies such as *huitlacoche* and *mole poblano*, has become a marker of cultural capital among upper-class foodies in the United States. The restaurants that serve this "alta cocina mexicana" are, of course, priced beyond the reach of working-class Latin American immigrants, many of whom have undoubtedly noted the irony of US American chefs like Bayless having achieved celebrity status by serving traditional peasant food like birria, a slow-braised goat with corn masa, to the likes of Barack Obama.[4] When *barbacoa* appears on the menus and in the cookbooks of purveyors of "alta cocina mexicana," it is almost invariably done in a central Mexican style. Kennedy, who has obtained the Order of the Aztec Eagle (the highest award given to foreigners by the Mexican government), lays out not only recipes but also rules for preparing *barbacoa*: "Barbacoa is a meat served on Sundays." While Kennedy allows for certain regional variations, she writes that it is almost always goat or lamb serving as the meat. The only exception she mentions is a suckling pig in the Maya style from the Yucatán.[5]

Food writers and chefs have adopted Kennedy's many books as a sort of literary canon for how, when, and what to prepare when cooking in the traditional Mexican style. This means, when it comes to *barbacoa*, there will be no *carne de res* (beef). Kennedy is simply reflecting a longstanding disdain residing on the Mexican side of borderlands culture, where a favorite dish is carne asada. As the Mexican revolutionary intellectual José Vasconcelos remarked in the early twentieth century, "Where carne asada begins, culture ends."[6]

At García's Mexican Food To-Go, as well as many other working-class Mexican food establishments in the southwestern United States and northern Mexico, however, *barbacoa* signifies the slow smoking of red meat with wood charcoal. The regional variations are not in the type of meat, but in the wood used to smoke the brisket. In northern Mexico and west Texas it is likely to be mesquite, while in the east, stretching into Oklahoma and Kansas, it is likely to be some combination of hickory and oak. Whether barbecued brisket should be served with white bread and pickles or flour tortillas and guacamole is a debate best left to food bloggers and internet partisans. Demands for food purity often undergird nationalist discourse, and I am much more concerned with how those demands cater to an invention of tradition rather than some essential authenticity. Indeed, the supposed authenticity of Texas barbecue as residing in the cut of the cow's brisket is, itself, a recent invention that came from Jewish butchers in the early part of the twentieth century.[7]

In this essay, I am concerned with the story people tell about the relation of barbecue to national and racial identities rather than the contours and elements of the food itself. I take as my point of theoretical departure Roland Barthes's approach to food as a system of signification in culture. "For what is food?" Barthes famously asked. Beyond a collection of products that provide nutrition, food is, for Barthes, "a system of communication, a body of images, a protocol of usages, situations, and behavior. . . . It is a real sign, perhaps the functional unit of communication."[8]

It does not take much research to find what the word and the practice of barbecue signify in English. Putting aside the Spanish history of *barbacoa* for a minute, an extensive search of "barbecue" on the internet demonstrates that to many food reviewers, chefs, and travel writers, barbecue is the quintessential US American food. One PBS show, *Barbecue America*, touted the cooking style as "the country's unique contribution to the culinary landscape."[9] The supposedly all-American identity of barbecue is ubiquitous in the media. "Barbecue is the most American of foods," proclaims food writer Dotty Griffith in *Celebrating Barbecue: The Ultimate Guide to America's Four Regions of 'Cue* (2002). "To hell with apple pie. If Congress decided to declare a national dish, barbecue should win by acclamation."[10] At the 2016 National Barbecue Association meeting held in Jacksonville, Florida, some five hundred people showed up to taste and discuss this supposedly unique US American foodway. One participant told the *Florida Times-Union* that barbecue was "the most American food you can get. This is our food."[11]

There is nothing unique about the image of cooked meat as a unifying symbol of the nation, of course. Across Latin America, similar representations of large-scale feasts stand in for the nation. In Argentina and Uruguay, meals of grilled meats known as *parrilladas* are also staging grounds for the performance of national unity. As Rebekah Pite notes, the *parrillada* is often lumped in together with other foods of mixed-race origins and practices to form a base of *comida criolla* (Creole food). During the 1960s and 1970s, around the same time Kennedy was compiling her recipes of traditional Mexican cooking, Argentine food writers started to turn away from their Eurocentric obsessions with French and Italian food and toward the "authentic" Argentina of the rural interior of the country.[12] *Parrilladas* have been celebrated in the poetry of Julio Cortázar and the *payadas* (folk songs) of Argentine troubadours. An Argentine *parrillada*, along with a Chilean or Bolivian asado, or a Brazilian churrasco, may serve similar roles in a national system of communication about the meaning of food in society, but I will not consider them here as barbecue/*barbacoa*, for the simple reason that the process of cooking is entirely different.

What makes barbecue/*barbacoa* distinct from other large-scale social events involving the cooking of meat lies in both the circuitous route it took through the Americas and the technology of its cooking; it is the indirect heat of the smoke and the flavor of the wood that cooks the meat in barbecue/*barbacoa*, rather than the direct flame as in an asado (grill) or a *parrillada*. This may seem like a technicality, but cooking with smoke requires a great deal more time than cooking with fire, thus prolonging the social aspect of barbecue/*barbacoa*.

Although the majority of this work deals with barbecue/*barbacoa* in narrative rather than the cooking process itself, it is worth noting that the indigenous technology of infusing smoke into the meat and rendering its fat through a slow burn was only sporadically practiced by Europeans before contact with indigenous peoples (mainly to smoke and/or cure fish).[13] Barbecue, as I will argue, is by dint of its creolized, hybridized nature an extension of Caribbean culture traversing several nations. The famous "barbecue belt" of the southern United States should more properly be represented as a Barbecue Sphere that encompasses all of the Caribbean nations, pushes north past the Carolinas and into southern

Virginia, then extends westward through the Gulf of Mexico, taking in most of Mexico, Texas, and Oklahoma, and ending somewhere in northwest Kansas. By rereading barbecue/*barbacoa* as a transculturated and inter-American foodway that still preserves much of its indigenous technology, its African flavoring and cooking techniques, as well as its Spanish ingredients, I hope that we can see beyond the narrow discourse of barbecue/*barbacoa* as US-centric culinary tradition and more properly center it as a decolonial practice within a system of communication.

Barbaric Barbecue: A Short Literary History

Barbecue has witnessed its share of false etymologies and nationalist ploys. For many years, it was believed that the word derived from a French term "de la barbe à queue" (from the beard to the tail). In *Barbecue: A Global History* (2014), Jonathan Deutsch and Megan Elias reproduce a nineteenth-century US American barbecue recipe that cites this spurious etymology.[14] The authors note that the idea of barbecue originating in Europe is a widely held belief. There are some obvious issues, however. Pigs, for one, lack beards, and their entire heads, not just their chins, are roasted on a spit.[15] The ubiquity of accounts of words such as "barbikew," "barbeque," and "barbacoa," from Panama to Florida, dating back to before there was any known contact between the French and those on the North American mainland, suggests that the word comes not from European sources but from indigenous American sources. As we shall see later, it is not only the word that filtered into Spanish and English, but the very technology of cooking.

The first mentions of *barbacoa* appear early in the colonial enterprise and show up independently of one another. The search for gold in Colombia led Spanish explorers close to the Pacific coast in the sixteenth century, where, along the way, they met a tribe calling itself the Barbacoas. Scholars posit that the name came from the houses on stilts that the indigenous people used. The language spoken was some form of Taíno or Arawak, leading us to another region in which *barbacoa* was documented.

Barbacoa also appeared in *crónicas* by Hernando De Soto, Gonzalo Fernández de Oviedo, and, possibly, Christopher Columbus. Let us examine these one by one. The case of Columbus and *barbacoa* is difficult to assess for a number of reasons. First of all, the word that Columbus uses in his 1493 letter is "babeque," which is very close to the English version (barbecue), but may have been simply the name of a place, rather than a way of cooking. Columbus had landed in the Bahamas when he heard that there might be gold in a place called Babeque. There was some dispute between Columbus and Martín Alonso Pinzón (captain of the Pinta) about where to go from the Bahamas. The natives there had told them something about the island Haiti (later named Hispaniola) but Pinzón wanted to go to Babeque. On the second voyage, Columbus may have spotted—and even smelled—his first actual barbecue. Reports from one of Columbus's men identified a sweet-smelling smoke from the shore of Cuba. We do not have the firsthand account of this encounter with a sweet smoke, but we do have a later telling of it by the *cronista* Andrés Bernáldez.

According to Bernáldez, Columbus's crew was hungry and wanted to see what the indigenous people were cooking, although the admiral urged them to remain on board. An initiative to pursue this smoke led to some consternation on board, but a group of men did find the source. The Spanish sailors initially marveled at the sight of an elaborate wooden structure that held foods above a low fire so that they would not burn. The fascination turned to disgust with they learned that the Taíno were not only barbecuing rabbits and fish but also serpents. "In many places there were many serpents, the disgusting and nauseating things which men ever saw, all with their mouths sewn up."[16] From the descriptions of horns and scales it seems apparent that the Spanish had encountered barbecued lizards or iguanas, which would have been unknown to them. Columbus ordered the men to seize the barbecued fish, which they promptly ate. The Taíno waved at the Spanish, urging them to come back for a feast, despite the theft. Columbus, according to Bernáldez, brought hawks' bells and "other trifling things" to the feast, which was well before the Pilgrims' (in)famous meal with indigenous people in North America and may have been the first intercultural barbecue in the history of the Americas. In any case, the alternation between fascination, desire, and disgust became a hallmark of European writing about American barbecue. As Andrew Warnes documents in *Savage Barbecue* (2008), white people have used barbecue/*barbacoa* as a symbol for all sorts of Eurocentric projections about American violence, barbarism, and debauchery. Even the word "buccaneer" seems to have been derived from a French corruption of barbecue, owing to the wooden masts on ships that resembled barbecue stilts.

The notion of barbecue/*barbacoa* entered the European consciousness more fully through the writings of the Spanish chronicler Gonzalo

Fernández de Oviedo, whose *Historia general y natural de las Indias* (1854) remained a touchstone for Spanish ideas about the Americas for centuries. Oviedo based much of what he knew about *barbacoa* from the writing on the De Soto expeditions. Mentions of *barbacoa* are not simply passing references in Oviedo's text; the word recurs in many different contexts. In the first instance, *barbacoa* is not a meat or even a style of cooking. It is a structure. Writing about the Taíno people in the Caribbean, Oviedo says that the *barbacoa* is a sort of scaffolding inside of which natives warehouse their maize. The *barbacoa* protected this essential food item from water and sun. "From this barbacoa," Oviedo wrote, "[young Indians] are constantly yelling and scaring away birds that come to eat the corn."[17]

The next iteration of *barbacoa* in Oviedo did refer to a cooking tool. "They had for lunch some hens that they call guanaxas, and cuts from deer that they had prepared on the barbacoa, which is like a grill."[18] Oviedo later takes up the subject of the use of the *barbacoa* as an important technique for cooking among people who lacked metal knives to cut up the meat. Barbecuing deer, wild turkey, and even reptiles served many functions. Slow cooking the meat indirectly helped preserve it, "since the climate is hot, and the meat quickly becomes damaged."[19]

It is curious that references to *barbacoa* as both a storage technology and a cooking method in Oviedo's text are represented without much of the moralizing, Eurocentric judgement found in other colonial *crónicas*. Scholars have noted that Oviedo's exhaustive history was written with a sort of "aesthetic eroticism" toward the natural environment of the Americas.[20] Oviedo's history contained none of the anthropomorphic monsters and wild natural dangers that existed in much speculative writing about the New World. When writing about *barbacoa*, Oviedo seems genuinely impressed by its ability to protect and preserve food. For the author, the imperative to lay out his firsthand observations of the New World took precedence over any overt ideology. This is not to say that there is not plenty of ideological work going on in Oviedo's writing about barbecue; like other *cronistas* he imagined a royal audience that would patronize his efforts. However, Oviedo did not use the *barbacoa* as a metaphor—as later writers would—for the "barbarism" of the native population.

The first barbecue/*barbacoa* as we know it today occurred—fittingly enough—in an area now known for slow-cooked pork. In 1540, somewhere in the Mississippi River Valley, either on the Arkansas or Mississippi side, the Hernando De Soto expedition paused as winter set in. Unlike the Pánfilo de Narváez expedition earlier, which had ended with all but a handful of explorers dead, De Soto brought livestock. Most importantly for this story, De Soto brought pigs, around two hundred of them. The De Soto chronicle was written by a crewmember known to history simply as a Gentleman of Elvas, after the eponymous town in Portugal. A Gentleman of Elvas makes mention of *barbacoas* as warehouses or house on stilts in locations throughout Florida and Georgia.

The indigenous people of this area (Muscogee, Euchee, Seminole, and perhaps some Cherokee) had a diet based on the "three sisters" of corn, beans, and squash. De Soto admired these peoples' cultivation of the crops and helped himself to much of the corn. As they proceeded westward toward the Mississippi River Valley, the cultivation methods changed, as did the people. When De Soto came to Chickasaw country, he found increasing hostility. In the *crónica* by a Gentleman of Elvas, it appears that there was mutual suspicion between De Soto and the chief of the Chickasaw. Both tried to deceive the other, although a Gentleman of Elvas rationalizes all of De Soto's deceptions and lies as part of his Christianizing project. Since the first ill-fated Spanish expeditions to Florida (the name given for the North American continent by sixteenth-century Spanish explorers), pigs had become a desired commodity by Native Americans. They adapted easily to their new environment, and the slow-smoking technique for deer, wild turkey, and reptiles was perfectly suited to the hog.

During De Soto's winter stay in Chickasaw country, someone decided to use the *barbacoa* infrastructure to cook one of the Spaniards' pigs. De Soto "invited the cacique, and certain principal Indians, and gave them hog's flesh to eat," a Gentleman of Elvas wrote. "And though they did not commonly use it, yet they were so greedy of it, that every night there came Indians to certain houses a crossbow shot from the camp, where the hogs lay, and killed, and carried away as many as they could."[21] Hog meat, in other words, became a symbol of Chickasaw weakness, and a self-fulfilling justification for killing those indigenous people who would eat it. The first southern barbecue was, then, born out of both technological innovation and extreme violence, perhaps yet another metaphor for what would later become the United States.

Other accounts of *barbacoa* make it clear that the word continued to refer either to the method of cooking or to the structure itself. The Oxford English Dictionary cites a J. W. Boddam-Whetham in 1879 thus: "For preservation, a barbecue is erected, and the fish are smoked over a fire."[22] In today's Barbecue Sphere there is no mistaking the noun version of barbecue/*barbacoa*. All semantic confusion has been eliminated by referring to the style of cooking as "barbecue" or "barbacoa," while referring to the apparatus as a "grill" or "parrilla." Outside the Barbecue Sphere, however, the semantic confusion persists, perhaps due to lack of exposure to the pronounced difference between cooking directly over a fire and the much more subtle and involved process of cooking indirectly with smoke. Even the barbecue historians Deutsch and Elias allow for barbecue to signify such practices as the South American asado, which utilizes fire, not smoke.[23]

In any case, the appeal of the end product caused delight and anxiety not only among the Spanish but also the English and French as they later encountered the practice elsewhere in the Americas. It may be from the French that the notion of barbecue as a cannibalistic practice first arises. An eighteenth-century French traveler by the name of Jean Bernard Bossu wrote of his time among the people of the "Akanças," presumably in the Mississippi River Valley. In a 1770 letter, Bossu wrote of the practice of "boucaner," which, upon careful inspection, greatly resembles a barbecue cookout. "The savages create a boucaner; that is, they pass smoke [over the meat]."[24] What disturbed Bossu, however, was the fact that this *boucaner* was done with human meat. Whether or not Bossu read Edmund Hickeringill's 1661 account, *Jamaica Viewed*, we cannot know, but it is clear that, at the time of Bossu's writing, the conflation of barbecuing and cannibalism was a trope among European observers. Hickeringill had spent time in Jamaica and wrote doggerel verse about the native population there, the decimated Caribs, who themselves were coming to be seen as cannibals:

> But usually their Slaves, when captive ta'ne,
> Are to the *English* sold; and some are slain,
> And their Flesh forthwith Barbacu'd and eat
> By them, their Wives and Children as choice meat.
> Thence are they call'd *Caribs*, or *Cannibals*;
> The very same that we *Man-eaters* call.[25]

The writings of both Hickeringill and Bossu emphasize the practice of slavery among native people in the Americas, further consolidating the conflation of barbecue/barbarian regardless of the local context. Many scholars have noted that while cannibalism was undoubtedly practiced in the Barbecue Sphere, it was probably not practiced by the Carib people.

For barbecue scholar Warnes, Hickeringill's writing on Jamaica had the effect of "othering" not only the natives who practiced barbecue, but also the whole culture that produced it. By the eighteenth century, it was clear that the act of barbecuing symbolized a form of "going native" among various European populations. Bossu, in his letter about the Mississippi River Valley, wrote that native people, whites, and Creoles had the tradition of having a *barboka*, which he describes as a "country festival . . . with an entire hog as the foundation, grilled on charcoal in the ground."[26]

As the English gradually replaced the Spanish and the French in Southeast, the associations of barbecue with barbarism became even more pronounced. Whereas the Spanish colonial project often allowed space for contact zones to create hybrid forms of food, music, dance, and even religion, the English (and later the US Americans) drew bright-line distinctions between themselves and the "barbarians." Warnes, considering the evolving notion of barbecue as barbarism in the Americas, writes that

> a long tradition of conflating barbecue and cannibalism flourishes across English-speaking cultures. When Joel Chandler Harris has Brer Fox threaten to "bobbycue" Brer Rabbit; when Herman Melville has an unnamed sailor tell Ishmael about the human "barbecues" of Queg's Polynesian home; when Robert Louis Stevenson, not long after a tour of California, nicknames his dubious cook Long John Silver "Barbecue"—in short, whenever English-speaking culture has turned to a favorite verb to evoke the cannibal act [this legacy] is once again accepted.[27]

The literary legacy of barbecue is quite different in Latin America. Even the act of cannibalism has been turned on its head to become a metaphor not for barbarism, but for creative innovation. The defining text of the Brazilian *modernismo*, the "Manifesto Antropófago" (Anthropophagist Manifesto), took the (supposed) cannibalism of the Tupi and Caraiba people to be the guiding spirit of Brazilian identity. "The absorption of the sacred enemy," Oswald de Andrade wrote, was an act of decolonization. Rather than a barbaric act, the ritual of cannibalism was reconfigured to be a symbol of eating that led to a profound transformation of the colonial subject. For the Brazilian, Andrade wrote, "Only cannibalism unites us. Socially, Economically. Philosophically."[28] The flow of the Caribs, Tupi, and other groups across Brazil was more important to him than the Portuguese in terms of a foundational identity. "Before two Portuguese men discovered Brazil, Brazil discovered happiness," he wrote, somewhat idealistically.

Here it is important to note that many of the indigenous flows of people in the southeastern United States did not move north to south, but south to north as well as west to east. The Caribs (or Karib, or "Caraiba," as De Andrade called them) and Arawaks moved into Florida and mixed with Muscogee (Creek) and Cherokee, who in turn layered their absorptions of European culture with Spanish, French, and, only much later, English words and traditions. The word "Seminole"—now the name of a tribe in modern Oklahoma—is a corruption of the Spanish word *cimarrón*, a word for a runaway slave. Modest vegetables like okra (a West African transplant), and simple cooking techniques like barbecue point to a hidden history and culture that unites the Caribs of Brazil with the Muscogee of Oklahoma and with the Taíno of Cuba. Simple foods and simple words can help us rethink the flow of culture from the Barbecue Sphere—from corn bread to tortillas, from barbecue to *barbacoa*, from okra to gumbo—in a concrete way to think past nationalist formations of culture. *Barbacoa* could not be contained by Spanish colonial writers like Oviedo any more than barbecue can be contained by purists insisting on the "authenticity" of Texas brisket, a foodway, we must remember, that employs a Taíno cooking method, a kosher cut of meat, and a Spanish-Moorish animal import.[29]

In a sense, the mixing of ingredients and traditions that characterizes barbecue mirrors other cultural products as well. John Shelton Reed, for example, famously remarked that jazz and barbecue sprang from the same cultural mixture and methodology of improvisation, of making do, of *resolver*, as it is said in Cuban Spanish. A good pit master does not stick to a recipe or precise measurements, but rather makes it up as she goes along, adding some wood smoke here, some extra sauce there, and, more than anything, enjoying the moment with others. Jazz, likewise, is born from improvisation and play between musicians. This may be why Miles Davis did not even like the word "jazz," preferring instead the term "social music," which allowed for Afro-Latin, rock, funk, and Spanish influences to seep in and transform sound.

Nationalism on the Grill

Although the Taíno created the technology and the word for barbecue/*barbacoa*, it has been on the move for more than five hundred years. After the English conflated barbecue with cannibalism, this style of cooking and eating was marginalized until the early days of the American republic, in which George Washington often wrote of large-scale barbecues to be held in the new nation. In the South, various mutations of barbecue took hold. German settlers in the Carolinas, for example, saw the barbecued hog as a vector for their mustard sauces. In Texas, barbecue overlapped with its Mexican cousin, *barbacoa*, and the cow—not the pig—became the main meat involved.

From Texas to Indian Territory to Arkansas, sweet and spicy sauces began to be served simultaneously, reflecting the coexistence of Anglo, African, Mexican, and indigenous cultures in those areas. It is here, in the Southwest, where the pig was replaced by the cow and where vaquero culture—derived from Moorish and Iberian influences—also shaped the foodways of the region. Today, the Southwest's two main regional cuisines are Tex-Mex and southern barbecue. These types of cooking are supposed to compete with one another over what is most "authentically" southwestern. Authenticity, however, is a red herring. The division between Tex-Mex and barbecue is a false one. In fact, one could even argue that the idea that any variety of Mexican food—whether it be Tex-Mex or central Mexican—is not American food but some kind of ethnic food is itself a rhetorical move to make the region's historical foundations in Hispanic/mestizo culture an "other." As many Mexican Americans are fond of saying when the discussion turns to immigration: "We didn't cross the border. The border crossed us." Corn bread, after all, is a close cousin to the tortilla, pulled pork a half-sibling to carnitas, and barbecue and *barbacoa* fraternal twins.

US American nationalists, however, have long worried about the Barbecue Sphere as "a mongrel culture," a miscegenated culture, while more modern conservative intellectuals have warned about the "browning" of America and the decline in Anglo-Protestant capitalist values. The African American critic Albert Murray, however, famously called the entire United States a "mulatto nation," one whose music, cooking, even speech patterns were tied up in a long history of mixing between Europe and Africa.[30] Despite the shared threads of cooking, singing, and improvising that run through various nations within the Barbecue Sphere, some Latin American intellectuals have tried to carve out a particular form of mixed-race nationalism from the region's hybrid cultures.

The great poet and political activist José Martí—working during a time of revolution and independence—conceived of the Americas as fundamentally divided in two: there was North America—primarily the United States—and "our mestizo America." In the context of late nineteenth-century Latin America, when the United States was entering its first imperial phase, the bifurcation of a hemisphere into one mixed-race, transculturated region and another based on manifest destiny and white supremacy represented a defensive posture that responded to the politics of the day. Martí, along with his intellectual heirs in the Cuban Revolution like Roberto Fernández Retamar, insisted that the obsession with race was an imposition from the North American empire. "There is no racial hatred," Martí wrote of mestizo America in his seminal essay "Nuestra América" (1891), "because there are no races."[31] The concept of a mestizo America was a powerful one throughout the Caribbean and Central America, a region in the crosshairs of the Great White Fleet, the United Fruit Company, and the US Marines during the late nineteenth and early twentieth centuries. A few years after the publication of "Nuestra América," the Nicaraguan poet Ruben Darío echoed many of Martí's thoughts in verse. The United States, he wrote in the poem "To Roosevelt," was an industrial machine of a nation, subjecting all local cultures to the brutal logic of capitalism:

> You are the United States,
> You are the future invader
> the naive America who has Indian blood,
> that still prays to Jesus Christ and still speaks Spanish.[32]

There were many US Americans who still had native blood as well, and others who were every bit as mestizo as a Cuban or a Mexican, but the United States as a political entity had forged a domestic and foreign policy with the explicit agenda to "kill the Indian, and save the man." Darío and Martí were rightly terrified of the coming of a new empire in the Western hemisphere and emphasized the solidarity of mestizo identity to oppose Martí's "Monster of the North." Simmering under the fears of cultural imperialism, however, was the slow burn of barbecue, a way of cooking, eating, and socializing—a way of life in other words—that made such easy distinctions between North and South, Anglo and Latin, much more complicated. Had they seen past the US propaganda, perhaps Martí and Darío would have seen a hidden history of transculturation that complicates the notion of US American culture as a monolith. Later intellectuals developed Martí's amorphous thoughts about a mestizo America into specifically nationalist projects, including the *indigenistas* of Mexico, the *modernistas* of Brazil, and Fernando Ortiz's theory of *cubanidad*.

Fernando Ortiz, widely considered the most important Cuban

anthropologist, wrote of the Taíno as a sort of substratum in the modern creation of *cubanidad*. "There must have been already among the Indians—especially among the Taínos, who were agrarian—some rudimentary cubanidad," Ortiz wrote in 1940, "born out of the social solidarity of their human group, of their rooting in the territory, of the cohesive identity of their peculiar culture and the consciousness of their ancestral unity. But it is doubtful that a Taíno group from Cuba would have felt its own historical personality to be distinct from that of their fellows and predecessors, the Taínos from Haiti. There is no doubt that Cuba's Taínos felt Taíno, but it is hard to ascertain whether they also felt *Cuban*."[33] Ortiz acknowledges the contributions of the Taíno people to modern Cuba's agricultural and linguistic foundations. After all, they were the first to cultivate tobacco—one of the two pillars of Cuban development (the other being sugar). But looming in the background of all of Ortiz's work was Cuba's neocolonial status under the hegemon of the United States, along with the rise of white ethnic nationalism in Europe. The Taíno did not thus lend much in the way of what the historian Van Wyck Brooks called a "usable past" to the spirit of *cubanidad*. Ortiz shared the view of many of his contemporaries that indigenous Cuba had largely been wiped out by Spanish colonization, a view that more recent scholars have begun to disprove.[34] For all of his short-sightedness about the continuing legacy of indigenous culture in Cuba, however, Ortiz did lay the groundwork for reconsidering the most basic elements of a culture—what it plants, cooks, and eats—as integral to more high-minded notions of nation-building. For Ortiz, Cuba was tobacco and sugar. Without those basic plants, the culture would be unrecognizable. The slow cook of a Cuban stew, the *ajiaco*, then served a similar function to the *barbacoa*: a food, yes, but also a system of communication, a semiotics of the constituent parts of the nation.

The southwestern United States, meanwhile, has long been a contested cultural contact zone among Spanish, indigenous, African, and Anglo-European cultures. Barbecue presents an interesting microcosm of this contact zone. In the area ceded to the United States by Mexico under the Treaty of Guadalupe Hidalgo in 1848, Mexican *barbacoa* coexists uneasily with German-style barbecue, while African American soul food cooks lean toward spicier pork-based dishes.

The racial fault lines in barbecue are simultaneously readily apparent in the region and yet rarely discussed. Until around 2019, US American celebrity barbecue chefs with television shows and cookbooks were almost universally non-Hispanic white. Aaron Franklin, Bobby Flay, John

Markus, and others parlayed cooking success into a mass cultural phenomenon, cashing in on an early twenty-first-century US American infatuation with barbecue. That all these celebrity chefs were, until recently, white men underscores the wider problem of a culture founded on cultural hybridity but that effaces the non-European elements of its foodways.[35] Texas food journalist Robb Walsh has been one of the few professional food writers willing to address the lacuna between the hybrid heritage of barbecue and its racially segregated contemporary reality. Discussing the almost all-white contestants at a Texas barbecue competition, Walsh writes that the "white-dominated contest is symptomatic of a larger racial divide that runs through the middle of Texas barbecue with far more serious consequences. This division wasn't the result of intentional racism either. It's just that, according to Texas mythology, barbecue belongs to white people."[36] Walsh, a barbecue historian, has documented the massive influence of African American pit masters in shaping Texas barbecue since the nineteenth century.

Food is a system of communication, yes. What a given food signifies over time and from place to place varies greatly. Lobster, once considered barely fit for a prisoner's meal in New England, became a symbol of wealth in the twentieth century. *Chapulines*, Mexican grasshoppers fried in chile and lime, were a peasant food before the paradigm-shifting Mexican restaurant Hugo's introduced them to a Houston audience in the early twenty-first century. US barbecue culture has come to signify a capitalistic, patriarchal, and culturally vapid version of the United States, an imagined community painted in red, white, and blue, served during the Super Bowl, and scarfed down between the all-important commercials for beer and cars. The rich, culturally hybrid history of barbecue has been rewritten to serve a capitalistic purpose cloaked in a superficial US American nationalism. This latest manifestation of barbecue/*barbacoa* is at odds with the food's origins, but those origins can thankfully be easily rediscovered on San Antonio's westside at Garcia's Mexican Food To-Go.

Notes

1. See Margath A. Walker, "Border Food and Food on the Border: Meaning and Practice in Mexican Haute Cuisine," *Social and Cultural Geography* 14, no. 6 (2013).
2. Jeffrey M. Pilcher, *Planet Taco: A Global History of Mexican Food* (New York: Oxford University Press, 2012), xiii.

3. See Mario Montaño, "Appropriation and Counterhegemony in South Texas: Food Slurs, Offal Meats, and Blood," in *Usable Pasts: Traditions and Group Expressions in North America*, ed. Tuleja Tad (Boulder: University Press of Colorado, 1997), 50–56, https://doi.org/10.2307/j.ctt46nrkh.7.
4. The Obama were frequent patrons of Bayless's Chicago restaurants.
5. Diana Kennedy, *Cocina esencial de México* (Mexico City: Oceano, 2012).
6. "El norte, donde comienza la carne asada," *Vanguardia*, September 3, 2014, https://vanguardia.com.mx/elnortedondecomienzalacarneasada-2156857.html.
7. Brisket is often considered the gold standard in barbecue cooking competitions with its cooking traditions rooted in the central Texas Hill Country. According to *Texas Monthly* journalist Daniel Vaughn, however, it was not until the late 1950s that brisket became a standard on menus in Texas meat markets. The earliest purveyors of brisket in Texas were Jewish butchers such as the Weil brothers of Corpus Christi. Vaughn writes, "It makes sense that Jewish immigrants would be the first ones to smoke specifically brisket in the States. The hind quarter of beef isn't Kosher unless the sciatic nerve is removed, and that is rarely done by butchers." Daniel Vaughn, "The History of Smoked Brisket," *Texas Monthly*, January 24, 2014, https://www.texasmonthly.com/bbq/smoked-brisket-history/.
8. Roland Barthes, "Toward a Psychosociology of Contemporary Food Consumption," in *Food and Culture: A Reader*, ed. Carole Counihan and Penny Van Esterik (London: Routledge, 2013), 24.
9. "Barbecue America," PBS, February 20, 2003, http://www.pbs.org/food/shows/barbecue-america/.
10. Dotty Griffith, *Celebrating Barbecue: The Ultimate Guide to America's Four Regions of 'Cue* (New York: Simon and Schuster, 2002).
11. Matt Soegrel, "Barbecue Experts Gather to Munch on 'the Most American Food You Can Get,'" *Florida Times-Union*, March 10, 2016, https://www.jacksonville.com/article/20160310/NEWS/801244726.
12. Rebekah Pite, "La Cocina Criolla: A History of Food and Race in Twentieth-Century Argentina," in *Rethinking Race in Modern Argentina*, ed. Paulina Alberto and Eduardo Elena (New York: Cambridge University Press, 2016).
13. See Andrew Warnes, *Savage Barbecue: Race, Culture, and the Invention of America's First Food* (Athens: University of Georgia Press, 2008).
14. Jonathan Deutsch and Megan J. Elias, *Barbecue: A Global History* (London: Reaktion Books, 2014).
15. Warnes, *Savage Barbecue*, 24.
16. Lionel Cecil Jane, ed., *Select Documents Illustrating the First Four Voyages of Columbus*, 2 vols. (London: Routledge, 2017).
17. Gonzalo Fernández de Oviedo y Valdés, *La historia general y natural de Las Indias* (Madrid: Real Academia de la Historia, 1854), 266. My translation.
18. Oviedo, *La historia*, 556.
19. Oviedo, *La historia*, 136.
20. Alexandre Coello de la Rosa, "Representing the New World's Nature: Wonder and Exoticism in Gonzalo Fernández de Oviedo y Valdes," *Historical Reflections / Réflexions Historiques* 28, no. 1 (2002): 73–92.
21. A Gentleman of Elvas, *A Narrative of the Expedition of Hernando de Soto into*

Florida (London: Richard Hackluyt, 1609), accessible at https://www.gutenberg.org/files/34997/34997-h/34997-h.htm.

22. *Oxford English Dictionary*, s.v. "Barbecue."
23. Deutsch and Elias, *Barbecue*, 32.
24. J. M. Carrière, "Indian and Creole Barboka, American Barbecue," *Language* 13, no. 2 (1937): 148–50, https://doi.org/10.2307/408723.
25. Thomas W. Krise, ed., *Caribbeana: An Anthology of English Literature of the West Indies, 1657–1777* (Chicago: University of Chicago Press, 1999), 45.
26. Quoted in Carrière, *Savage*, 149.
27. Warnes, *Savage Barbecue*, 46.
28. Oswald de Andrade and Leslie Bary, "Cannibalist Manifesto," *Latin American Literary Review* 19, no. 38 (July–December 1991), 38.
29. Cattle were introduced to Spain via north Africa.
30. Albert Murray, *The Omni-Americans: Some Alternatives to the Folklore of White Supremacy* (New York: E. P. Dutton, 1970), 22.
31. José Martí, "Our America," accessible at https://writing.upenn.edu/library/Marti_Jose_Our-America.html.
32. Rubén Darío, "To Roosevelt," accessible at https://www.poets.org/poetsorg/poem/roosevelt.
33. Fernando Ortiz, "The human factors of *cubanidad*," *HAU: Journal of Ethnographic Theory* 4, no. 3 (Winter 2014): 455–80.
34. See, for example, Maximilian Forte, ed., *Indigenous Resurgence in the Contemporary Caribbean: Amerindian Survival and Revival* (Bern, Switzerland: Peter Lang, 2016).
35. See the Fox News article purporting to list "America's Most Influential BBQ Pitmasters and Personalities," all twelve of whom are white men. "America's Most Influential BBQ Pitmasters and Personalities," Fox News, accessed December 10, 2018, https://www.foxnews.com/food-drink/americas-most-influential-bbq-pitmasters-and-personalities.
36. Robb Walsh, "Texas Barbecue in Black and White," in *Cornbread Nation* 2, ed. Lolis Eric Elie (Oxford, NC: Southern Foodways Alliance, 2004), 50.

EPILOGUE

Why Gastronarratives Matter

MARÍA PAZ MORENO

Food and culture are inextricably tied together, and they are also tied to the written word, as one of the most efficient ways of human expression and knowledge transmission. The study of the central role played by food in human societies, with rules and rituals that go beyond the mere preparation and consumption of nutrients to fill a biological need, as well as its written manifestations, allows us to gain valuable insights into human culture. As this volume on gastronarratives shows, the deeply intertwined relationship between food, culture, and literature is of paramount importance in the Spanish-speaking world. The academic field of food studies, which has been growing by leaps and bounds in recent years, has helped us examine food and everything that surrounds it from new, interesting perspectives, by integrating analytical tools from different disciplines. The study of literature, traditionally confined within rigid theoretical frames, has particularly benefited from this trend, having recently been incorporated into the field of cultural studies, of which food studies is a most fruitful branch. The boundaries of the genre have been expanded in the process, and as a result scholars are now approaching literary texts with new eyes, examining their connections to food and its numerous cultural manifestations.

As Edward O. Wilson points out in his influential book *Consilience: The Unity of Human Knowledge* (1999), food-related cultural practices are present in every human society and have very likely been there since the beginning of human civilization itself.[1] Wilson cites American anthropologist George P. Murdock, who in 1945 coined the term "universals of culture" to refer to the social behaviors and institutions present in every one of the hundreds of societies studied to that time. He listed sixty-seven such universals, among which he included cooking, family-feasting, food taboos, and mealtimes. It can be argued that many food traditions and their cultural manifestations, from modes of preparation and consumption to food avoidance and fasting, are Darwinian in origin. They evolved independently in separate societies to guarantee the survival of the group within their environmental and historical context. In Wilson's view, what is truly unique about human evolution in comparison to other species is that "a large part of the environment shaping it has been cultural. . . . Members of past generations who used their culture to best advantage, like foragers gleaning food from a surrounding forest, enjoyed the greatest Darwinian advantage."[2] Furthermore, the culture of each society is shaped by these universals and a series of rituals and customs, from the sharing of food and fermented beverages, to music, storytelling, religious beliefs, etcetera, all of which combine to shape and strengthen the identity of the group.[3] Even though food is equally necessary for survival for all human groups, the sophisticated cultural system that develops around it is different for each group, depending on environmental, genetic, and other factors, and is essential to the construction of that society and the definition of the group's identity.

These ideas, rooted in anthropological theories as well as Darwin's theory of evolution, can be very useful when applied to humanistic studies to illuminate the role of food as a decisive factor in human evolution, as well as a building block of society and one of its most powerful identity-building elements. This is why the study of food discourses and modes of production, preparation, and consumption in relation to the social, political, and cultural aspects can be so revealing. All kinds of food-related texts, both literary and non-literary—such as cookbooks or restaurant menus—are worthy of study and can provide us with valuable insights about the society in which they originated. This flexibility of the field and its many possibilities is what constitutes its greatest potential. Researchers of food studies ought to cross previously impassable boundaries to work from multidisciplinary approaches, combining tools from literary theory, sociology, linguistics, anthropology, history, and other disciplines, encompassing both the humanities and the natural sciences. This approach has the potential to produce groundbreaking research that can help us better understand the role that food, both as a biological need and an important component of a complex social and cultural system, plays in human existence.

While substantial work has been undertaken in this area in the

English-speaking world, the field of Latin American and Spanish Peninsular literature has been slower at catching up. Nevertheless, a number of pioneer studies have successfully started to chart this new territory, and especially since the 1990s, scholars of cultural studies focusing on Latin America have turned to the connections between food, literary production, and culture for new insights into the multifaceted nature of their relationship. The analysis of food as related to problematic issues in the Latin American context, such as colonialism, immigration, gender, ethnicity, and power, among others, is providing us with highly illuminating and fruitful lines of research. In addition to these, the process of nation-building that often underlies the concept of a "national cuisine," the symbolic meaning of such concept and its ties to the idea of national identity, is another topic of much critical attention, having been and continuing to be explored by many scholars.

The essays compiled in this issue under the concept of gastronarratives are valuable examples of the potential of the emerging field of food studies when applied to Latin America and the meaning of food in its many textual productions. The texts that provide the starting point for analysis include colonial manuscripts, travel literature, convent recipe writing, novels, short stories, etiquette manuals, and cookbooks, thus covering different epochs and a wide geographic range spanning all of Latin America. In this context, issues of race, power, and gender emerge as central. This new volume follows in the footsteps of a number of pioneer studies that helped raise a new awareness about the implications of food for Latin American cultural studies. Just to name a few: *Food, Politics, and Society in Latin America*, published in 1985; *Conquista y comida: Consecuencias del encuentro de dos mundos* (1996); and more recently, the work of scholars like Jeffrey Pilcher, author of *¡Que vivan los tamales!* (1998) and *Planet Taco* (2012), Steve Striffler and Mark Moberg's *Banana Wars* (2003), and Rebecca Earle's *The Body of the Conquistador* (2012).[4] The *Cincinnati Romance Review* monographic volume that I edited in 2012 was devoted to the topic, *Writing about Food: Culinary Literature in the Hispanic World*, and my first book on the subject, *De la página al plato*, published in the same year, reflected my own increasing interest in the subject and a desire to help fill important voids in the field.[5] Specifically, the *Cincinnati Romance Review* issue was born out of an attempt to survey the existing interest on the topic and gauge critics' engagement with it, and to get a better grasp of the status quo of the existing research on food and culture of the Spanish-speaking world. Mainly focused on works of literature and encompassing research on both Spain and Latin America, the volume included the work of prominent researchers who had pioneered studies on the subject.

Gastronarratives matter because they tell stories that may otherwise go untold. By providing us with a reading between the lines, we are made aware of the subtleties of ideological discourses embedded in apparently "innocent" texts such as cookbooks, gastronomy treaties, or literary works where food plays a role. Current research continues to explore the topics mentioned earlier, but is also delving into new ones, some of which are highly relevant to contemporary challenges. To this end, future investigations should deepen the connection between the humanistic and scientific approaches to the study of food; research will be needed to highlight the ecological impact of a changing world on our food traditions. Given that the culture of food is largely modeled by the environment, future studies will no doubt have to examine the impact of our planet's changing climate as reflected in the literature and in the new cultural food practices that will develop. Challenges include the diminished availability of resources, such as water and its impact on agriculture, and the scarcity of certain commodities caused by excessive rain, drought, plagues, or the disappearance of pollinating insects that aid in the production of fruit. The ecological impact of these challenges and our ability to adapt to them will result in changing food habits, new or modified traditions, dishes, food rituals, perhaps even the emergence of new food taboos. New social realities may be born out of this as well.

How soon and in what manner can we expect to start seeing these adaptations in the food-related body of literature? What will become of the ancient food traditions of those peoples whose ancestral homelands are no longer habitable or are unable to provide enough food, and who may find themselves displaced and forced to relocate to new environments? It is only a matter of time before new literary and textual manifestations begin to reflect this new reality. We know that migration movements by human groups have historically resulted in changes in food culture, often related to ingredients and dishes brought along with the moving populations. Processes of colonization, conquest, and counter-colonization in the form of immigration have historically acted as forces of gastronomic change all over the world. It is a never-ending, continuous process that may now be entering a new phase.

This is not a far-fetched scenario. A 2016 report by the Food and Agriculture Organization of the United Nations (FAO) alerted that the impact of climate change in Latin America and the Caribbean, which is already experiencing some noticeable adverse effects, will be "considerable" due the region's "economic dependence on agriculture, the low adaptive capacity of its population and the geographical location of some of its countries."[6] According to this report, Bolivia, Ecuador, El Salvador, Honduras, Nicaragua, Paraguay, Peru, and the northeast regions of Brazil will endure the most severe impact. This is already resulting in significant challenges for the food security of these country's populations, as main crops that have traditionally been the base of the local diets (such as rice, potatoes, and corn) and others of economic importance as exports (such as coffee and sugar cane) are being impacted by climate change. As this trend continues, some traditional agricultural systems these populations have relied upon for centuries may be at risk, as the FAO reports states that "changes in the distribution of rainfall throughout the year could endanger the production of milpa (agroecosystem with simultaneous maize, beans, and squash crops)."[7] Although it is impossible to predict with certainty the evolution and impact of these changes, it seems clear that they are on the not-so-distant horizon. Finding the balance to adapt to a new climatic reality while maintaining food traditions of great cultural significance will be a major challenge. As studies like the ones included in this volume show, issues surrounding food in relation to social and economic structures and historical processes will continue to be the subject of much future research. Finally, the relevance of food and its discourses cannot be underestimated, as it continues to reflect the ever-evolving reality of Latin America and the narratives that shape and define it as a historically complex and multilayered cultural space.

Notes

1. Edward O. Wilson, *Consilience: The Unity of Knowledge* (New York: Random House, 1999).
2. Wilson, *Consilience*, 180.
3. Wilson, *Consilience*, 142.
4. John C. Super and Thomas C. Wright, eds., *Food, Politics, and Society in Latin America* (Lincoln: University of Nebraska Press, 1985); Janet Long, ed., *Conquista y comida: Consecuencias del encuentro de dos mundos* (Mexico City: Universidad Nacional Autónoma de México, 1996); Jeffrey M. Pilcher, *¡Que vivan los tamales! Food and the Making of Mexican Identity* (Albuquerque: University of New Mexico Press, 1998); Jeffrey M. Pilcher, *Planet Taco. A Global History of Mexican Food* (New York: Oxford University Press, 2012); Mark

Moberg and Steve Striffler, *Banana Wars: Power, Production, and History in the Americas* (Durham, NC: Duke University Press, 2003); Rebecca Earle, *The Body of the Conquistador: Food, Race, and the Colonial Experience in Spanish America, 1492–1700* (Cambridge: Cambridge University Press, 2013).

5. María Paz Moreno, ed., *Writing about Food: Culinary Literature in the Hispanic World*, Special issue, *Cincinnati Romance Review* 34 (Fall 2012), and María Paz Moreno, *De la página al plato. El libro de cocina en España* (Gijón, Spain: Trea, 2012).
6. *Food and Nutrition Security and the Eradication of Hunger. CELAC 2025: Furthering Discussion and Regional Cooperation* (United Nations ECLAC; F AO; ALADI, 2016), 71, accessed December 8, 2018, https://www.cepal.org/en/publications/40355-food-and-nutrition-security-and-eradication-hunger-celac-2025-furthering.
7. *Food and Nutrition*, 79.

BIBLIOGRAPHY

Introduction: Toward the Construction of a Latin American Gastronarrative

Acosta de Samper, Soledad. *La mujer: revista quincenal exclusivamente redactada para señoras y señoritas* 1 (January–June 1880); 5, no. 59–60 (May 1881). https://soledadacosta.uniandes.edu.co/items/show/638.

Alarcón, Daniel. "Contra la gastronomía peruana." In *Radio Ambulante*, January 3, 2017. Podcast, 25:56. http://radioambulante.org/audio/contra-la-gastronomia-peruana-2.

Appadurai, Arjun. "How to Make a National Cuisine: Cookbooks in Contemporary India." *Comparative Studies in Society and History* 30, no. 1 (1988): 3–24.

Austin, Elisabeth. "Reading and Writing Juana Manuela Gorriti's *Cocina Ecléctica*: Modeling Multiplicity in Nineteenth-Century Domestic Narrative." *Arizona Journal of Hispanic Cultural Studies* 12, no. 1 (2009): 31–44.

Barthes, Roland. "Toward a Psychosociology of Contemporary Food Consumption." In *Food and Culture*, edited by Carole Counihan and Penny Van Esterik, 28–35. New York: Routledge, 2008.

Christou, Maria. *Eating Otherwise: The Philosophy of Food in Twentieth-Century Literature*. Cambridge: Cambridge University Press, 2017.

Coward, Rosalind. "Naughty but Nice: Food Pornography." In *Ethics: A Feminist Reader*, edited by Elizabeth Frazer, Jennifer Hornsby, and Sabina Lovibond, 132–38. Oxford: Blackwell, 1992.

Eagleton, Terry. "Edible Écriture." In *Consuming Passions: Food in the Age of Anxiety*, edited by Sian Griffiths and Jennifer Wallace, 203–8. Manchester: Mandolin, 1998.

Gorriti, Juana Manuela. *Cocina ecléctica*. In *Obras completas*. Vol. 3. Salta, Argentina: Fundación del Banco del Noroeste, 1994.

Lee, Michael Parrish. *The Food Plot in the Nineteenth-Century British Novel*. London: Palgrave Macmillan, 2016.

Ortiz, Fernando. *Contrapunteo cubano del tabaco y el azúcar*. Havana: J. Montero, 1940.

Parkhust Ferguson, Priscilla. "A Cultural Field in the Making: Gastronomy in 19th-Century France." *The American Journal of Sociology* 104, no. 3 (1998): 597–641.

Scott, Nina. "La comida como signo: Los encuentros culinarios de América." In *Conquista y comida: Consecuencias del encuentro de dos mundos*, edited by Janet Long, 145–54. Mexico City: Universidad Nacional Autónoma de México, Instituto de Investigaciones Históricas, 1996.

———. "Measuring Ingredients: Food and Domesticity in Mexican Casta Paintings." *Gastronomica* 5, no. 1 (2005): 70–79.

———. "Rigoberta Menchú and the Politics of Food," *ReVista Harvard Review of*

Latin America, Spring 2021, https://archive.revista.drclas.harvard.edu/book/rigoberta-mench%C3%BA-and-politics-food.
Tobin, Ronald. "Thought for Food: Literature and Gastronomy." Talk delivered at UC Santa Barbara in November 2008. https://www.uctv.tv/shows/Thought-for-Food-Literature-and-Gastronomy-16255.

Chapter 1: Food, Power, and Discursive Resistance in Tahuantinsuyu and the Colonial Andes

Brading, D. A. "The Incas and the Renaissance: The Royal Commentaries of the Inca Garcilaso de la Vega." *Journal of Latin American Studies* 18, no. 1 (1986): 1–23.
Castro-Klarén, Sara. "Dancing and the Sacred in the Andes: From Taqui-Oncoy to Rasu-Ñiti." In *New World Encounters*, edited by Stephen Greenblatt, 159–76. Berkeley: University of California Press, 1993.
Cieza de León, Pedro. *Crónica del Perú: el señorío de los Incas*. Edited by Franklin Pease. 1550. Reprint, Caracas: Biblioteca Ayacucho, 2005.
Covarrubias Orozco, Sebastián de. *Tesoro de la lengua castellana, o española*. Madrid: Imprenta Luís Sánchez, 1611. http://fondosdigitales.us.es/fondos/libros/765/16/tesoro-de-la-lengua-castellana-o-espanola/.
Earle, Rebecca. *The Body of the Conquistador: Food, Race and the Colonial Experience in Spanish America*. Cambridge: Cambridge University Press, 2012.
Garcilaso de la Vega, El Inca. *Comentarios reales*. 1609. Reprint, Mexico City: Porrúa, 1998.
González Echevarría, Roberto. *Celestina's Brood: Continuities of the Baroque in Spanish and Latin American Literature*. Durham, NC: Duke University Press. 1993.
Gose, Peter. *Invaders as Ancestors: On the Intercultural Making and Unmaking of Spanish Colonialism in the Andes*. Toronto: University of Toronto Press, 2008.
———. "The State as a Chosen Woman: Brideservice and the Feeding of Tributaries in the Inka Empire." *American Anthropologist* 102, no. 1 (2000): 84–97.
Guaman Poma de Ayala, Felipe. *The First New Chronicle and Good Government: On the History of the World and the Incas up to 1615*. Translated by Roland Hamilton. Austin: University of Texas Press, 2009.
———. *El primer nueva corónica y buen gobierno*. Edited by John Murra and Rolena Adorno. Translated by J. L. Urioste. 3 vols. Mexico City: Siglo XXI, 1980. First published in 1615.
Jiménez de la Espada, Marcos. *Relaciones geográficas de Indias: Perú, 1577–1586*. Vol. 1. Edited by José Urbano Martínez Carreras. Madrid: Atlas, 1965.
Krögel, Alison. *Food, Power, and Resistance in the Andes*. Lanham, MD: Lexington Books, 2011.
Kubler, George. "The Quechua in the Colonial World." In *Handbook of South American Indians: The Andean Civilizations*, edited by J. H. Steward, 2:331–410. Washington, DC: Smithsonian Institution, 1946.
Mannheim, Bruce. *The Language of the Inka since the European Invasion*. Austin: University of Texas Press, 1991.
Mazzotti, José Antonio. *Coros mestizos del Inca Garcilaso: resonancias andinas*. Lima: Fondo de Cultura Económica, 1996.

Murra, John. *La organización económica del estado Inca*. Mexico City: Siglo XXI, 1983.
Ortega, Julio. "Discourse of Abundance." Translated by Nicolás Wey Gómez. *American Literary History* 4, no. 3 (1992): 369–85.
———. "Guaman Poma y el discurso de los alimentos." In *Reflexiones lingüísticas y literarias: Literatura, II*, edited by Rafael Olea Franco, James Valender, and Rebeca Barriga Villanueva, 139–52. Mexico City: Centro de Estudios Lingüística y Literatura, Colegio de México, 1992.
———. "Leer y describir: el Inca Garcilaso y el sujeto de la abundancia." In *El hombre y los Andes: homenaje a Franklin Pease G.Y.*, edited Javier Flores Espinoza and Rafael Varón Gabai, 1:397–408. Lima: Pontificia Universidad Católica del Perú Fondo Editorial, 2000.
———. *Transatlantic Translations: Dialogues in Latin American Literature*. London: Reaktion Books, 2006.
Ramírez, Susan Elizabeth. *To Feed and Be Fed: The Cosmological Bases of Authority and Identity in the Andes*. Redwood City, CA: Stanford University Press, 2005.
Silverblatt, Irene. "Imperial Dilemmas, the Politics of Kinship, and Inca Reconstructions of History." *Comparative Studies in Society and History* 30, no. 1 (1988): 83–102.
———. *Moon, Sun and Witches: Gender Ideologies and Class in Inca and Colonial Peru*. Princeton, NJ: Princeton University Press, 1987.
Socolow, Susan Migden. *The Women of Colonial Latin America*. New York: Cambridge University Press, 2000.
Spalding, Karen. *Huarochirí: An Andean Society under Inca and Spanish Rule*. Redwood City, CA: Stanford University Press, 1984.
Stern, Stephen J. "The Variety and Ambiguity of Native Andean Intervention in Markets." In *Ethnicity, Markets, and Migration in the Andes: At the Crossroads of History and Anthropology*, edited by Brooke Larson and Olivia Harris, 73–100. Durham, NC: Duke University Press, 1995.
Wachtel, Nathan. *The Vision of the Vanquished: The Spanish Conquest of Peru through Indian Eyes, 1530–1570*. Translated by Ben Reynolds and Siân Reynolds. New York: Harper and Row, 1977.
Zamora, Margarita. *Language, Authority, and Indigenous History in the Comentarios reales de los Incas*. New York: Cambridge University Press, 1988.

Chapter 2: The Potato

Arguedas, José María. "Huk Doctorkunaman Qayay." In *Temblar/Katatay*, 50–57. Lima: Instituto Nacional de Cultura, 1972.
Arnold, Denise Y., and Juan de Dios Yapita, eds. *Madre melliza y sus crías/ Ispall Mama wawampi: Antología de la papa*. La Paz, Bolivia: Hisbol/ILCA, 1996.
Asociación de Defensa y Desarrollo de las Comunidades Andinas del Perú and the Instituto de Extensión Agrícola de la Universidad de Hohenheim de Alemania. *Taller Campesino sobre la papa: Costumbres y perspectivas, Lima, 4–9 de septiembre de 1989*. Lima: [1989?].
Brush, Stephen B., Heath J. Carney, and Zózimo Huamán. "Dynamics of Andean Potato Agriculture." *Economic Botany* 35, no. 1 (1981): 70–88.
Carroll, Amy Sara. "From *Papapapá* to *Sleep Dealer*: Alex Rivera's Undocumentary

Poetics." In *Political Documentary Cinema in Latin America*, edited by Antonio Traverso and Kristi Wilson, 211–27. New York: Routledge, 2016.

Castellanos, Juan de. *Historia del Nuevo Reino de Granada*. Edited by Antonio Paz y Mélia. Vol. 1. Madrid: Imp. A. Pérez Dubrull, 1886. First published in 1589.

Cieza de León, Pedro de. *Primera parte de la chronica del Perú*, ch. XL. Antwerp, Belgium: Editorial Juan Steelsio, 1554.

Clayton, Michelle. *Poetry in Pieces: César Vallejo and Lyric Modernity*. Berkeley: University of California Press, 2011.

Cobo, Bernabé. *Historia del nuevo mundo*. Edited by Marcos Jiménez de la Espada. Vol. 1. Seville, Spain: Imprenta de E. Rasco, 1890. First published in 1652.

Cruz Ch'uktaya, Maxmiliano. "Papa tarpuy." In *La sangre de los cerros / Urcukunapayawarnin: Antología de la poesía quechua que se canta en el Perú*, edited by Rodrigo Montoya, Eduardo Montoya, and Luis Montoya, 63–64. Lima: Centro Peruano de Estudios Sociales; Mosca Azul; Universidad Nacional Mayor de San Marcos, 1987.

Doutriaux, Miriam. "Power, Ideology and Ritual: The Practice of Agriculture in the Inca Empire." *Kroeber Anthropological Society Papers* 85 (2001): 91–108.

Earle, Rebecca. *The Body of the Conquistador: Food, Race and the Colonial Experience in Spanish America*. Cambridge: Cambridge University Press, 2012.

———. *Potato*. New York: Bloomsbury Publishing, 2019.

Franco, Jean. *César Vallejo: The Dialectics of Poetry and Silence*. Cambridge: Cambridge University Press, 1976.

Garcilaso de la Vega, El Inca. *Comentarios reales de los Incas*. Edited by Aurelio Miró Quesada. 2 Vols. Caracas: Fundación Biblioteca Ayacucho, 1985. First published in 1609.

Gutiérrez, Raymundo, and César Valencia, eds. *Las papas nativas de Canchis: un catálogo de biodiversidad*. Lima: Servicios Gráficos JMD, 2010.

Guaman Poma de Ayala, Felipe. *El primer nueva corónica y buen gobierno*. Edited by John V. Murra and Rolena Adorno. Translated by Jorge L. Urioste. 2001. http://kb.dk./permalink/2006/poma/info/en/frontpage.htm. First published in 1615.

Harrison, Regina. *Signs, Songs, and Memory in the Andes: Translating Quechua Language and Culture*. Austin: University of Texas Press, 1989.

Hawkes, J. G. "On the Origin and Meaning of South American Indian Potato Names." *Linnean Society of London Botanical Journal* 53 (1947): 205–50.

———. *The Potato: Evolution, Biodiversity and Genetic Resources*. Washington, DC: Smithsonian Institution Press, 1990.

Hawkes, J. G., and J. Francisco-Ortega. "The Early History of the Potato in Europe." *Euphytica* 70 (1993): 1–7.

Kinder, David H., Karen R. Adams, and Harry J. Wilson. "*Solanum Jamesii*: Evidence of Cultivation of Wild Potato Tubers by Ancestral Puebloan Groups." *Journal of Ethnobiology* 37, no. 2 (2017): 218–40.

Llosa, Claudia, dir. *La teta asustada* (The Milk of Sorrow). 2009; Lima: Olive Films, 2010. DVD.

Marks, Laura U. *The Skin of the Film: Intercultural Cinema, Embodiment, and the Senses*. Durham, NC: Duke University Press, 2000.

Mitre, Eduardo. "La papa." In *La luz del regreso*. La Paz, Bolivia: Servicio Gráfico Quipus, 1999.

Murra, John V. "Rite and Crop in the Inca State." In *Culture and History: Essays in Honor of Paul Radin*, edited by Stanley Diamond, 393–408. New York: Columbia University Press, 1960.
Neruda, Pablo. "A la papa." In *Obras completas*, 1:1299. Buenos Aires: Losada, 1967.
Ortega, Julio. "Las papas." Translated by Regina Harrison. *The Boston Globe Magazine*, February 1988. Reprinted in *Global Cultures: A Transnational Short Fiction Reader*. Edited by Elizabeth Young-Bruehl, 30–34. Middleton, CT: Wesleyan University Press, 1994.
Pagden, Anthony. *The Fall of Natural Man: The American Indian and the Origins of Comparative Ethnography*. Cambridge: Cambridge University Press, 1982.
Reader, John. *Potato: A History of the Propitious Esculent*. New Haven, CT: Yale University Press, 2009.
Rivera, Alex, dir. *Papapapá*. 1995; United States: SubCine, 1997. DVD.
Rojas, Adriana. "Mother of Pearl, Song and Potatoes: Cultivating Resilience in Claudia Llosa's *La teta asustada/Milk of Sorrow* (2009)." *Studies in Spanish & Latin American Cinemas*, 14, no. 3 (2017): 297–314.
Rowe, John Howland. "Eleven Inca Prayers from the Zithua Ritual." *Kroeber Anthropological Society Papers*, nos. 8–9 (1953): 82–99.
Salaman, Radcliffe N. *The History and Social Influence of the Potato*. 1949. Reprint, Cambridge: Cambridge University Press, 1985.
Sauer, Carl O. *Seeds, Spades, Hearths, and Herds*. 1952. Reprint, Cambridge, MA: MIT Press, 1975.
Smith, Andrew F. *Potato: A Global History*. London: Reaktion Books, 2011.
Spooner, David. "Roadmaps to the Origins of the Potato." In *International Year of the Potato 2008: New Light on a Hidden Treasure*, 115–16. Rome: Food and Agriculture Association of the United Nations, 2008.
The Huarochirí Manuscript: A Testament of Ancient and Colonial Andean Religion. Translated by Frank Salomon and Jorge L. Urioste. Austin: University of Texas Press, 1991.
Vallejo, César. "Telúrica y magnética" from *Poemas humanos*. In *Obra poética completa*, edited by Enrique Ballón Aguirre, 135–36. Caracas: Fundación Biblioteca Ayacucho, 1985.
Velerio-Holguín, Fernando. "Pilgrimage and Gastronomy." In *Gabriel García Márquez in Retrospect: A Collection*. Edited by Gene H. Bell-Villada, 147–64. Lanham, MD: Lexington Books, 2016.
Vich, Cynthia. "De estetizaciones y viejos exotismos: apuntes en torno a *La teta asustada* de Claudia Llosa." *Revista de Crítica Literaria Latinoamericana* 40, no. 80 (2014): 333–44.
Zuckerman, Larry. *The Potato: How the Humble Spud Rescued the World*. Boston: Faber and Faber, 1998.

Chapter 3: The Culinary World of Sor Juana Inés de la Cruz

Asbaje y Ramírez de Santillana, Juana Inés de. *Obras completas*. Mexico City: Porrúa, 2018.
Carmagnani, Marcello. "La organización de los espacios americanos en la monarquía española, siglos XVI-XVIII." In *Las Indias Occidentales. Procesos de*

incorporación territorial a las Monarquías Ibéricas. Siglos XVI a XVIII, 333–57. Mexico City: Red Columnaria, Colegio de México, 2012.

Corona Ortega, Diana Salomé. *Gastronomía novohispana: un enfoque filológico*. Mexico City: Universidad Nacional Autónoma de México, 2011.

Curiel Monteagudo, José Luis. *Virreyes y virreinas golosos de la Nueva España*. Mexico City: Porrúa, 2004.

De la Cruz, Sor Juana Inés. *Obras completas. Comedias, sainetes y prosa*. Edited by Alfonso G. Salceda. Mexico City: Fondo de Cultura Económica; Instituto Mexiquense de Cultura, 1994.

———. "Answer by the poet to the most illustrious Sister Filotea de la Cruz." Translation by William Little, 2008. https://docplayer.net/34355203-Answer-by-the-poet-to-the-most-illustrious-sister-filotea-de-la-cruz-1-by-sor-juana-ines-de-la-cruz-1691.html.

Enriqueta, Quiróz. "Comer en Nueva España. Privilegios y pesares de la sociedad en el siglo XVIII." *Historia y Memoria*, no. 8 (2014): 19–58.

Garza Marcué, Rosa María, and Cecilia Vázquez Ahumada. *Mujeres construyendo un mundo: las recetas del convento de Santa Mónica en Puebla*. Puebla, Mexico: Instituto Nacional de Antropología e Historia, Benemérita Universidad Autónoma de Puebla, 2017.

Gómez García, Lidia E. "La fundación de la Nobilísima Ciudad Puebla de los Ángeles." In *La Puebla de los Ángeles en el Virreinato*, edited by Sigrid María Louvier Nava, 12–27. Puebla, Mexico: UPAEP; Fundación Amparo IAP, 2016.

Lavín, Mónica. *Sor Juana en la cocina*. Mexico City: Clío, 2000.

Lavín, Mónica, and Ana Benítez Muro. *Sor Juana en la cocina*. Mexico City: Grijalbo, 2010.

Lavrin, Asunción. "Santa Teresa en los conventos de monjas de Nueva España." *Hispania sacra* 67, no. 136 (2015): 505–29.

Loreto López, Rosalva. "Prácticas alimenticias en los conventos de mujeres en la Puebla del siglo XVIII." In *Conquista y comida: Consecuencias del encuentro de dos mundos*, edited by Janet Long, 481–503. Mexico City: Universidad Nacional Autónoma de México, 2003.

Loreto López, Rosalva, and Ana Luisa Benítez Muro. "Un bocado para los ángeles: la cocina en los conventos." In *Cocina Virreinal Novohispana II*. Mexico City: Clío, 2000.

Montanari, Massimo. *El hambre y la abundancia. Historia y cultura de la alimentación en Europa*. Barcelona: Crítica, 1993.

Morino, Angelo. *El libro de cocina de Sor Juana Inés de la Cruz*. Translated by Juan Pablo Roa. Bogotá: Norma, 2001.

Muriel, Josefina. *Conventos de monjas en la Nueva España*. Mexico City: Editorial Santiago, 1946.

———. *Cultura femenina novohispana*. Mexico City: Universidad Nacional Autónoma de México, Instituto de Investigaciones Históricas, 2000.

———. "Presentación." In *Libro de cocina. Convento de San Jerónimo*, edited by Josefina Muriel and Guadalupe Pérez de San Vicente, 7–11. Toluca, Mexico: Instituto Mexiquense de Cultura, 1996.

Paz, Octavio. *Sor Juana Inés de la Cruz o las trampas de la fe*. Mexico City: Seix Barral, 2005.

Pérez de San Vicente, Guadalupe. "Sor Juana y su libro de cocina." In *Memoria del Coloquio Internacional Sor Juana Inés de la Cruz y el pensamiento novohispano*, 341–49. Toluca, Mexico: Instituto Mexiquense de Cultura; Universidad Autónoma del Estado de México, 1995.

Quiroz Muñoz, Enriqueta. "Del mercado a la cocina." In *Historia de la vida cotidiana en México*, edited by Pilar Gonzalbo Aizpuru. Vol. 3, *El siglo XVIII: entre tradición y cambio*, 17–44. Mexico City: Colegio de México; Fondo de Cultura Económica, 2005.

Rubial García, Antonio. "Las órdenes mendicantes evangelizadoras en Nueva España y sus cambios estructurales durante los siglos virreinales." *Históricas Digital Serie Novohispana* 83 (2012): 215–36.

Spell, Lota M. *Cuatro documentos relativos a Sor Juana*. Mexico City: Imprenta Universitaria, 1947.

Vera Báez, Paola Jeannete. "Cultura gastronómica mexicana." In *El Arca del Gusto México. Productos, saberes e historias del patrimonio gastronómico*, edited by Paola Jeannete Vera Báez, Guadalupe Xóchitl Malda Barrera, and Dauro Mattia Zocchi. Puebla, Mexico: Slow Food Editore; Universidad Popular Autónoma del Estado de Puebla; Universidad Autónoma de Querétaro, 2018.

———. "Tradición cultural gastronómica de Puebla." In *Encuentro con la Historia. Puebla a través de los siglos*, edited by Marco Antonio Rojas Flores, Pedro Ángel Palou Pérez, and Víctor Bacre Parra, 4:367–86. Puebla, Mexico: Investigaciones y Publicaciones A.C., 2015.

———. "Viandas para el alma y ayunos para el cuerpo: Del refectorio y la olla de comunidad." In *Los conventos del siglo XVI de Puebla y Morelos*, edited by Francisco Javier Pizarro Gómez, José Antonio Quintana Fernández, Rosa Perales Piqueres, and María Pía Benítez de Unánue, 191–203. Puebla, Mexico: Universidad Popular Autónoma del Estado de Puebla, 2018.

Chapter 4: Immigrants, Elites, and Identities

Arona, Juan de. *La inmigración en el Perú, monografía histórico-crítica*. Lima: Imprenta del Universo de C. Prince, 1891. https://hdl.handle.net/2027/uc1.b3455103.

"El banquete de la colonia suiza." *Actualidades*. September 21, 1907. https://hdl.handle.net/2027/coo.31924100624653.

Bardales, Juan José. "Comandante Jorge Broggi." *La Bomba Lima* (blog). August 6, 2015. https://labombalima.blogspot.com/2015/08/jorge-broggi.html.

Bonfiglio, Giovanni. *Los italianos en la sociedad peruana: una visión histórica*. 2nd. ed. Lima: Saywa, 1994.

———. "Migración y empresarialidad en el Perú." http://usmp.edu.pe/idp/wp-content/uploads/2015/11/migracin_y_empresarialidad_para-web.pdf.

———. *La presencia europea en el Perú*. Lima: Fondo Editorial del Congreso del Perú, 2001.

Bunle, Henri. "Migratory Movements between France and Foreign Lands." In *Internal Migrations, Volume II: Interpretations*, edited by Walter F. Willcox, 201–36. New York: National Bureau of Economic Research, 1931. http://www.nber.org/chapters/c5110.

"Five O'Clock Tea." *El Mundo Ilustrado*, July 30, 1904.
Fuentes, Manuel Atanasio. *Guía de domicilio de Lima para el año de 1864*. Lima: imprenta del autor, 1863. https://catalog.hathitrust.org/Record/009833590.
Goebel, Michael. "Reconceptualizing Diasporas and National Identities in Latin America and the Caribbean, 1850–1950." In *Immigration and National Identities in Latin America*, edited by Nicola Foote and Michael Goebel, 1–27. Gainesville: University Press of Florida, 2014.
Juárez López, José Luis. *Engranaje culinario: La cocina mexicana en el siglo XIX*. Mexico City: Conaculta, 2012.
Martínez Carreño, Aída. *Mesa y cocina en el siglo XIX: Colombia*. Bogotá: Ministerio de Cultura, 1990.
Matto de Turner, Clorinda. *Herencia (novela peruana)*. Edited by Mary Berg. Buenos Aires: Stock Cero, 2006.
Molero Denegri, Sofia Indira. "La construcción sociocultural de la gastronomía china en Lima: siglo XIX-XXI." PhD diss., Universidad Nacional Mayor de San Marcos, 2010.
El Mundo Ilustrado, July 31, 1904.
"Los dos claveles." *El Mundo Ilustrado*, September 18, 1904.
Niembro Gaona, María, and Rodolfo Téllez Cuevas. "Historia y mestizaje de México a través de su gastronomía." *Culinaria* 4 (July–December 2012), 30–58. http://web.uaemex.mx/Culinaria/culinaria_historia/cuatro_ne/pdfs/historia_del_mestizaje.pdf.
Novo, Salvador. *Cocina mexicana. Historia gastronómica de la ciudad de México*. Mexico City: Porrúa, 2010.
Orlove, Benjamin, ed. *The Allure of the Foreign: Imported Goods in Postcolonial Latin America*. Ann Arbor: University of Michigan Press, 1997.
Orlove, Benjamin, and Arnold J. Bauer. "Giving Importance to Imports." In *The Allure of the Foreign: Imported Goods in Postcolonial Latin America*, edited by Benjamin Orlove, 1–29. Ann Arbor: University of Michigan Pres, 1997.
Palma, Clemente. "El porvenir de las razas en el Peru." Bachelor's thesis, Universidad Nacional Mayor de San Marcos, 1897. http://cybertesis.unmsm.edu.pe/handle/20.500.12672/338.
Pérez Siller, Javier, and Chantai Cramaussel, eds. *México Francia: Memoria de una sensibilidad común; siglos XIX–XX*. Vol. 2. Mexico City: Centro de Estudios Mexicanos y Centroamericanos, 1993. http://doi.org/10.4000/books.cemca.836.
Pilcher, Jeffrey M. *¡Que vivan los tamales! Food and the Making of Mexican Identity*. Albuquerque: University of New Mexico Press, 1998.
Prantl, Adolfo, and José L. Groso. *La ciudad de México: Novísima guía universal de la capital de la República de México*. Mexico City: J. Buxó y Cia, 1901. http://books.google.com/books?id=EvhKAAAAMAAJ&oe=UTF-8.
Prieto, Guillermo. *Memorias de mis tiempos*. Mexico City: Imprenta de la Viuda de Bouret, 1906.
Restrepo, Cecilia M. *La alimentación en la vida cotidiana del Colegio Mayor de Nuestra Señora del Rosario 1776–1900*. Bogotá: Editorial Universidad del Rosario, 2009.
Sánchez, Luis Alberto. *Valdelomar: su tiempo y su obra*. Lima: Inpropesa, 1987.
"Servicio de mesa." *El Mundo Ilustrado*, July 30, 1904.

Torres Bautista, Mariano Enrique. "Vivir a la francesa en México. La familia Maurer y su establecimiento en el México anterior al Porfiriato." In *Extraños en tierra ajena: migración, alteridad e identidad, siglos XIX, XX y XXI*, edited by Raquel Barceló Quintal, 55–73. Mexico City: Plaza y Valdés, 2009.

Uribe, María Susana Victoria. "La minuta del día: Los tiempos de comida de la elite capitalina a principios del siglo XX." *Historia y grafía* 34 (January–June 2010). http://www.scielo.org.mx/scielo.php?script=sci_arttext&pid=S1405-09272010000100002.

Chapter 5: Native Food and Male Emotions

Ahmed, Sara. *The Cultural Politics of Emotion*. Edinburgh: Edinburgh University Press, 2014.

Ancízar, Manuel. *Peregrinación de Alpha por las provincias del Norte*. Bogotá: Imprenta de Echeverria Hermanos, 1853.

Appelbaum, Nancy. *Mapping the Country of Regions: The Chorographic Commission of Nineteenth-Century Colombia*. Chapel Hill: University of North Carolina Press, 2016.

Boussingault, Jean-Baptiste. *Memorias del explorador francés Jean-Baptiste Boussingault, que describe los momentos más relevantes de su vida y hace mención de sus logros como explorador y científico*. Bogotá: Banco de la República, 1985.

Earle, Rebecca. *The Body of the Conquistador: Food, Race and the Colonial Experience in Spanish America, 1492–1700*. Cambridge: Cambridge University Press, 2014.

Holton, Isaac F. *New Granada: Twenty Months in the Andes*. New York: Harper & Brothers, 1857.

Isaács, Jorge. *María*. 1866. Reprint, Madrid: Sociedad General Española de Librería, 1983.

Lopez Rodriguez, Mercedes. *Blancura y otras ficciones raciales en los Andes Colombianos del siglo XIX*. Madrid: Iberoamericana Veurvert, 2019.

Peluffo, Ana. *En clave emocional. Cultura y afecto en América Latina*. Buenos Aires: Prometeo Libros, 2016.

Reclus, Elisée. *Viaje a la Sierra Nevada de Santa Marta*. Bogotá: Biblioteca Popular de la Cultura, 1992.

Samper, José María. *Filosofía en cartera: colección de pensamientos sobre religión, moral, filosofía, ciencias sociales, historia, literatura, poesía, bellas artes, caracteres, viajes, etc. en prosa y en verso*. Bogotá: Imprenta de La Luz, 1887.

Sánchez, Efraín. *Ramón Torres Méndez, pintor de la Nueva Granada*. Bogotá: Fondo Cultural Cafetero, 1987.

Smith, Mark. *How Race Is Made: Slavery, Segregation, and the Senses*. Chapel Hill: University of North Carolina Press, 2006.

Tompkins, Kyla Wazana. *Racial Indigestion: Eating Bodies in the 19th Century*. New York: New York University Press, 2012.

Villa-Flores, Javier, and Sonya Andrea Lipsett-Rivera. *Emotions and Daily Life in Colonial Mexico*. Albuquerque: University of New Mexico Press, 2014.

Chapter 6: A Matter of Taste

Austin, Elisabeth. "Reading and Writing Juana Manuela Gorriti's *Cocina Ecléctica*: Modeling Multiplicity in Nineteenth-Century Domestic Narrative." *Arizona Journal of Hispanic Cultural Studies* 12, no. 1 (2009): 31–44.

Arcondo, Aníbal. *Historia de la alimentación en Argentina. Desde los orígenes hasta 1920*. Córdoba, Argentina: Ferreyra Editor, 2002.

Belasco, Warren. *Food: The Key Concepts*. Oxford: Berg Publishers, 2008.

Biltekoff, Charlotte. *Eating Right in America: The Cultural Politics of Food and Health*. Durham, NC: Duke University Press, 2013.

Bourdieu, Pierre. *La distinción: criterios y bases sociales del gusto*. Barcelona: Taurus, 1998.

Colombi, Beatriz. *Viaje Intelectual: Migraciones y desplazamientos en América Latina, 1880–1915*. Rosario, Argentina: Beatriz Viterbo, 2004.

Elias, Norbert. *The Civilizing Process*. Oxford: Basil Blackwell, 1978.

Elichondo, Margarita. *La comida criolla: memorias y recetas*. Buenos Aires: Ediciones del Sol, 2008.

Gorriti, Juana Manuela. *Cocina ecléctica*. Buenos Aires: Lajouane, 1890.

González Stephan, Beatriz. "Modernización y disciplinamiento. La formación del ciudadano: del espacio público y privado." In *Esplendores y miserias del siglo XIX: Cultura y sociedad en América Latina*, edited by Beatriz González Stephan, 431–56. Caracas: Monte Ávila, 1994.

Jagoe, Eva-Lynn. "Familial Triangles: Eduarda Mansilla, Domingo Sarmiento, and Lucio Mansilla." *Revista Canadiense de Estudios Hispánicos* 29, no. 3 (Spring 2005): 507–24.

Jáuregui, Carlos. *Canibalia: Canibalismo, calibanismo, antropofagia cultural y consumo en América Latina*. Madrid: Iberoamericana, 2008.

Lojo, María Rosa. Introduction to *Recuerdos de viaje*, by Eduarda Mansilla, 11–37. Córdoba, Argentina: Buena Vista, 2011.

Longone, Jan. "From the Kitchen." *The American Magazine and Historical Chronicle* 3–4 (1987): 34–43.

Mansilla, Eduarda. *Recuerdos de viaje*. Buenos Aires: Stockcero, 2006.

Masiello, Francine. "Lost in Translation: Eduarda Mansilla de García on Politics, Gender, and War." In *Representing the Spanish American Essay: Women Writers of the 19th and 20th Centuries*, edited by Doris Meyer, 68–79. Austin: University of Texas Press, 1995.

Martí, José. "Coney Island." In *En los Estados Unidos. Escenas norteamericanas*. Alicante, Spain: Biblioteca Virtual Miguel de Cervantes. http://www.cervantesvirtual.com/obra-visor/en-los-estados-unidos-escenas-norteamericanas--0/html/fef234ce-82b1-11df-acc7-002185ce6064_11.htm.

———. José Martí to Manuel Mercado, May 18, 1895. In *Obras Completas*. 8:182. Havana: Editorial Nacional de Cuba, 1965.

Mennell, Stephen. *All Manners of Food: Eating and Taste in England and France from the Middle Ages to the Present*. Oxford: Basil Blackwell, 1987.

Miseres, Vanesa. *Mujeres en tránsito: Viaje, identidad y escritura en Sudamérica (1830–1910)*. Chapel Hill: North Carolina Studies in the Romance Languages and Literatures, 2017.

Peluffo, Ana. *En clave emocional: cultura y afecto en América Latina*. Buenos Aires: Prometeo, 2016.
Perry, Charles. "As American As Roasted Oysters." *Los Angeles Times*, December 26, 2011. http://articles.latimes.com/2001/dec/26/food/fo-oyster26.
Pilcher, Jeffrey M. "Eating à la Criolla: Global and Local Foods in Argentina, Cuba, and Mexico." *IdeAs* 3 (2012): 1–18.
Pratt, Mary Louise. *Imperial Eyes: Travel Writing and Transculturation*. London: Routledge, 2017.
Rodó, José Enrique. *Ariel. Motivos de Proteo*. Caracas: Biblioteca Ayacucho, 1976.
Royte, Elizabeth. "The Mollusk that Made Manhattan." *The New York Times*, March 5, 2006. https://www.nytimes.com/2006/03/05/books/review/the-mollusk-that-made-manhattan.html.
Sarmiento, Domingo. *Viajes*. Madrid: Fondo de Cultura Económica, 1993.
Scatena Franco, Stella Maris. *Peregrinas de outrora. Viajantes latino-americanas no século XIX*. Florianópolis, Brazil: Editora Mulheres, 2008.
Spicer-Escalante, Pablo. Introduction to *Recuerdos de viaje*, by Eduarda Mansilla, vii–xxiii. Buenos Aires: Stockcero, 2006.
Stein, Jordan. "How an Old Sherry Drink Defined an Era of American History." *Saveur*, December 29, 2015. https://www.saveur.com/sherry-cobblerdrink-of-an-era.
Szurmuk, Mónica. *Women in Argentina: Early Travel Narratives*. Gainesville: University Press of Florida, 2000.
Urraca, Beatriz. "'Quien a Yaqueeland se encamina . . .': The United States and Nineteenth-Century Argentine Imagination." *Ciberletras* 1, no. 2 (2008). http://www.lehman.cuny.edu/ciberletras/v01n02/Urraca.htm.
Viñas, David. *De Sarmiento a Dios. Viajeros argentinos a USA*. Buenos Aires: Sudamericana, 1998.

Chapter 7: Homemaking in 1950s Mexico

Aguilar-Rodríguez, Sandra. "Industrias del hogar: mujeres, raza y moral en el México posrevolucionario." *Revista de Historia Iberoamericana* 9, no. 1 (2016).
Anaya, Anita. "Por una humanidad feliz." In *Almanaque Dulce*. Mexico City: Unión Nacional de Productores de Azúcar, 1952.
Arendt, Hannah. "Race-Thinking before Racism." *The Review of Politics* 6, no. 1 (1944): 36–73.
Buck, Sarah A. "The Meaning of the Women's Vote in Mexico 1917–1953." In *The Women's Revolution in Mexico, 1910–1953*, edited by Stephanie Mitchell and Patience A. Schell, 79–98. Lanham, MD: Rowman & Littlefield, 2007.
Castellanos Guerrero, Alicia, Jorge Gómez Izquierdo, and Francisco Pineda. "Racist Discourse in Mexico." In *Racism and Discourse in Latin America*, edited by Teun A. Van Dijk, 217–58. Plymouth, UK: Lexington Books, 2009.
Elias, Megan. *Stir It Up: Home Economics in American Culture*. Philadelphia: University of Pennsylvania Press, 2010.
"Editorial." *Mujeres de Hogar*, August 1951.
"Entre nosotras y en voz baja." *Mujeres de Hogar*, August 1950.

French-Fuller, Katharine. "Gendered Invisibility, Respectable Cleanliness: The Impact of the Washing Machine on Daily Living in Post-1950 Santiago, Chile." *Journal of Women's History* 18, no. 4 (2006): 79–100.

Kamminga, Harmke, and Andrew Cunningham. *The Science and Culture of Nutrition, 1840–1940*. Clio Medica 32. Amsterdam: Rodopi, 1995.

Kiki. "Recetario práctico de cocina." *Mujeres de Hogar*, August 1950.

Madame 1, no. 1 (September 1950).

Meyer, Lorenzo. "La encrucijada." In *Historia general de México*, edited by Daniel Cosío Villegas. Mexico City: Colegio de México, 1998.

Moreno, Julio. *Yankee Don't Go Home! Mexican Nationalism, American Business Culture, and the Shaping of Modern Mexico, 1920–1950*. Chapel Hill: University of North Carolina Press, 2003.

Navarrete, Federico. *Las relaciones inter-étnicas en México*. Mexico City: Universidad Nacional Autónoma de México, 2004.

Pilcher, Jeffrey M. "Josefina Velázquez De León: Apostle of the Enchilada." In *The Human Tradition in Mexico*, edited by Jeffrey M. Pilcher, 137–48. Wilmington, DE: SR Books, 2003.

———. *¡Que vivan los Tamales! Food and the Making of Mexican Identity*. Albuquerque: University of New Mexico Press, 1998.

"Que sabe usted de IEM." *Mujeres de Hogar*, June 1951.

Schell, Patience A. *Church and State Education in Revolutionary Mexico City*. Tucson: University of Arizona Press, 2003.

Schwartz Cowan, Ruth. *More Work for Mother: The Ironies of Household from the Open Hearth to the Microwave*. New York: Basic Books, 1983.

Spencer, Herbert. *The Principles of Biology*. 2 vols. London: Williams and Norgate, 1864.

Stepan, Nancy Leys. *The Hour of Eugenics: Race, Gender, and Nation in Latin America*. Ithaca, NY: Cornell University Press, 1991.

Stern, Alexandra Minna. "From Mestizophilia to Biotypology: Racialization and Science in Mexico 1920–1960." In *Race and Nation in Modern Latin America*, edited by Nancy P. Appelbaum, Anne S. Macpherson, and Karin Alejandra Rosemblatt, 187–210. Chapel Hill: University of North Carolina Press, 2003.

Suárez y López Guazo, Laura Luz. *Eugenesia y racismo en México*. Mexico City: Universidad Nacional Autónoma de México, 2005.

Tuñón Pablos, Julia. *Women in Mexico: A Past Unveiled*. Austin: University of Texas Press, 1999.

Vaughan, Mary Kay. "Modernizing Patriarchy: State Policies, Rural Households, and Women in Mexico 1930–1940." In *Hidden Histories of Gender and the State in Latin America*, edited by Maxine Molyneux and Elizabeth Dore, 194–214. Durham, NC: Duke University Press, 2000.

———. *The State, Education, and Social Classes in Mexico, 1880–1928*. DeKalb: Northern Illinois University Press, 1982.

Vaughan, Mary Kay, and Heather Fowler-Salamini, eds. *Women of the Mexican Countryside, 1850–1990: Creating Spaces and Shaping Transitions*. Tucson: University of Arizona Press, 1994.

Chapter 8: Sense of Place and Gender in Rosario Castellanos's "Cooking Lesson"

Beauvoir, Simone de. *The Second Sex*. Translated by H. M. Parshley. New York: Vintage Books, 1989.

Castellanos, Rosario. "Lección de cocina." In *Álbum de familia*, 7–22. Mexico City: Joaquín Mortiz, 1971.

———. *A Rosario Castellanos Reader: An Anthology of Her Poetry, Short Fiction, Essays, and Drama*. Edited by Maureen Ahern. Translated by Maureen Ahern et al. Austin: University of Texas Press, 1988.

———. *El eterno femenino*. Mexico City: Fondo de Cultura Económica, 1975.

———. *The Eternal Feminine*. Translated by Diane E. Marting and Betty Tyree Osiek. In *A Rosario Castellanos Reader: An Anthology of Her Poetry, Short Fiction, Essays, and Drama*, 273–362. Austin: University of Texas Press, 1988.

Duncan, Nancy. *BodySpace: Destabilising Geographies of Gender and Sexuality*. New York: Routledge, 1996.

Fishburn, Evelyn. "'Dios anda en los pucheros': Feminist Openings in Some Late Stories by Rosario Castellanos." *Bulletin of Hispanic Studies* 72, no. 1 (January 1995): 97–110.

Foucault, Michel. "Of Other Spaces." Translated by Jay Miṣkowiec. *Diacritics* 16, no. 1 (Spring 1986): 22–27.

Genette, Gérard. *Narrative Discourse: An Essay in Method*. Ithaca, NY: Cornell University Press, 1980.

Gilbert, Sandra M., and Susan Gubar. *The Madwoman in the Attic: The Woman Writer and the Nineteenth Century Imagination*. New Haven, CT: Yale University Press, 2000.

Llanos Mardones, Bernardita. "Self-Portrait and Female Images in Rosario Castellanos." *Torre de Papel* 9, no. 3 (Fall 1999): 54–70.

Ludmer, Josefina. "Tretas del débil." In *La sartén por el mango: encuentro de escritoras latinoamericanas*, edited by Patricia Elena González and Eliana Ortega, 47–54. Río Piedras, Puerto Rico: Ediciones Huracán, 1984.

Massey, Doreen. *Space, Place and Gender*. Cambridge: Polity Press, 1994.

Mulvey, Laura. "Visual Pleasure and Narrative Cinema." *Media and Cultural Studies*, edited by Meenakshi Gigi Durham and Douglas M. Kellner, 342–52. Malden, MA: Blackwell Publishing, 2006.

Ozaryún, Kemy. "Beyond Histeria: 'Haute Cuisine' and 'Cooking Lesson' Writing as Production." In *Splintering Darkness: Latin American Women Writers in Search of Themselves*, edited by Lucía Guerra Cunningham, 87–110. Pittsburgh: Latin American Literary Review Press, 1990.

Paz, Octavio. *The Labyrinth of Solitude: Life and Thought in Mexico*. New York: Grove Press, 1961.

Porter, Susie. *From Angel to Office Worker: 1890–1950*. Lincoln: University of Nebraska Press, 2018.

Pitt-Rivers, Julian. "Postscript: The Place of Grace in Anthropology." In *Honor and Grace in Anthropology*, edited by J. G. Peristiany and Julian Pitt-Rivers, 215–46. Cambridge: Cambridge University Press, 1992.

Rimmon-Kenan, Shlomith. *Narrative Fiction: Contemporary Poetics*. London: Methuen, 1983.

Rodríguez, Ismael, dir. *Nosotros los pobres* (We the Poor). 1948; Mexico City: Películas Rodríguez y Cinematográfica Rodríguez, 2009. DVD.
Rose, Margaret. *Parody: Ancient, Modern, and Postmodern*. Cambridge: Cambridge University Press, 1993.
Showalter, Elaine. *The Female Malady: Women, Madness and English Culture, 1830–1980*. London: Virago, 1987.
Zeitz, Eileen M. "Técnica e ideología en 'Lección de cocina.'" In *Actas del VIII Congreso de la Asociación Internacional de Hispanistas II*, edited by David Kossoff, Ruth H. Kossoff, Geoffrey Ribbans, and José Amor y Vázquez, 765–71. Madrid: Istmo, 1986.

Chapter 9: Lemons, Oregano, Satisfaction, and Hopeless Melancholy

Alleyne, Mervyn. *The Construction and Representation of Race and Ethnicity in the Caribbean and the World*. Kingston, Jamaica: University of West Indies Press, 2002.
André, María Claudia. *Chicanas and Latin American Women Writers Exploring the Realm of the Kitchen as a Self-Empowering Site*. Lewiston, NY: Edwin Mellon Press, 2001.
Birmingham-Pokorny, Elba. "'The Page on Which Life Writes Itself': A Conversation with Mayra Santos Febres." In *Daughters of the Diaspora: Afra-Hispanic Writers*, edited by Miriam DeCosta-Willis, 451–61. Kingston, Jamaica: Ian Randle, 2003.
———. "Reclaiming the Female Body, Culture, and Identity in Mayra Santos Febres's 'Broken Strand.'" In *Daughters of the Diaspora: Afra-Hispanic Writers*, edited by Miriam DeCosta-Willis, 462–69. Kingston, Jamaica: Ian Randle, 2003.
Chiclana y González, Arleen. "The Body of Evidence: Body-Writing, the Text and Mayra Santos Febres' Illicit Bodies." In *Unveiling the Body in Hispanic Women's Literature*, edited by Renée Scott and Arleen Chiclana y González, 161–86. Lewiston, UK: Edwin Mellen Press, 2006.
Classen, Constance. "The Witch's Senses: Sensory Ideologies and Transgressive Femininities from the Renaissance to Modernity." In *Empire of the Senses*, edited by David Howes, 70–84. New York: Berg, 2005.
Classen, Constance, David Howes, and Anthony Synnott. *Aroma*. London: Routledge, 1994.
Corbin, Alain. *The Foul and the Fragrant*. Cambridge, MA: Harvard University Press, 1986.
Drobnick, Jim. Preface in *The Smell Culture Reader*, edited by Jim Drobnick, 13–17. New York: Berg, 2006.
Herz, Rachel. "I Know What I Like. Understanding Odor Preferences." In *The Smell Culture Reader*, edited by Jim Drobnick, 190–203. New York: Berg, 2006.
Mavor, Carol. "Odor di Femina. Though You May Not See Her, You Can Certainly Smell Her." In *The Smell Culture Reader*, edited by Jim Drobnick, 277–88. New York: Berg, 2006.
Mosby, Dorothy. "'The Erotic as Power': Sexual Agency and the Erotic in the Work of Luz Argentina Chiriboga and Mayra Santos Febres." *Cincinnati Romance Review* 30 (2011): 83–98.

Niebylski, Dianna. *Humoring Resistance: Laughter and the Excessive Body in Latin American Women's Fiction*. Albany: State University of New York Press, 2004.
Ortiz, María Inés. "La gastronomía como metáfora de la identidad en la literatura puertorriqueña del siglo XX." PhD diss., University of Cincinnati, 2007.
Pérez, Carmen. "'Marina y su olor' y 'Hebra rota': Lo maravilloso y lo mítico." *Exégesis* 15, no. 43 (2002): 59–64.
Porteous, J. Douglas. "Smellscape." In *The Smell Culture Reader*, edited by Jim Drobnick, 89–106. New York: Berg, 2006.
"Puerto Rico 2000: Resumen de características de la población y vivienda." Washington, DC: US Census Bureau, 2002. https://www.census.gov/prod/cen2000/phc-1-53-SPAN.pdf.
Rivera Villegas, Carmen. "La celebración de la identidad negra en 'Marina y su olor' de Mayra Santos Febres." *Espéculo* 27 (2004). http://www.ucm.es/info/especulo/numero27/marina.html.
Santos Febres, Mayra. "Marina y su olor." In *Pez de vidrio*, 41–50. Río Piedras, Puerto Rico: Huracán, 1996.
Scott, Renée. *What Is Eating Latin American Women Writers? Food, Weight, and Eating Disorders*. Amherst, NY: Cambria Press, 2009.
Smith, Mark. *How Race Is Made: Slavery, Segregation, and the Senses*. Chapel Hill: University of North Carolina Press, 2006.
West-Durán, Alan. "Puerto Rico: The Pleasures and Traumas of Race." *Centro Journal* 17, no. 1 (2005): 46–69. https://www.redalyc.org/pdf/377/37717103.pdf.
Watson, Lyall. *Jacobson's Organ and the Remarkable Nature of Smell*. New York: Plume, 2001.

Chapter 10: Exquisite Paradise

Abarca, Meredith. "Receta de una memoria sensorial para tamales: Eduardo Machado." In *Comidas Bastardas. Gastronomía, tradición e identidad en América Latina*, edited by Ángeles Mateo del Pino and Nieves Pascual Soler, 387–407. Santiago: Editorial Cuarto Propio, 2013.
Allende, Isabel. *Afrodita: cuentos, recetas y otros*. New York: HarperLibros, 1997.
Barthes, Roland. *S/Z: An Essay*. New York: Hill and Wang, 2000.
———. "Toward a Psychosociology of Contemporary Food Consumption." In *Food and Culture: A Reader*, edited by Carole Counihan and Penny Van Esterik, 28–35. New York: Routledge, 2008.
Blanqué, Andrea. *La piel dura*. Buenos Aires: Planeta, 1999.
Bourdieu, Pierre. *Distinction: A Social Critique of Judgement of Taste*. London: Routledge, 1986.
Caldo, Paula. "En la radio, en el libro y en la televisión, Petrona enseña a cocinar. La transmisión del saber culinario, Argentina (1928–1960)." *Edução Unisinos* 20, no. 3 (September–December 2016): 319–27.
———. "Leer, comprar y cocinar. Una aproximación a los aportes de los *recetarios* de cocina en el proceso de construcción de las mujeres amas de casa y consumidoras, Argentina 1880–1940." *Revista Sociedad y Economía* no. 24 (January–June 2013): 47–70.
———. "Pequeñas cocineras para grandes amas de casa . . . La propuesta pedagógica

de Ángel Bassi para las escuelas argentinas, 1914–1920." *Temas de Mujeres* 5, no. 5 (2009): 33–50.

———. "Recetas, ecónomas, marcas y publicidades: la educación de las mujeres cocineras de la sociedad de consumo (Argentina, 1920–1945)." *Arenal* 20, no. 1 (January–June 2013): 159–90.

Castellanos, Rosario. *Álbum de familia*. Mexico City: Joaquín Moritz, 2012.

Earle, Rebecca. "European Cuisine and the Columbian Exchange." *Food and History* 7, no. 1 (2010): 3–10.

———. *The Body of Conquistador: Food, Race, and the Colonial Experience in Spanish America, 1492–1700*. Cambridge: Cambridge University, 2012.

———. "Food, Colonialism and the Quantum of Happiness." *History Workshop Journal* 84 (October 2017): 170–93.

Esquivel, Laura. *Íntimas suculencias, tratado filosófico de la cocina*. Madrid: DeBolsillo, 2015.

Ferrero, Adrián. "Entrevista a Hebe Uhart." *Confluencia* 30, no. 2 (Spring 2015): 179–85.

Few, Martha. "Chocolate, Sex, and Disorderly Women in Late-Seventeenth and Early-Eighteenth Century Guatemala." *Ethnohistory* 52, no. 4 (2005): 673–87.

Gandulfo, Petrona C. de. *El libro de Doña Petrona. 1000 Recetas Culinarias por Petrona C. de Gandulfo*. Buenos Aires: Editorial Atlántida, 1944.

Gorodischer, Angélica, and Ana Sampaolesi, eds. *Locas por la cocina*. Buenos Aires: Biblos, 1997.

Korsmeyer, Carolyn. *El sentido del gusto. Comida, estética y filosofía*. Barcelona: Paidós, 2002.

Krögel, Alison. *Food, Power, and Resistance in the Andes: Exploring Quechua Verbal and Visual Narratives*. Plymouth, UK: Lexington Books, 2012.

Lévi-Strauss, Claude. "The Culinary Triangle." In *Food and Culture: A Reader*, edited by Carole Counihan and Penny Van Esterik, 40–47. New York: Routledge, 2008.

Mastretta, Ángeles. "La cocina de Marichu." *Nexos*, February 1, 1992. https://www.nexos.com.mx/?p=6435.

Mateo del Pino, Ángeles, and Nieves Pascual Soler, eds. *Comidas Bastardas. Gastronomía, tradición e identidad en América Latina*. Santiago: Editorial Cuarto Propio, 2013.

Maurette, Pablo. *El sentido olvidado. Ensayos sobre el tacto*. Buenos Aires: Mardulce, 2015.

Mercado, Tununa. "Antieros." In *Ocampo, Pizarnik, Shua y otras. Damas de letras. (Cuentos de escritoras argentinas del siglo XX)*, edited by María Moreno, 3–10. Buenos Aires: Libros Perfil, 1998.

Montecino Aguirre, Sonia. *La olla deleitosa*. Santiago: Catalonia, 2005.

Pérez, Inés. *El hogar tecnificado. Familias, género y vida cotidiana 1940–1970*. Buenos Aires: Biblos, 2012.

Pite, Rebekah E. *La mesa está servida. Doña Petrona C. De Gandulfo y la domesticidad en la Argentina del siglo XX*. Buenos Aires: Edhasa, 2016.

Ponte, Antonio José. *Las comidas profundas*. Rosario, Argentina: Beatriz Viterbo, 2010.

———. "¿Quién va a comerse lo que esa mujer cocina?." *Ddc*, March 2, 2012. http://www.diariodecuba.com/cultura/1330677346_1206.html.

Poulain, Jean-Pierre. *The Sociology of Food: Eating and the Place of Food in Society*. New York: Bloomsbury Academic, 2017.
Sampaolesi, Ana. "Pachacamac." In *Locas por la cocina*, edited by Angélica Gorodischer and Ana Sampaolesi, 144–48. Buenos Aires: Biblos, 1997.
———. "Sal en el bife." In *Locas por la cocina*, edited by Angélica Gorodischer and Ana Sampaolesi, 163–65. Buenos Aires: Biblos, 1997.
Ramírez, Churampi. "Who Is Afraid of . . . Chicha?." In *Comidas Bastardas. Gastronomía, tradición e identidad en América Latina*, edited by Ángeles Mateo del Pino and Nieves Pascual Soler, 269–85. Santiago: Editorial Cuarto Propio, 2013.
Speranza, Graciela. Prologue in *Relatos reunidos*, by Hebe Uhart, 2–15. Buenos Aires: Alfaguara, 2010.
Sutton, David. *Remembrance of Repasts: An Anthropology of Food and Memory*. Oxford: Berg, 2001.
Traversa, Oscar, ed. *Cuerpos de papel II. Figuraciones del cuerpo en la prensa 1940–1970*. Buenos Aires: Santiago Arcos Editor, 2007.
Uhart, Hebe. *Relatos reunidos*. Buenos Aires: Alfaguara, 2010.
Pitts-Taylor, Victoria. *The Brain's Body: Neuroscience and Corporeal Politics*. Durham, NC: Duke University Press, 2016.
Zubiaurre, Maite. "Culinary Eros in Contemporary Hispanic Female Fiction: From Kitchen Tales to Table Narratives." *College Literature* 33, no. 3 (Summer 2006): 29–51.

Chapter 11: The Poetics of Gastronomic History

Bielsa, Esperança. *The Latin American Urban Crónica: Between Literature and Mass Culture*. Lanham, MD: Lexington Books, 2006.
Browne, Walden. *Sahagún and the Transition to Modernity*. Norman: University of Oklahoma Press, 2000.
Brulotte, Ronda L., and Alvin Starkman. "Caldo de Piedra and Claiming Pre-Hispanic Cuisine as Cultural Heritage." In *Edible Identities: Food as Cultural Heritage*, edited by Ronda Brulotte and Michael A. Di Giovine, 109–23. London: Routledge, 2016.
Coffey, Mary K. *How Revolutionary Art Became Official Culture: Murals, Museums, and the Mexican State*. Durham, NC: Duke University Press, 2012.
Corona, Ignacio, and Beth E. Jorgensen, eds. *The Contemporary Mexican Chronicle: Theoretical Perspectives on the Liminal Genre*. Albany: State University of New York Press, 2002.
Delgado Moya, Sergio. *Delirious Consumption: Aesthetics of Consumer Capitalism in Mexico and Brazil*. Austin: University of Texas Press, 2017.
Fitzpatrick, Joan. "Food and Literature: An Overview." In *Routledge International Handbook of Food Studies*, edited by Ken Albala, 122–34. London: Routledge, 2013.
Gelpí, Juan G. *Ejercer la ciudad en el México moderno*. Buenos Aires: Corregidor, 2017.
Guerrero, Javier. "Continente vulgar. Salvador Novo en Hollywood." *Revista de Estudios Hispánicos* 51 (2017): 11–44.

———. *Tecnologías del cuerpo. Exhibicionismo y visualidad en América Latina.* Madrid: Iberoamericana Vervuert, 2014.

Juárez López, José Luis. *Nacionalismo culinario. La cocina mexicana en el siglo XX.* Mexico City: Consejo Nacional para la Cultura y las Artes, 2008.

Lefebvre, Henri. *Critique of Everyday Life: The One-Volume Edition.* Translated by John Moore and Gregory Elliott. London: Verso, 2014.

———. *Rhythmanalysis: Space, Time and Everyday Life.* Translated by Stuart Elden and Gerald Moore. London: Bloomsbury, 2013

Levine, Caroline. *Forms: Whole, Rhythm, Hierarchy, Network.* Princeton, NC: Princeton University Press, 2015.

Long, Mary K. "Writing the City: The Chronicles of Salvador Novo." In *The Contemporary Mexican Chronicle: Theoretical Perspectives on the Liminal Genre*, edited by Ignacio Corona and Beth E. Jorgensen, 181–200. Albany: State University of New York Press, 2002.

Monsiváis, Carlos, ed. *A ustedes les consta. Antología de la crónica en México.* Mexico City: Era, 2003.

Moraña, Mabel. "Baroque/Neobaroque/Ultrabarroque: Disruptives Readings of Modernity." In *Hispanic Baroques: Reading Cultures in Contexts*, edited by Nicholas Spadaccini and Luis Martín-Estudillo, 242–81. Nashville: Vanderbilt University Press, 2005.

Novo, Salvador. *Cocina mexicana. Historia gastronómica de la ciudad de México.* Mexico City: Porrúa, 2010.

———. *Nueva grandeza mexicana. Ensayo sobre la ciudad de México y sus alrededores en 1946.* Mexico City: Consejo Nacional para la Cultura y las Artes, 1992.

Poot Herrera, Sara, ed. *En gusto se comen géneros. Congreso Internacional Comida y Literatura.* 3 vols. Mérida, Mexico: Instituto de Cultura de Yucatán, 2003.

Sánchez Prado, Ignacio M. "Diana Kennedy, Rick Bayless and the Imagination of 'Authentic' Mexican Food." *Bulletin of Spanish Studies* 97, no. 4 (2019): 567–92.

———. "The Pre-Columbian Past as a Project: Miguel León Portilla and Hispanism." In *Ideologies of Hispanism*, edited by Mabel Moraña, 40–61. Nashville: Vanderbilt University Press, 2005.

Sherman, John W. "The Mexican 'Miracle' and Its Collapse." In *The Oxford History of Mexico*, edited by William H. Beezley and Michael C. Meyer, 537–68. Oxford: Oxford University Press, 2000.

Weis, Robert. "Por la verdad del Osito Bimbo. Intelectuales de élite, la cultura nacional y la industrialización de la comida en México." *Brújula* 1, no. 1 (2002): 94–103.

Chapter 12: Food, Hunger, and Identity in Martín Caparrós's Travel Writing

Angulo Egea, María. "El realismo intransigente del periodismo literario de Martín Caparrós. Compromiso político, sentido histórico y voluntad de estilo." In *Estudios sobre el Mensaje Periodístico* 22, no. 2 (2016): 627–45.

Caparrós, Martín. *Larga distancia.* Buenos Aires: Seix Barral, 2004.

———. *El hambre.* Buenos Aires: Planeta, 2014.

———. *El interior.* Buenos Aires: Seix Barral, 2009.

———. *Una luna. Diario de hiperviaje.* Barcelona: Anagrama, 2009.

Coward, Rosalind. *Female Desires: How They Are Sought, Bought, and Packaged.* New York: Grove Weidenfeld, 1985.

Kavadlo, Jesse. "*Fear Factor*: Pornography, Reality Television, and Red State America." In *Pop-Porn: Pornography in American Culture*, edited by Ann C. Hall and Mardia J. Bishop, 99–110. Westport, CT: Praeger, 2007.

Moreno, María. "El pintor de la vida moderna." Radar Libros, *Página 12*, September 14, 2003. https://www.pagina12.com.ar/diario/suplementos/libros/10-737-2003-09-14.html.

Prieto, Adolfo. *Los viajeros ingleses y la emergencia de la literatura argentina. 1820–1850*. Buenos Aires: Sudamericana, 1996.

Rotker, Susana. *La invención de la crónica.* Buenos Aires: Letra Buena, 1992.

Valeri, Renée. "Travel." In *Encyclopedia of Food and Culture*, edited by Solomon H. Katz. New York: Scribner, 2003.

Chapter 13: American Counterpoints

"America's Most Influential BBQ Pitmasters and Personalities." Fox News, March 29, 2015. Accessed December 10, 2018. https://www.foxnews.com/food-drink/americas-most-influential-bbq-pitmasters-and-personalities.

Andrade, Oswald de, and Leslie Bary. "Cannibalist Manifesto." *Latin American Literary Review*, 19, no. 38 (July–December 1991): 38.

Barthes, Roland. "Toward a Psychosociology of Contemporary Food Consumption." In *Food and Culture: A Reader*, edited by Carole Counihan and Penny Van Esterik. New York: Routledge, 2013.

"Barbecue America." PBS. February 20, 2003. http://www.pbs.org/food/shows/barbecue-america/.

Carrière, J. M. "Indian and Creole Barboka, American Barbecue." *Language* 13, no. 2 (1937): 148–50.

Darío, Rubén. "To Roosevelt." https://www.poets.org/poetsorg/poem/roosevelt.

Deutsch, Jonathan, and Megan J. Elias. *Barbecue: A Global History*. London: Reaktion Books, 2014.

Fernández de Oviedo y Valdés, Gonzalo. *La historia general y natural de Las Indias.* Madrid: Real Academia de la Historia, 1854.

Gentleman of Elvas. *A Narrative of the Expedition of Hernando de Soto into Florida.* London: Richard Hackluyt, 1609. https://www.gutenberg.org/files/34997/34997-h/34997-h.htm.

Griffith, Dotty. *Celebrating Barbecue: The Ultimate Guide to America's Four Regions of 'Cue*. New York: Simon and Schuster, 2002.

Kennedy, Diana. *Cocina esencial de México*. Mexico City: Oceano, 2012.

Krise, Thomas W., ed. *Caribbeana: An Anthology of English Literature of the West Indies, 1657–1777*. Chicago: University of Chicago Press, 1999.

Jane, Lionel Cecil, ed. *Select Documents Illustrating the First Four Voyages of Columbus*. 2 vols. London: Routledge, 2017.

Martí, José. "Our America." https://writing.upenn.edu/library/Marti_Jose_Our-America.html.

Montaño, Mario. "Appropriation and Counterhegemony in South Texas: Food Slurs, Offal Meats, and Blood." In *Usable Pasts: Traditions and Group Expressions in North America*, edited by Tuleja Tad, 50–67. Boulder: University Press of Colorado, 1997. http://doi.org/10.2307/j.ctt46nrkh.7.

Murray, Albert. *The Omni-Americans: Some Alternatives to the Folklore of White Supremacy*. New York: E. P. Dutton, 1970.

Ortiz, Fernando. "The human factors of *cubanidad*." *HAU: Journal of Ethnographic Theory* 4, no. 3 (Winter 2014): 455–80.

Pilcher, Jeffrey M. *Planet Taco: A Global History of Mexican Food*. New York: Oxford University Press, 2012.

Pite, Rebekah. "La Cocina Criolla: A History of Food and Race in Twentieth-Century Argentina." In *Rethinking Race in Modern Argentina*, edited by Paulina Alberto and Eduardo Elena. New York: Cambridge University Press, 2016.

Soegrel, Matt. "Barbecue Experts Gather to Munch on 'the Most American Food You Can Get.'" *Florida Times-Union*, March 10, 2016.

Warnes, Andrew. *Savage Barbecue: Race, Culture, and the Invention of America's First Food*. Athens: University of Georgia Press, 2008.

Vaughn, Daniel. "The History of Smoked Brisket." *Texas Monthly*, January 24, 2014. https://www.texasmonthly.com/bbq/smoked-brisket-history/.

Walker, Margath A. "Border Food and Food on the Border: Meaning and Practice in Mexican Haute Cuisine." *Social and Cultural Geography* 14, no. 6 (2013).

Walsh, Robb. "Texas Barbecue in Black and White." In *Cornbread Nation 2*, edited by Lolis Eric Elie. Oxford, NC: Southern Foodways Alliance, 2004.

CONTRIBUTORS

SANDRA AGUILAR-RODRÍGUEZ is an associate professor in Latin American history at Moravian University. She completed her undergraduate degree at the Universidad del Claustro de Sor Juana in Mexico City. She was granted an MPhil in Latin American Studies from the University of Oxford and a PhD in women's studies from the University of Manchester in the United Kingdom. She was a postdoctoral fellow at Lehigh University. Her research focuses on food, race, gender, class, and modernization in twentieth-century Mexico. Her work has been published both in the United States and Latin America in various journals and books, such as the *Radical History Review, The Americas, Revista de Historia Iberoamericana, Revista de Estudios Sociales*, and the edited books *Technology and Culture in Twentieth Century Mexico* and *El hambre de los otros. Ciencia y políticas alimentarias en Latinoamérica, siglos XX y XXI*. She is a member of the Red de Estudios Históricos y Sociales de la Nutrición y Alimentación en América Latina (REHSNAL), a network of scholars who focus on the historical study of food and nutrition in Latin America, and a member of the editorial advisory board of the journal *Global Food History*.

RUSSELL COBB is an associate professor in Modern Languages and Cultural Studies at the University of Alberta, where he teaches Latin American studies and comparative literature. His work bridges the worlds of creative nonfiction and traditional cultural histories of the Greater Caribbean, including the US American South. As a writer of creative nonfiction and popular history, he works on transculturation between African, European, and indigenous cultures, including cuisine and music. His writing has appeared in *Slate*, *NPR*, the *New York Times*, and *The Nation*, among other places. Cobb's books include *The Great Oklahoma Swindle: Race, Religion, and Lies in America's Weirdest State* (2020), *Hearts in Darkness* (2013), and the edited collection *The Paradox of Authenticity in a Globalized World* (2014).

ROCÍO DEL AGUILA is an associate professor in the Modern and Classical Languages and Literatures Department at Wichita State University. Her research interests are nineteenth-century literature, postcolonial identities, gender studies, and food studies. She has published articles on food representation in texts by women writers and has presented about cooking traditions, the Asian diaspora, and Latin American foodways, including her TEDx talk *Cooking Communities*. She is the founder of *Migrant Kitchens*—a project about immigration, tradition, and empowerment through recipes—and directed the documentary *Cocin(ando) Wichita* (2019). She has taught courses about literature and food that incorporated nontraditional approaches to teaching and experiential learning.

REGINA HARRISON, a specialist in Andean literature and Quechua, the language of the Incas, is professor emerita of Latin American literatures and comparative literature at the University of Maryland. Her first book, *Signs, Songs, and Memory in the Andes: Translating Quechua Language and Culture* (1989), won the Kovacs Award (Modern Language Association) and honorable mention for the Latin American Studies Association Bryce Wood Book Prize. Her semantic study of Quechua confession manuals, *Sin and Confession in Colonial Peru* (2014), funded with a fellowship from the John Simon Guggenheim Memorial Foundation, was awarded the Bainton Book Prize in History from the Sixteenth Century Society. She also has authored books and articles on Ecuadorian literature, notably *Entre el tronar épico y el llanto elegíaco: simbología indígena en la poesía ecuatoriana* (1996) and *Historia, arte y música en el manuscrito "La perla mystica," Quito (1700–1718)* (2019). A filmmaker, Harrison directed *Cashing in on Culture: Indigenous Communities and Tourism* (2002); she later filmed and directed *Mined to Death* (2005), winner of the Latin American Studies Association's Award in Film, in Potosí, Bolivia. *Gringo Kullki: From Sucres to Dollars in Ecuador* (2015), in Quichua with English subtitles, is her most recent documentary.

ALISON KRÖGEL is an associate professor of Andean literary and cultural studies at the University of Denver, where she teaches courses on contemporary and colonial Andean literature, as well as Quechua language and culture courses. Her research includes studies of the roles played by food and cooks in Andean literatures and cultures, Quechua- and Kichwa-language poetry and oral traditions, and the challenges faced by Quechua sheepherders working on the mountain plains of Wyoming and Colorado. A recipient of a Fulbright research grant to

Ecuador (2013–14), she has published the books *Musuq Illa: Poética del harawi en runasimi (2000–2020)* (2021) and *Food, Power, and Resistance in the Andes: Exploring Quechua Verbal and Visual Narratives* (2010), as well as numerous articles in literary-studies and anthropology journals. Her work has also appeared in edited volumes such as *The Cambridge Companion to Latin American Poetry*, *Cine Andino*, and *The Routledge History of Food*, and she is the editor of Musuq Illa, a multilingual, digital humanities collective focused on Quechua-language poetry.

MERCEDES LOPEZ RODRIGUEZ is an associate professor of colonial Spanish American literature in the Department of Languages, Literatures, and Cultures at the University of South Carolina. Her research focus stems from a long interest in the representation of difference and the emergence of new cultural practices amid contexts of conflict in Latin America, with a specific interest in the Andean region. Her scholarly research lies at the intersection of literary studies, ethnography, history, and art history. She is the author of two books, *Blancura y otras ficciones raciales en los Andes colombianos del siglo XIX* (Iberoamericana Veuvert, 2019) and *Tiempos para rezar y tiempos para trabajar* (ICANH, 2001). These works examine how racial categories have been textually constructed, suggesting that the production of social difference through texts is an essential problem for both Andean and literary studies. She is now working on a new book titled *Sensing and Feeling the Other: Hearing, Smelling, Tasting, and Touching Emotions in Colombia 1850–1970*. She is also currently working on the lives of Colombian immigrants in South Carolina, exploring the impact of the last five decades of the internal conflict on the lives of those who fled the violence in their country.

VANESA MISERES is an associate professor in the Department of Romance Languages and Literatures at the University of Notre Dame. She specializes in nineteenth- and early-twentieth-century Latin American literature with a particular focus on women writers, travel writing, and war literature, as well as gender, cultural, and food studies. She is the author of *Mujeres en tránsito. Viaje, identidad y escritura en Sudamérica* (Chapel Hill: North Carolina Studies in the Romance Languages, 2017). She has studied, published, and presented on food and feminism and the role of food in travel writing to and from Latin America. She has also taught several courses related to food in Latin America, incorporating nontraditional approaches to teaching using blogs and social media as well as collectively creating podcasts, blogs, and cookbooks with students.

ELIZABETH MONTES GARCÉS is an associate professor in the division of Spanish and Italian studies at the University of Calgary, Canada. Her area of specialization is women's writing in Latin America and world cinema. To date she has published three books with Peter Lang and the University of Calgary Press: *Los mecanismos de representación en la narrativa de Fanny Buitrago* (1997), *Relocating Identities in Latin American Culture* (2007), and *Violence in Contemporary Argentinean Literature and Film: 1989–2005* (2010). She has also published several articles in the journals *Revista Canadiense de Estudios Hispánicos, Texto Crítico, Revista de Estudios Colombianos, Letras Femeninas*, and many others. She has participated in conferences and symposia in Canada, the United States, Europe, and Latin America. She is a senior researcher at the Latin American Research Centre at the University of Calgary. Her most recent projects include a monographic special issue of *Revista Canadiense de Estudios Hispánicos* on the representation of women in Latin American and Spanish comics that was released in November 2019, and the chaper "Thriller and Performance in Costa-Gavras's State of Siege," published in the edited volume *The Films of Costa-Gavras: New Perspectives* (2020).

MARÍA PAZ MORENO is a native of Spain. She is professor of Spanish in the Department of Romance Languages and Literatures at the University of Cincinnati. She is coeditor of the academic journal *Cincinnati Romance Review*. Moreno's research focuses on Spanish contemporary poetry, women poets, and food studies, specializing in culinary literature and cookbooks. She is the author of landmark works on the writer Juan Gil-Albert, among them the monograph *El culturalismo en la poesía de Juan Gil-Albert* and the edition of his complete poetry. In the field of food studies she has authored numerous articles and two books: *De la página al plato: El libro de cocina en España* (Trea, 2012), and *Madrid: A Culinary History* (Rowman & Littlefield, 2018). In 2012 she edited a monographic volume of *Cincinnati Romance Review* entitled *Writing about Food: Culinary Literature in the Hispanic World.*

NINA B. NAMASTE is an associate professor of Spanish in the Department of World Languages and Cultures at Elon University in North Carolina. She earned a PhD in Hispanic literature from Indiana University, with a particular emphasis on twentieth-century theater from Spain, Mexico, Argentina, and Chile. Her core research focuses on culinary imagery as a means to express issues of race, class, and gender identity formation, though she has also published on the intersection between globalization and national identity in contemporary Spanish and Spanish American fictional works. She has had discipline-specific articles published in *Contemporary Theatre Review*, *Gestos*, and *Letras Femeninas*, among other journals and collected volumes. For three years she organized a yearly interdisciplinary conference on food in Oxford and led the Making Sense of Food Project. She currently co-organizes the biannual Meaning of Food conference in Greensboro (https://meaningoffoodconference.com/). She teaches courses about food and identity formation, genders and sexualities studies, and the general studies curriculums at Elon.

IGNACIO M. SÁNCHEZ PRADO is the Jarvis Thurston and Mona Van Duyn Professor in the Humanities at Washington University in St. Louis. A scholar of Mexican literature, cinema, and culture, he has published seven authored books and over one hundred academic articles. His most recent books are *Strategic Occidentalism: On Mexican Fiction, the Neoliberal Book Market and the Question of World Literature* (Northwestern University Press, 2018), and *Intermitencias alfonsinas. Estudios y otros textos (2004–2018)* (Universidad Autónoma de Nuevo León, 2019). He has also edited fourteen critical collections, including *A History of Mexican Literature* (with Anna Nogar and José Ramón Ruisánchez, Cambridge University Press, 2016) and the forthcoming *Mexican Literature as World Literature* (Bloomsbury, 2021). His public writing has appeared in the *Washington Post*, *Los Angeles Review of Books*, *El Universal*, and other publications. He was the Kluge Chair in the Countries and Cultures of the South at the Library of Congress during the summer of 2021.

LEE SKINNER is dean of Newcomb-Tulane College at Tulane University and professor of Spanish in the Department of Spanish and Portuguese. She is the author of *Gender and the Rhetoric of Modernity in Spanish America, 1850–1910* (University Press of Florida, 2016) and *History Lessons: Refiguring the Historical Novel in Nineteenth Century Spanish America* (Juan de la Cuesta, 2006), and has published numerous articles on nineteenth-century Spanish American narrative and nonfiction in journals including *Latin American Research Review*, *Revista de Estudios Hispanicos*, *Bulletin of Hispanic Studies*, and *Hispanic Review*. She is currently writing a cultural history of food and eating in Spanish America from 1825 to the present.

ÁNGEL T. TUNINETTI is the Armand E. and Mary W. Singer Professor in the Humanities at West Virginia University. A native of Argentina, he obtained his PhD at Washington University in St. Louis. His main area of research is travel literature to and from Latin America, especially in the Southern Cone region. He has published two books: *Otras intenciones, otras miradas: textos complementarios a una excursión a los indios ranqueles* (Universidad Nacional de Río Cuarto, Argentina, 2017) and *Nuevas tierras con viejos ojos: Viajeros españoles y latinoamericanos en Sudamérica, siglos XVIII y XIX* (Ediciones Corregidor, Buenos Aires, 2001) and many articles on travel writing and Latin American literature. As a Fulbright scholar and specialist, he has completed fellowships in Paraguay working on the internationalization of higher education. At WVU he teaches "Seminar on Latin American Culture: Panorama Culinario de América Latina." Sponsored by the Consortium for North American Higher Education Collaboration, Tuninetti and Paola Jeannete Vera Báez have team-taught classes on food, and their students have worked collaboratively on a blog highlighting different regional cuisines and videos showcasing traditional Latin American dishes.

KARINA ELIZABETH VÁZQUEZ has a BA in sociology from the University of Buenos Aires and a doctorate in Latin American literature from the University of Florida. She directs the Spanish Community-Based Learning Program at the University of Richmond in Virginia. She is the author of *Fogwill: Realismo y mala conciencia* (Circeto, 2009) and *Aprendices, obreros y fabriqueras: el trabajo industrial en la narrativa argentina del siglo XX* (Biblos, 2013); coeditor of *Insomne pasado: lecturas críticas sobre Latinoamérica colonial. Un homenaje a Félix Bolaños* (F&G 2016); and the translator to Spanish of the graphic novel *Darkroom: A Memoir in Black and White* by Lila Quintero-Weaver (UA Press, 2018). Her interests are literary and visual representations of work; the representations of food, cooking, and domestic service in Latin America; experiential learning; and graphic novels. She has published extensively on Latin America, particularly on Argentine narrative, Peronism, labor, film, and pedagogy. She is currently working on a coedited volume on the Argentine writer Aurora Venturini.

PAOLA JEANNETE VERA BÁEZ is a culinary anthropologist and professor at the Universidad Popular Autónoma del Estado de Puebla (UPAEP) Faculty of Gastronomy. She has master's degrees in anthropology and history, and she is a PhD candidate in Mesoamerican studies. She has published several ethnographies and articles about the anthropology of food and the Mexican gastronomic culture. Her area of specialization is the culinary semiotic system made up of the set of texts identified in the collective memory of Mexican culture.

INDEX